W9-BWK-324

FAMILY AND FAVELA

Recent Titles in
Contributions in Latin American Studies

Modernization and Stagnation:
Latin American Agriculture into the 1990's
Michael J. Twomey and Ann Helwege, editors

State Formation in Central America: The Struggle
for Autonomy, Development, and Democracy
Howard H. Lentner

Cuba and the Future
Donald E. Schulz, editor

Ambivalent Anti-Colonialism: The United States and the Genesis of West Indian
Independence, 1940–1964
Cary Fraser

Mexico Faces the 21st Century
Donald E. Schulz and Edward J. Williams, editors

Authoritarianism in Latin America since Independence
Will Fowler, editor

Colombia's Military and Brazil's Monarchy: Undermining the Republican Foundations
of South American Independence
Thomas Millington

Brutality and Benevolence: Human Ethology, Culture, and the Birth of Mexico
Abel A. Alves

Ideologues and Ideologies in Latin America
Will Fowler, editor

FAMILY AND FAVELA

*The Reproduction of Poverty
in Rio de Janeiro*

JULIO CÉSAR PINO

Contributions in Latin American Studies, Number 10

GREENWOOD PRESS
Westport, Connecticut • London

Library of Congress Cataloging-in-Publication Data

Pino, Julio César.
   Family and favela : the reproduction of poverty in Rio de Janeiro
/ Julio César Pino.
      p. cm.—(Contributions in Latin American studies, ISSN
1054–6790 ; no. 10)
   Includes bibliographical references (p.   -) and index.
   ISBN 0–313–30362–2 (alk. paper)
   1. Poverty—Brazil—Rio de Janeiro—History—20th century.
2. Poor—Brazil—Rio de Janeiro—History—20th century. 3. Family—
Economic aspects—Brazil—Rio de Janeiro—History—20th century.
4. Squatter settlements—Brazil—Rio de Janeiro—History—20th
century. 5. Households—Brazil—Rio de Janeiro—History—20th
century. 6. Working class—Brazil—Rio de Janeiro—History—20th
century. I. Title. II. Series.
HC189.R4P56   1997
330.981'53064—dc21   96–47433

British Library Cataloguing in Publication Data is available.

Library of Congress Catalog Card Number: 96–47433
ISBN: 0–313–30362–2
ISSN: 1054–6790

First published in 1997

Greenwood Press, 88 Post Road West, Westport, CT 06881
An imprint of Greenwood Publishing Group, Inc.

Printed in the United States of America

The paper used in this book complies with the
Permanent Paper Standard issued by the National
Information Standards Organization (Z39.48–1984).

10 9 8 7 6 5 4 3 2 1

Copyright Acknowledgments

The author and publisher gratefully acknowledge permission for use of the following material:

Excerpts from Julio César Pino, "The Dark Mirror of Modernization: The Favelas of Rio de Janeiro
in the Boom Years, 1948–1960," *Journal of Urban History* 22, no. 4 (May 1996), pp. 419–453,
copyright © 1996 by Sage Publications, Inc. Reprinted by permission of Sage Publications, Inc.

Excerpts from Julio César Pino, "Labor in the Favelas of Rio de Janeiro, 1940–1969," *Latin American Perspectives*, forthcoming, copyright © by Sage Publications, Inc. Reprinted by permission of
Sage Publications, Inc.

Excerpts from Julio César Pino, "Urban Squatter Households in Rio de Janeiro, 1940–1969," *Locus*
8, no. 2 (Spring 1996), pp. 135–167. Reprinted by permission of *Locus*.

Excerpts from the Moura Family Papers, Rio de Janeiro. Reprinted by permission of Maria Coeli.

For Julio, Juliana, Lissette, Mia, and Rio

Ille terrarum mihi praeter omnis
Angulus ridet
—Horace, *Odes*, vi. 13

Poor naked wretches, wheresoe'er you are,
That bide the pelting of this pitiless storm,
How shall your houseless heads and unfed sides,
Your loop'd and window'd raggedness, defend you
From seasons such as these? . . .
Expose thyself to feel what wretches feel,
That thou mayst shake the superflux to them,
And show the heavens more just.

—Shakespeare, *King Lear*, Act III, Scene IV

Contents

Illustrations

TABLES

MAPS

Acknowledgments

Short of printing out the UCLA Faculty Guide and the Rio de Janeiro telephone book, let me single out some individuals for heartfelt thanks: Bradford Burns, for comments and consideration; Eulalia Lobo, for introductions in Rio de Janeiro; Dr. Helio Aguimaga, key to the favelas; Doracy of CPMAIC, without whom this project would never have left the ground; Ricardo and Laisinha of the Brazilian Institute of Municipal Administration; Gilda Blank and Olga Bronstein, for combing through their files on my behalf; Vera Campello and Dona Flora, for use of the Fundação Leão XIII archives; José Artur Rios, for his newspaper collection and his lovely, indispensable secretaries, for their time; Vitor Valla, for his exhaustive bibliography on the favelas; Alcimir Gomes of Cordovil; Maria Coeli de Moura, for access to her father's papers; Dona Wanda of the Fundação Leão XIII in Bràs de Pina, for setting up interviews with the residents; Jorge Dionisio de Barros, a historian in his own right; Dona Lucilene of the Posto Camela Dutra at Jacarézinho; Padre Nelson, for use of his papers; João Gomes Filho, for his monthly budget; and the staff of the Biblioteca Nacional and the library at the Pontífica Universidade Católica.

My research in Brazil during 1989–1990 was sponsored by the Fulbright-Hays Dissertation Abroad Fellowship of the Department of Education. I particularly want to thank Nilza Waldeck and Senhor Rocha of the Fulbright offices in Rio de Janeiro and Brasília, respectively, for their hospitality.

Introduction

The eyes are the first thing you notice—much too large for an infant. Then you notice the skimpy diaper and white sailor's cap. Clearly, Senhor Jorge was no ordinary baby. The photo he shows me is proof that even as an infant he showed signs of the alertness that marks his twilight years. Next he hands me a receipt: "Casa Nova Aurora, Furniture in all styles—Bedrooms, Kitchens, Living Rooms, Carpets and Sofas. We received from Sr. DB the amount of . . . on this date 22 of September 1947." "Look at this yellow paper," he says. "Federal District, Elevator Operator's Card; Ficha 3947 belongs to JDB, Rio de Janeiro, 27 of May 1953." More bills: "Société Anonyme du Gaz de Rio de Janeiro, Serviço de Energia Elétrica e Gas. Service until 3 of March, 1961, debt: $Cr. 650.00." One last item, in which a man's life is summarized on a green and white card:

Union for the Defense and Betterment
of the Favela of Brás de Pina. Sr. JDB.
Profession: mechanic.
Civil Status: married.
Place of Birth: Minas Gerais, Brasil, 12/12/1921 .

The documents testify that as husband, father, laborer, customer, and citizen, Senhor Jorge was reproduced by the society into which he was born. Economic systems and political regimes establish and perpetuate themselves at the daily level, and without a discussion of whom the laborer marries, works for, owes money to, or how he interacts with other members of his social class, any examination of poverty is doomed to produce what Shakespeare called "airy nothing." The use and abuse of men and women, their passage through institutions and their developing consciousness of themselves as members of both family household and social class is the underlying theme of this work. The *favelas* (squatter settlements) of Rio de Janeiro, with their teeming masses trapped in misery, are the perfect site for an investigation of how social inequality is reproduced in Brazil.

Economists, sociologists, anthropologists, and even psychologists have investigated poverty in Brazil from almost every conceivable angle. What can a historian add? The answer is that a new study is needed because a change of optics has become necessary—a shift of focus away from individual cases and toward household studies. Economist José Pastore attests to the importance of the family in understanding Brazil:

After all, 91% of Brazilians live in family households. The household is therefore the laboratory where different strategies are combined to arrive at the final level of well-being of the family and each of its members. It would be difficult to imagine in Brazil a household where one member was rich and the other poor. More common is the "community-chest" where each member collaborates to the proportion of his work and earnings. . . . the final social situation of society is the product of these family arrangements.[1]

The problem addressed in this book is the place of the family in Brazilian underdevelopment in the twentieth century, using the squatters of the city of Rio de Janeiro as test subjects. Until recently, the study of the family in Brazil has been almost exclusively the domain of anthropologists and sociologists. Most have focused on the family as a juridical and cultural unit.[2] On the other hand, economic historians dealing with the forging of the working class in Brazil have rarely paid attention to the household.[3] An analysis of family and class in Brazil can help bridge the gap separating microscopic studies of lone individuals from macroscopic analyses of social class.

Social classes result from the successful reproduction of the relations of production in any society. The relations of production encompass all the conditions necessary for the mode of production to be reproduced. A social class is not a collection of individuals but the product of the historical transition from one economic system to another. A working class is formed when producers are denied access to the means of subsistence and are forced to hire themselves out. This social relation of production between labor and capital must be reproduced if capitalism is to survive.[4]

The two most important settings for the reproduction of social classes are the work place and the home. In the workplace the capitalist, by buying labor power, produces subjective or abstract wealth—"which exists in the physical body of the worker, and is separated from its own means of objectification and realization; in short the capitalist produces the worker as wage-laborer."[5] The worker produces objective wealth in the form of capital, which is concrete and specified. The worker is reproduced by being provided with wages that help purchase goods and services for the recomposition of his or her labor power, but only in the amount necessary for subsistence. Producers must simultaneously be deprived of the true worth of their labor power if they are to put it at the continual disposal of the owners of capital. The production and reproduction of the wagelaborer are thus the *sine qua non* of the capitalist mode of production.

The household is the other major location where the worker is reproduced. The reproduction of laborpower at home is subject to means of control different from, but related to, those that workers experience as producers. Feminist authors have enhanced our understanding of the reproduction of the working class by pointing to the factor of gender—how sex and class barriers reinforce one another through the exploitation of labor that takes place inside the household. Marx's analysis of the extraction of surplus value, which derives from his theory of socially necessary labor time, leaves little room for an analysis of noncapitalist production carried on inside the home. A new approach to the connections between sex and class is necessary, one that considers how labor is reproduced through the household.[6]

The first purpose of this work is to enhance our comprehension of the reproduction of the working class in Brazil after 1930, using the family household as the systematic unit of analysis. It is the household that allocates members to the labor force and decides how income shall be shared and spent. How can we comprehend the growth of the modern Brazilian economy and the efficacy of government welfare services in housing, education, and health if we don't study the matter from the perspective of the family?

Second, the work explores the structure of the contemporary Brazilian family. Many tomes have been devoted to this topic in the disciplines of sociology, anthropology, and psychology. What has been missing is the historian's touch—a sketch of the family in evolution through time. The picture most academics have drawn is a still life, a faint rendering of the patriarchal clans depicted by Gilberto Freyre and other authors. In the twentieth century the family has been studied in a historical vacuum, without reference to the increased role of the state and the profound changes in the Brazilian economy since the 1930s.

The third aim is to reacquaint the reader with the history of Rio de Janeiro. Much can be learned of the city's transformation into a twentieth-century metropolis by studying the process of urban development from the bottom up, witnessing the consequences of modernization through the eyes of the poor. Were they merely passive spectators to the upheavals of city and national life during these years, or did they attempt to become a political force in their own right? The crucial reason to focus on Rio de Janeiro is the chance to study the incorporation of the rural worker into the urban economy and the growth of squatter settlements peopled by the migrant poor. The Rio de Janeiro Municipal Planning Agency (IPLAN-RIO) reports that in 1991 the city contained 661 favelas housing 962,793 people in 239,678 shanties.[7] Many assume that the working class of Rio de Janeiro and the favelados are two distinct groups. In fact they are Siamese twins separated by the ignorance and prejudice of most observers. One more reason for this study is to reunite squatters and laborers.

A history of the squatter poor in Rio de Janeiro is, of course, not unprecedented. Janice Perlman covered similar terrain in *The Myth of Marginality: Urban Poverty and Politics in Rio de Janeiro*, which focused on favela formation in the 1960s.[8] While breaking new ground in dealing with issues like survival strategies devised by the poor, this pioneering volume still used the individual as the unit of analysis, throwing only a slight glance at the family in the favela. Perlman's book is one of many studies published since the 1970s that refute the theory of marginality—the notion that the shantytown dwellers constitute an outcast group of feuding individuals shut off from urban society.[9] Instead, the shantytown should be seen as a functioning community closely connected to the metropolis. The perspective of this book is that the participation of the poor in community life takes place through the family. Many researchers have made the false distinction between "marginals" and "workers" because they have failed to explore how the destitute are integrated within the city.

Recently, many American journalists have wondered in print how the average Brazilian copes with astronomical inflation and unemployment. What they do not grasp is that inflation, low wages, and loss of jobs impact on the whole family. The link between household and social class is what has been missing from the literature on the urban poor.[10] Another problem with much of the literature is that the poor are not seen as members of a generation, "confronting personal and political problems that mark them off from their predecessors."[11] A study of lower-income families makes sense only if it focuses on an extended time period meaningful to the subjects and manageable by the researcher. The generation analyzed here encompassed a critical cycle of Brazilian history stretching from the dictatorship of GetúlioVargas starting in 1930, and his drive to industrialize the country, to the period of military rule following the coup of 1964 and the much-touted "Brazilian economic miracle."

How can the experience of poverty during these years be re-created for the contemporary reader? In a thousand little ways the poor leave records of themselves that speak to the historian. Birth, marriage, and death certificates document the structure of the favela family. Labor cards, with details on age, employment history, technical skills, and salary, offer evidence to judge whether the urban poor are marginals or an integral part of the city economy. Health reports attest to the physical condition of the labor force and the special problems of women and children. Labor union pamphlets provide clues about job conditions and employee grievances. Land deeds reconstruct the process of building and expanding the shanty. Records of welfare and charity organizations tell us how far down the social ladder government and private services reached. Handbills passed out by candidates for election indicate the political concerns of the favela residents.

The research for this study was conducted in the city of Rio de Janeiro in 1989–1990. The most important information came from the private papers of individuals who lived in the favelas or were involved in the supervision of the squatter settlements. Favelados brought me home records on household expenditures, employment, and political activity. In the three favelas where I chose to do field research, I was given access to the files of the residents' association. I also consulted the archives of city officials and Catholic Church personnel who dealt with the favelas in the 1940s and 1950s. Engineers and urban planners involved in favela renewal projects in the 1960s turned over their original surveys. I personally interviewed many original settlers of the favelas. Gaining access to firsthand material was not in itself a sufficient reason to have spent a year in Brazil.

Something more important was involved in my project; the opportunity to study what the Gouncourt brothers, early French social historians, called "intimate history." The project was not simply a look for documents but a search for people. It offered a chance to find out how favelados cope with their condition and, through joint action, make history. On-site inspection of the living and working quarters of the favelados was the key that unlocked the mystery surrounding Rio's poor, a group often talked about but little understood.

Four major hypotheses are considered in this historical study:

1. Was there a causal relationship between economic underdevelopment and household structure?
2. Were poor households integrated into the urban workforce?
3. How was income redistributed inside the household, whose members might be unemployed or underemployed? Was social mobility possible for the favelados?
4. How did the poor view the world around them, and how did the city regard the poor? What sort of political activity arose from the clash between city and squatter settlement?

The book begins with a review of the functions of family and household in contemporary society, and then presents a short history of the family in Brazil. Chapter 2 surveys the industrialization of Rio de Janeiro after 1930 and the creation of the subproletariat that came to live in the favelas. Chapter 3 gives an overview of the explosive growth of squatter settlements in Rio de Janeiro from 1948 to 1960. Chapters 4–7 chronicle changes in household structure, economic activity, living standards, and politics in three favelas—Praia do Pinto, Brás de Pina, and Jacarézinho—from 1940 to 1969.

This is the story of millions of human beings who were forgotten by society and, until recently, ignored by historians. The most surprising thing I encountered in the course of my research was the degree to which middle- and upper-class *Cariocas* (citizens of Rio de Janeiro) ignored the very existence of the favela, unless they felt threatened by crime emanating from the shantytowns. Ralph Ellison spoke of the American Negro as the "invisible man." The favela is the invisible Rio de Janeiro. Yet, for the most part it was favelados who built the skyscrapers and residential apartments of the rich, cleaned their houses, raised their children, and bore the brunt of the city's economic decline after 1930. The favela is the perfect metaphor for the city; many Brazilians concur that their *cidade maravilhosa* is becoming a "mega-favelopolis."[12] This study may provide some answers as to whether Rio de Janeiro and Brazil can enter the twenty-first century without shantytowns.

1

The Family

No component of society is more difficult to define or harder to portray simply through statistics than the family. Several years ago, a group of scholars specializing in Latin America established a criterion that has come into wide acceptance.

The family is a group of people who bear a kinship relation, either consanguinity or fictive, to one another, and perceive that connection as the basis of a mutual and usually exclusive bond; and deal with each other accordingly, engaging in exchange of various goods (such as affection, esteem, emotional support and material items) as a result of that bond.[1]

The definition of the family that these authors adopt is cultural, genealogical, and behavioral. While certainly valid, this view fails to capture the evolution of the family institution across time and its interaction with the rest of society. A historical materialist explanation, based on the role of the family within the mode of production, is more useful. Throughout the history of class societies, the family has served four main functions: the biological unit through which the community is repopulated; a productive unit sending men, women, and children into the workforce; a social force transmitting both the dominant and popular culture to offspring; and a political link between ruling groups and subordinates. Each function complements the others. Claude Meillassoux writes: "The domestic community (or its modern transformation, the family) is the only economic and social system which manages the physical reproduction of human beings, the reproduction of the producers and the social reproduction at large through a comprehensive set of institutions."[2] The family physically produces labor power under the guidelines and restrictions set by the existing mode of production and relations of production, and, in turn, the perpetuation of the economic system is explained by the methods through which the means of production, social relations of production, and family organization are reproduced. Frederick Engels was one of the first to sketch the evolution of the family from hunter-gatherer communities, whose members were loosely associated by bonds of personal dependence, to the nuclear family households, whose birth, he claimed, coincided with the dawn of the capitalist era.[3] This is not to say that the family at any one time corresponds exactly to the demands of the mode of production. The family existed under slavery and feudalism. It persists under capitalism and the so-called socialist societies of today. What changes through time is the relative importance of its four major functions of biological reproduction of the labor force, economic production, social adaptation, and political control. This chapter examines the role of the family in modern capitalist society as it serves these four functions, with a focus on the history of the family in Brazil.

It is important first of all to distinguish the family from the household. The Brazilian national census of 1950, the first to count squatter families, defined the family as "a group of persons related among themselves, as well as those living in a state of dependence, subordination, or hospitality under a head, all living in the same dwelling, including individuals living alone." In the 1960 census "family" gave way to "family group," which maintained the criteria of the old definition but also included "a grouping of at the most 5 persons, living in a private dwelling, without being linked by ties of kinship or domestic dependency."[4] The difference between family and household is crucial to understanding how poor families are reproduced. Marianne Schmink argues for a distinction based on economic functions. Social relations are what define the family, she states, while "the household or (domestic unit) refers to a coresident group of persons who share most aspects of consumption, drawing on and allocating a common pool of resources (including labor) to ensure their material reproduction."[5] Drawing on this definition, this study contends that the contemporary household corresponds to the economic, social, and political needs of capitalism, especially in the underdeveloped countries. The modern household reproduces the marginalization of women and children, the unequal production and distribution of wealth and political power, and the ideology of the ruling class in capitalist society.

FAMILY AND HOUSEHOLD IN CLASS SOCIETY

Biological reproduction and economic production are linked in determining the composition of the family in class society. Family size and structure are to a great extent dependent on employment and income. Limiting the number of offspring is one way working-class families can enjoy a minimum of comfort, but this option must be balanced against the need to produce more members to increase household income. The frequency of biological reproduction is therefore closely tied to the cycle of the insertion of family members in the workforce, which in turn generates new levels of consumption and creates new conditions for the production of new family members.

The biological reproduction of the family is also a political question because historically men not only have owned the means of production but have also exerted control over women's bodies and held most of the legal rights over children. Biological differences form the origin of inequality between male and female, and the subordination of women and children is not simply the epiphenomenon of class society. Women who lack control of the means of both production and reproduction are at the mercy of the economy and biology. The contemporary unit of biological reproduction for many workers, the nuclear family household, plays a special role in the oppression of women and children and the perpetuation of capitalism. While in precapitalist societies men, women, and children were contracted as one unit to carry out productive tasks, often working as a team, under capitalism it is the individual who is hired, and the family becomes primarily a unit of consumption. In the workforce, women usually earn less money than men, thereby lowering the costs of production to the employer. At home the wife's performance of domestic work, without having an equal say in the allocation of the household earnings, reinforces patriarchy. The exclusion of women from well-compensated economic activity and the subordination of the female and her children inside the home is therefore necessary to the continuation of the male-dominated capitalist system.

The economic functions of the household differ according to the modes of production, and changes in household occupational structure are related to changes in the productive structure. Peripheral capitalist economies such as Brazil are characterized by uneven and combined development of the productive forces. Advanced modes of production coexist with outmoded ones, and the two are interwoven. Old methods of production never entirely disappear but are forced to conform to advanced ones located in the more developed areas of the national economy. Artisan production, for example, a task performed by the family in subsistence economies, does survive in peripheral capitalist societies. But such activity, rather than simply satisfying the demands of the immediate group, may instead be aimed at the growing consumer market of low-income sectors in the large cities.[6]

This uneven and combined development of the economy and the labor market is reproduced within the home. Household members may be occupied in different forms of capitalist production, both industrial and preindustrial, formal and informal, archaic and modern.

Any given household may include workers of different structural characteristics and wage potential, who pool their earnings to different degrees; salaried employees in different formal sector occupations, self-employed workers in the informal market, and unpaid family workers. A low-income flow tends to provoke an intensification of the household's income-generating strategy, which often leads to a greater internal heterogeneity of class and occupational positions within the domestic unit.[7]

Since in the underdeveloped world there is no pure capitalist form of economic organization that precludes less advanced forms, the combined nature of urban industrial development means great diversity in occupations and sources of income for the household.

Working families measure their material well-being by their capacity to purchase consumer products.The consumption of goods and services through the redistribution of income from salaried and nonsalaried sources by household members forms the material basis for physical reproduction. The household head designs a hierarchy of spending, that is indicative of the material needs of the entire unit. This household budget, expressed as the cost of reproduction, is the measure of the the unit's ability to expand earning power to meet ever increasing needs. While the decision to enter the workforce is made individually, with the husband consulting or commanding the participation of women and children, decisions on how to spend earnings generated from work are made jointly, if not always democratically, inside the home.

The most obvious way to expand consumption is to raise the household income by utilizing every member to generate income to complement that earned by the head. "For family strategies of economic survival, family components begin to function like a reserve army of labor to be mobilized according to the contingencies that affect the household consumption fund."[8] Another method by which the cost of reproduction may be lowered is to make consumption less costly. There are both institutional and noninstitutional ways to do this. If the problem is lack of adequate housing at affordable prices, the family can turn to a government housing agency for a loan or hire neighbors to construct a new dwelling. Low-income families, who often lack access to government services, are more likely to employ informal methods to lower consumption costs, but a more common strategy is to combine institutional and noninstitutional means to cut expenses.[9]

The household unit, rather than the individual, is the best gauge of the welfare in any society, but especially in those where a majority lives below the poverty line. Simon Kuznets has proposed that income inequality does not necessarily decline as a consequence of economic growth in underdeveloped countries, in fact, it may become more pronounced.

There is no empirical evidence to check this conjunctural implication, but it is suggested by the absence in these areas of the dynamic forces associated with rapid growth that in the developed countries checked the upward trend of the upper income shares that was due to the cumulative effect of continuous concentration of past savings; and it is also indicated by the failure of the political and social systems of the underdeveloped countries to initiate the governmental or political practices that effectively bolster the weak positions of lower income classes. Indeed, there is a possibility that inequality in the secular income structure of underdeveloped countries may have widened in recent decades.[10]

Household consumption patterns thus furnish the truest measurement of income inequality in the Third World.

But the study of income distribution and consumption of goods and services by household yields few significant data if the inequalities that exist inside the home are not taken into account, such as the ratio of productive members to nonproductive, the availability of jobs for women and children, and the authority of the household head in allocating resources. The condition of class is lived through the institution of the family, and the household reproduces the authoritarian relationship between classes under capitalism. In the home there is an exchange of services between family members, related to the respective insertion of each in the labor force. The household head, usually male, is the principal salary earner, and is in many cases freed from household tasks. The female is frequently the only domestic producer of use values. She maintains the home, may engage in domestic production for outsiders, and has the additional task of rearing children. Children are expected to contribute to the household income and concentrate on study to improve family prospects in the next generation. The contribution made by each member to the collective survival of the unit seems to be the decisive element in determining what his or her domestic tasks shall be. The household, in this sense, is an agency by which capitalist relations of production are reproduced outside the workplace.

The division of labor inside the home and the redistribution of income shapes the way workers view themselves and their public role in class society. At first glance, household living puts severe restrictions on the political activity of working families. The head must earn money to provide for the material reproduction of self and household. But remuneration is often not sufficient, and he will join with others in similar predicaments to press for better wages and working conditions. Conflict with the ruling class accentuates the contradiction already present inside the home, pitting the head against those family members dependent on him. The family, in this regard, dissuades collective action on the part of labor against capital. A further impediment to collective political action by labor is that families tend to see their place in the economy as related to access to the means of consumption instead of production. "Since in industrial societies access to consumption and access to production are autonomous activities, linked only at the level of salary, participation in production, despite it being constructed around a fundamental relation, which opposes labor to capital, is evaluated primarily in terms of the salary that it generates."[11] Workers in capitalist societies in the first stages of a developing class consciousness limit their demands on capital to greater purchasing power, and the family household reinforces reformist politics.

There is a distinction, however, between real and possible class consciousness. Real consciousness is effective consciousness—what a social class knows about a given reality during a certain period in a given place. Possible consciousness is the most profound political expression feasible under an existing economic regime and determined historical conditions. "It is the maximum reality a social class can know without clashing with the existing economic and social interests."[12] The family household expands the limits of possible class consciousness. Workers in capitalist society evaluate their economic condition by comparing salary and consumption needs of their household and those of relatives, neighbors, and friends. In this way, working families project their future roles inside the existing socioeconomic order and gain a greater sense of common predicaments.

Class consciousness among workers is also enhanced by the bonds of exploitation. Under capitalism, women and children are incorporated into the workforce alongside men on an individual basis, which would tend to weaken the sense of common identity. Yet proletarianization can also forge new ties between them that were not possible in precapitalist societies. The strong parallels of the fate of all three are clearly evident. The male worker is segregated in his factory; the female, when unemployed, is segregated in the home; and the children, if not working, are segregated at school. The male is supervised by the factory boss; the female, by her husband; and children, by adults. Male workers, women, and children also suffer from unequal access to goods and public services, from education to leisure.[13]

A triangle of social class inequality, male supremacy, and state regulation of domestic life needs to be reinforced if a new generation of workers is to be produced. In modern capitalist society the family supposedly has no political interests apart from the polity, no special qualities or privileges that the state need recognize and respect. A dialectical process is at work whereby the political rights of the family are taken away at the same time that the state insists on the identity and unity of interests of family and polity. The family is relegated to the private sphere, and no longer may family interests be put before those of the state.[14] But while the family is removed from politics, politics is not removed from the family. The growing role of the state in regulating family life under late capitalism is evident, for example, in the Brazilian Civil Code in effect until 1962, which enshrined the rights of the husband over his wife and children. "Prior to 1962 the Civil Code maintained the division of labor, and also gave legal status to the lack of differentiation between the family and the polity. The authority of the state was used to guarantee the continued subordination of Brazilian women."[15] A study of urban poverty must elucidate the ways by which the modern state tries to reproduce the working-class family through legislation, education, religion, and propaganda.

THE BRAZILIAN FAMILY IN HISTORY

Historians may elaborate a set of criteria that enables them to profile the family, but they must resist the temptation to reify their subject. They must abandon the idea that there is a "model" family from which all others diverge, and instead consider how social class, race, gender, geography, and culture combine to reproduce the family. This approach, however, runs against the main trend of family studies in Brazil. Until recently, most studies of the Brazilian family, rather than cataloging the diversity of kinship combinations through time, stressed the continuity and the monolithic character of the patriarchal extended family from the colonial era to the present. Oliveira Vianna, whose work may be taken as representative of modern Brazilian scholarship on the subject, argues that the "senhorial" family served as the organizing principle for colonial laws and political institutions while dismissing the *povo-massa* (rural folk) hinterland, black, and urban plebeian families as unworthy of attention.[16] Treating the patriarchal family and clan in isolation from the rest of society exhibits class and race bias, relegating the vast majority of Brazilians to a mimetic existence. The mechanical application of economic determinism by such scholars also makes us wary. It fails to consider how regional diversity and the outreach of state power influence family formation. Above all, this perspective ignores how sex, race, and class interact in a number of complicated ways to determine family organization.

The proper approach to the history of the Brazilian family is one that takes into account both the constraints on family organization and reproduction imposed by the mode of production, and the creativity of domestic groups in struggling for survival. It must re-create of the environment around the family, weighing such factors as economics, geography, culture, and religion, and then discuss the economic, social, political, and sexual functions of each family member. Historians must also consider alternatives to the predominant form of family organization, such as families composed of unmarried women with children. A summary of the evolution of the Brazilian family from the colonial period, beginning in 1500, to the military coup of 1964 makes clear the contradictions of family formation in underdeveloped societies.[17]

Gilberto Freyre's classic *Casa grande e senzala: Formação da família brasileira sob o regime da economia patriarcal* argued that the patriarchal extended family of the colonial Northeast, which served as the prototype of the modern Brazilian family, was the natural product of an economic regime built around the *engenho* (plantation) and the *fazenda* (large landed estate). Its *raison d' être* was to ensure that landed property remained intact for future generations.The patriarchal family, gathered in the *casa grande* (big house), functioned to pool resources and manpower to develop a vast land that tiny Portugal could not otherwise hold. The family also served as the most important unit of capital and credit in the colony through lending institutions that allowed less prosperous settlers to purchase slaves, oxen, and tools. Wealthy families controlled colonial politics by dominating city councils through nepotism. The patriarchs also fostered the cult of *machismo*, meaning male domination in politics, the martial arts, and religion.

Freyre terms the system of sexual and family life that prevailed among the upper classes in colonial Brazil "polygamous patriarchalism." The master father-husband had an "official family" formed through marriage to a woman from the upper class, plus an "unofficial family" of slaves, mistresses, illegitimate children, male and female relatives, and *agregados*—men and women residing on his property and tied to him by economic bonds and *compradrio* (godparenthood). In this way the master could enjoy sexual pleasure from his slaves, and political obedience from his godchildren and agregados while ensuring the continuity of property ownership.[18]

Freyre's vision is not so much wrong as limited. Like Vianna, he assumed that conditions and practices in the seventeenth-century Northeast formed the model for the rest of Brazil, regardless of class, race, or even geographical differences among the population.[19] But even if we restrict ourselves to the Northeast, significant differences are found in family composition. The white lower class of *lavradores* (small landholders) made up a substantial part of the rural population, a fact ignored by Freyre's dichotomy of the "masters and the slaves." These protoplanters supplied the engenho owners with sugar in return for occupancy of land. Typically, the engenho owner would lease land to sons, nephews, and sons-in-law, and the two families would henceforth be united by blood, money, politics, and compadrio. But the category of lavrador also included Catholic priests, militiamen, converted Jews, and wealthy widows. They constituted an economically important complement to the casa grande that did not copy its lifestyle or family structure.

The same was true of wage workers. Salaried employees who resided on the engenho included professionals with skills necessary to running the plantation, along with lawyers, chaplains, urban agents of the plantation owner, and physicians. The big house might also employ artisans of every sort, from blacksmiths to carpenters and masons, who stayed on the master's premises for the entire year. Unskilled labor was contracted on a short-term basis. Blacks, whites, and *pardos* (mulattoes) were found in all wage categories, as were immigrants. Most wage laborers stayed single for the duration of their service, so that neither monogamous marriage nor "polygamous patriarchy" prevailed among the majority of residents of the big house at any one time.[20]

A large number of Brazilians under the colony and empire, both male and female, belonged to the category of the vagrant poor. These were often recently emancipated men and women without clear legal status. Perhaps half of the Brazilian population of 12 million at the end of the nineteenth century could be so classified. Their ranks included freed slaves, mulattoes, Indians, and other nonwhites. The men were usually migrant workers economically idle for most of the year. Many of the women were prostitutes. Extralegal unions were the norm among this vast group, with common law marriages and consensual unions temporarily linking poor men and women.[21]

Female-headed households, especially among the poor, apparently were more common in colonial and imperial Brazil than was previously thought. Studying the rural areas of the state of São Paulo from 1765 to 1836, Elizabeth Kuznesof found a preponderance of single-headed households, with female-headed households comprising 31.41 percent of the total by 1836. This trend was related to the shift from subsistence to commercial agriculture and the new economic activities open to women in a market economy. There was a definite correlation between family structure and social class. Women who headed households were typically engaged in the least remunerative economic activities, such as sewing, spinning, and quilt making, and matrifocality became more common as economic conditions for working women worsened.[22]

Slaves made up one-third of the Brazilian population at the end of the colonial period, and in this category, too, the historian of the family finds surprises. The instability and disorganization traditionally attributed to slave families may not have existed after all. Slave families were legally recognized under Portuguese law. Slaves could marry slaves or free persons, though interracial marriage was forbidden. Husbands and wives had the right not to be separated at sale, though this did not apply to children and their parents. The Crown had an obvious interest in protecting the slave family and promoting marriage. The family unit was economically more efficient than the lone young bachelor, and there was less likelihood of escape or rebellion on the part of a slave father and husband. Still, given the weakness of Crown authorities in the countryside, which granted virtual autonomy to the fazenda and plantation owners, many married slaves were separated by sale, and slave women were sexually abused.

A greater impediment to slave marriage was demographic imbalance. In most areas of Brazil, male slaves outnumbered females by three or four to one, so that finding an eligible partner for matrimony might take years. In addition, marriage was expensive. The secular clergy often charged high sums for the ceremony. In fact, few slaves were ever married by the Church. Rather, they married with the master's blessing, usually in a ceremony performed according to African or Creole customs. Most slaves, whether born in Africa or the New World, married within their own race and ethnic group. Slave men tended to marry in their late twenties; women did so in their teens or early twenties. On average the male partner was five years older than the female. Mixed marriage was apparently not common. In the province of Minas Gerais, only 12 percent of marriages in the nineteenth century involved members of different races. African-born slaves apparently practiced endogamy as inter-linear marriage was forbidden by custom.[23]

Matrifocal families evidently were common among slaves and emancipated blacks, but this was not a sign of dysfunction or marginalization from the rest of society. Based on evidence extracted from wills and census figures for Vila Rica in the parish of Ouro Preto in Minas Gerais from 1804 to 1838, Donald Ramos found that single females who headed households were usually darker skinned than married women, and ex-slaves were more likely to give birth out of wedlock than white women. But this was not unusual. The great majority of adult free women—white, mulatto, Creole, and African-born—living in the parish in 1804 were not married, and 45 percent of all households were headed by women.[24]

Slaves enlarged the concept of the family by developing kinship ties and pseudo kinship networks to cope with their desperate situation. On the plantation godparenthood and coparenthood, both common to the peoples of Africa, served the purpose of socialization and provided financial aid to the less fortunate. In the large cities the *irmandades* (lay brotherhoods) sponsored by the Catholic Church reinforced such ties and gave slaves, free blacks, and mulattoes a degree of autonomy by permitting them to assemble, gather funds, and elect leaders.[25]

The abolition of slavery in 1888 and the proclamation of the First Republic in 1889 ushered in a new political era, but the economy of Brazil remained bound to agricultural monoculture, and the nation witnessed only a slow degree of urbanization. Yet important changes were underway that transformed family life. The rise of centralized political authority concentrated in political parties and bureaucracies caused the urban family to withdraw from the public sphere to the private. The growth of metropolitan centers, the emergence of a middle class, and greater opportunities to attain an education, at least for males, contributed to a partial loss of patriarchal power over wives and children. The wife's status was strengthened with the gradual disintegration of the "unofficial family" in both countryside and city, but women were still excluded from higher education and lacked many legal rights. This period was also marked by a separation between parents and children, in-laws, and other relatives when it came to living arrangements, visits, celebrations, and ceremonies. But a system of mutual obligations based on bloodlines, friendship, and labor did survive. Meanwhile, the ideal of the European bourgeois nuclear family spread among the upper classes in

Brazil, in part due to the influence of positivism on the elites.[26]

The First Republic also saw the rise of a large rural proletariat formed largely through European immigration and the incorporation of former slaves. The immigrants' attachment to monogamous marriage and paternalistic extended families was introduced into rural Brazil. But this type of family organization no longer fit the needs of Brazilian capitalism. Verena Stolcke has studied nineteenth-century coffee production in the rural areas of São Paulo based on the *colonato*: a task and piece rate system of remuneration. Originally the husband made decisions on how family labor was allocated, following a sexual division of labor. But women enjoyed some say in decisions regarding participation in the workforce and income distribution based on their contribution to the family workload. Following the transition to wage labor, beginning around the turn of the century, the position of women within the family was undermined. Females no longer performed the tasks of food crop cultivation and harvest for family subsistence, and instead became the reserve army of labor for the household, performing occasional wage labor to supplement the husband's income. Wage labor broke the solidarity inside the household of men, women, and children, and between households and kin groups.[27]

For blacks, abolition and the end of the monarchy gave them the freedom to sink to the very bottom of society. Black men in the Northeast lost agricultural jobs in the transition from the plantation to the industrialized sugar factory run on wage labor. At the same time immigrants denied them places on the coffee plantations and in industry. Black women were even worse off. Those who had previously worked in the plantation fields or served as domestics saw their jobs vanish. Many turned to prostitution. The whole period witnessed a decline in their social position vis-a-vis black males. Yet the repercussions for the black family from this tragic state of affairs is subject to great debate. The sociologist Florestan Fernandes asserts that marriage and family organization among blacks following abolition was virtually nonexistent. He claims the cruel heritage of slavery led to an unwillingness to find steady work on the part of black males, instability in male-female relationships, a low value placed on virginity, little inclination to formalize marriage and legalize families, widespread consensual unions, frequent changes of partners, and reliance on extended kinship networks, all of which hindered family formation and community solidarity.[28]

Recent scholarship suggests that black families were more stable than previously supposed. George Reid Andrews, in his study of blacks in São Paulo after 1888, finds a strong attachment to family values, with black marriage rates only slightly lower than for whites before turn of the century. The true obstacles to family formation among blacks derived not from the inherited culture of slavery but from the inability of newly freed men and women to find permanent employment at wages that could support a large household. White racism and the tendency of blacks to fight back against abuses by employers kept blacks on the lowest rungs of society, not any cultural inclination toward family disorganization.[29]

The drive toward modernization in Brazil launched by Getúlio Vargas after 1930 made social class a more important factor than race in determining family structure. The term "modernization" has traditionally been used by historians to mean the process of copying the economic stages of growth experienced by the advanced capitalist countries, an important component of which was the weakening of class inequalities. Yet a more accurate appraisal of the Vargas revolution would see it as the most important step in the formation of a dependent capitalist economy in Brazil, promoting industrialization through close integration with the United States but maintaining the social relations of production of the past largely intact. Modernization has also been taken to include a surge in urbanization, as happened in the United States and Great Britain in the nineteenth century. But whereas in those lands industrialization kept pace with urbanization, in Brazil the latter outran the former. Both these developments, modernization without significant change in social relations and urbanization unmatched by industrialization, were the results of what was earlier termed the uneven and combined development of the Brazilian economy. The consequences for family structure among the upper, middle and rural and urban working classes were profound.[30]

The industrialization and urbanization of Brazil brought about a shrinkage in household size in all social classes, but for different reasons. Increased social mobility for men and greater educational opportunities for women, along with more frequent practice of birth control, seem to have been decisive for the white middle and upper classes, while the need to reduce expenses to keep up with inflation was the major factor for low-income groups. But the function and structure of the family varied by economic condition. Upper-class families maintained extended structures because of modernization. Industrialization did not weaken the hold of the landed oligarchy over the economy, since in many cases that oligarchy successfully fused with the industrial bourgeoisie. Large kinship networks were still necessary to obtain jobs for family members, because competition for employment was more fierce in the city than in the countryside. The centralization and bureaucratization of the political system under Vargas did not significantly dilute clientelism but in some ways made family connections more important for attaining political office. Urbanization did not cause upper-class families to break off extended kinship ties but in some cases made them more valuable than before in keeping property and political influence intact.[31]

The imbalance between industrialization and urbanization also led to complex kinship arrangements among the middle class. Members of the middle class entered into marriage more freely than did the upper classes, for whom economic considerations still limited the choice of partner. Legal marriages became common among the middle class in part to gain access to city services. Husbands and wives now partook of cultural activities together, in contrast to the segregation practiced in the countryside. The middle-class wife assumed greater independence within the household thanks to easier access to education and the entry of large numbers of females into the workforce. Still, the husband maintained legal control over property, and divorce and abortion were strictly forbidden. The bourgeois nuclear family thus took the form of a conjugal rather than an economic unit, but with important restrictions on the liberty of the wife.

The complete breakup of the extended family among the urban middle class, predicted by modernization theorists in view of similar developments in the advanced capitalist countries, did not happen in Brazil. Family connections were especially important to second generation jobseekers and aspirants to political office. The extended family did not disappear but was instead modified. Even if members were no longer living under the same roof, the extended family could be kept alive through the use of the automobile and the telephone. For those in the middle class who did shed the extended family, solidarity between nuclear families living in the same neighborhood replaced kinship networks.[32]

The urban working class of Brazil, white, black, and pardo, grew tremendously as a result of the rural exodus that followed the Great Depression of 1929. Among the migrant poor living in the city, marriage was more unstable than in the countryside. One important reason is that in Brazil, individual migration by males was the common pattern, in contrast to the migration of whole families then occurring in countries like Mexico. The failure of many migrants to fully integrate with the city and the obstacles to social mobility made formal marriage impractical. Few workers had the material resources to commit themselves to the maintenance of an entire family for a lifetime. Consequently, it was not uncommon for the migrant husband to have two families, the "official" one left behind in the village of his birth, including wife and children, and the "unofficial" one formed in the city. The "unofficial" family functioned much like the legally constituted family, but with a greater degree of separation, polygamy, polyandry, and informal divorce. Consensual unions were common between members of the urban working class, as was religious marriage without a civil ceremony. But whether in a formal or an informal arrangement, the nuclear family prevailed among urban workers. The absence of property eliminated the need to preserve an inheritance. The loss of access to land weakened extended family ties. Land in the countryside had served not only to feed the family but also as the focal point for group identity and aspirations, a function lost in the urban world. The geographical mobility of urban workers also favored nuclearization. Employers valued urban workers for their capacity to shift from one job site to another, weakening any sense of family identification with the home. The living arrangements available to the migrants in slums and favelas contained no room for extended families, as did the shantytowns of rural Brazil. The "freedom" to sell one's labor power gave the worker greater liberty in family structures, undermining the sense of obligation to distant family members. Finally, the whole purpose of the rural exodus was anti family. Migrants were drawn to the city in part because the government promised to provide education, health care, and recreation facilities—all activities performed by the family in the countryside. If the extended family survived among urban workers, it did so by splitting into rural and urban branches, or by loosening the ties that joined members, so that fewer activities were undertaken in common.[33]

In rural Brazil, upper-class families continued to dominate the economic, political, and social scene from their great estates even after 1930. Though the household consisting of three generations living under one roof was a thing of the past, intralocal family networks remained as strong as ever. Interlocal connections, however, weakened as the growth of cities in the interior led to fewer contacts between kin and closer identification between individuals and urban institutions.

Two factors nevertheless assured family stability. First, almost all family members were born locally, and by custom newlyweds continued to reside for a time either on the family premises or in the same neighborhood. Second, nearly all the great families could trace their genealogy and property rights back for several centuries, so that property considerations remained important in keeping the family intact. But even within the upper class household, socioeconomic forces were at work that undermined the extended family. Income growth provided the means, and the growth of cities nearby the opportunity, to pursue work and other activities outside the home. Interestingly, in one famous case study of upper-class families in rural São Paulo, Oracy Nogueira found that it was the elderly, and not young people, who often opted to leave the household for permanent residence in hotels and boardinghouses as soon as they gained sources of income besides the dole of the patriarch.[34]

Closer integration with the market and the city also caused disruption in white, black, and pardo lower-class rural families. The *caipira* (rural poor) extended family survived, but many of the practices that had held it together in the past were deteriorating. Contract for work on an individual basis was the principal reason for decay, but other factors were at work as well. The *mutirão*, the tradition of mutual help among country folk, gradually disappeared in competition with wage labor. Housing elderly relatives and agregados in one place was now much less frequent. But patriarchal conditions still prevailed among many of the rural poor. Marriage in many cases was decided by parents. For economic reasons, matrimony was still a must for rural girls, but less so for young men, who had the option of working in the city. In some cases, as the extended family crumbled compradrio took its place, and these ties were often transferred to urban areas after migration.[35]

CONCLUSION

This brief sketch of the evolution of the Brazilian family sets the backdrop for an analysis of favela households. This study is an attempt to combine family, urban, and labor history to understand the reproduction of poverty in an underdeveloped country. It cannot be supposed that any one type of household structure corresponds to an underdeveloped capitalist economy, but there are links between under-development and the family that the historian must explore. Mariza Correa sketches the outlines of such an approach. "There is nothing to indicate that forms of family organization mechanically follow the dominant line of economic and social development of a region. It is necessary to study in detail the intricate ways in which political, economic and social forms articulate themselves and interweave. Family organization may complement an economic trend or it may contradict it."[36]

Research on the family and development in advanced capitalist societies provides no simple answer to the complexities of the relationship between family and economy. Peter Laslett argues that industrialization in Western Europe had no significant impact on family size. Eli Zaretsky holds that families grew smaller as factory work replaced domestic labor. Michael Anderson's study of nineteenth-century Lancashire led him to conclude that industrialization may actually lead to an increase in family size, depending on patterns of rural migration to the cities and wage levels. Turning this argument on its head, William Goode proposes that the nuclear family preceded and aided the process of industrialization.[37] But all agree that the connection of the family to the economy cannot be understood without reference to the various social classes that constitute modern capitalism. Brazilian sociologist Carmen Cinida Macedo concurs: "The analysis of the family should encompass an identification of the real practice of various classes, and reconstituting such practice by reference to the whole [of society], gain an understanding of the particular meaning family life assumes in each case."[38] It is impossible to comprehend the condition of the working class in Brazil without reference to the family. It would be equally futile to study the family in Brazil without analyzing how the family is enmeshed in the relations of production. What follows is an analysis of the political economy of Rio de Janeiro during the era of favela formation from 1930 to 1960, in order to comprehend the economic background of family formation among the Carioca poor.

2

The City

Successful family formation was made difficult for many workers in Rio de Janeiro after 1930 due to shrinking job opportunities and worsening living conditions. The contradictions in the economic development of Rio de Janeiro from 1930 to 1960 and the forging of the proletariat and subproletariat who populated the favelas are the twin themes of this chapter. It is my purpose to show that squatter settlements were the natural outcome of the industrialization of Rio de Janeiro and of the inability of industry, commerce, and the service sector to provide enough jobs for a burgeoning population. The working class in Rio grew to massive numbers as a result of the rural exodus that began after the depression of 1929 and the installation of the Getúlio Vargas regime following the revolution of 1930. But the chances of finding steady work at a salary sufficient to provide for a family actually decreased during this time. The most important development in the labor force was the formation of an informal working class. This subproletariat was an unorganized segment of the labor force confined to sporadic participation in the job market at unskilled and low-wage work, shuttling back and forth between the formal and informal economies. How this came to pass is comprehensible only when the economic history of Rio de Janeiro is examined from the perspective of the global, national, and local economies. Ultimately, it was Brazil's place in the international division of labor that denied hundreds of thousands of men and women full-time participation in the workforce of Rio de Janeiro and forced them to live in shantytowns.

UNEVEN AND COMBINED DEVELOPMENT

The creation of a world market during the age of European expansionism reoriented the subsistence economies of Asia, Africa, and Latin America toward agroexport production. Raw materials from the periphery were then unequally exchanged for European manufactured goods. This process is termed "uneven development." The peripheral regions henceforth had to adopt the economic features of the advanced nations in order to secure a place in the global market. Their economic survival depended on skipping historical stages through the import of technology from the core nations. Yet peripheral nations remained poor because only the export sector was developed; the backward subsistence sector was not eradicated but combined with the modern in a parasitic relationship. This phenomenon is termed "combined development": the interweaving of capitalist and precapitalist modes of production, expressed in property relations by the alliance of the industrial bourgeoisie with agrarian interests.[1]

Industrialization in the periphery has central features different from those of the core region. The modern industrial sector develops with a heavy dose of foreign investment. This sector provides a higher rate of return than industry in the advanced countries. The state also plays a greater role in industrial investment than in comparable phases of development in Europe and North America. The relationship of class forces explains the peculiarities of peripheral industrialization. A cheap industrial labor force gives peripheral production comparative advantage in competition with the developed nations; hence low living standards are a necessity for industrialization. Furthermore, industrial technology imported from the advanced countries is capital-intensive; it will not absorb the masses of the unemployed but will increase their number. Consumer goods in the periphery are mostly for purchase by the upper-income strata and imported to the detriment of domestic industry. As a result, the bulk of the population is shut out of the domestic consumer market, and the income gap between rich and poor will grow over time. The working population, excluded from both job and consumer markets, must be detached from politics as well. There is a strong connection between peripheral industrialization and authoritarianism, as evidenced in Chile under Augusto Pinochet in the 1970s and South Korea's military dictatorship of the 1960s.[2]

Brazil after 1930 offers an interesting case study of peripheral industrialization. State intervention in the economy under President Getúlio Vargas (1930–1945) paved the way for a new model of capital accumulation called import-substitution industrialization (ISI). Agroexports were the scaffolding of industrialization under Vargas. The maintenance of latifundia served ISI by providing cheap food to the urban masses and denying land to rural workers, who were forced to flee to the cities looking for work. But this rural exodus did not result in the formation of a large class of wage laborers, as happened during the industrial revolution in the advanced countries. The 1930s and 1940s in Brazil instead witnessed higher employment growth in the tertiary sector because ISI could not provide enough industrial jobs for the urban poor. The failure of industrialization in Brazil to create a large labor force with steady jobs is a case of incomplete proletarianization. This development forced a revival of the informal urban economy, featuring part-time work in petty production and services. The informal labor sector, with its high rates of unemployment and underemployment, lowered the cost of reproduction to capital by further depressing wages. Brazil from 1930 to 1960 experienced urbanization without full industrialization, and the growth of an informal labor market alongside without full industrialization, and the growth of an informal labor market alongside the formal.[3]

WHERE IS RIO DE JANEIRO?

The importance of Rio de Janeiro in Brazilian economic history makes it a prime showcase of uneven and combined development in the Third World. On New Year's Day of 1502, Portuguese sailors entered Guanabara Bay, and mistakenly thinking they had come across the mouth of a large river, called the new land Rio de Janeiro. The confusion on the part of the mariners was quite natural. The boundaries and status of Rio de Janeiro have shifted with time. Permanent settlement of the city dates to 1565. The Portuguese Crown declared Rio the seat of the Viceroyalty of Brazil in 1763, replacing Salvador de Bahia. During the Brazilian Empire (1822–1889) the city of Rio de Janeiro was detached from the state of Rio de Janeiro and converted into a "neutral municipality" to serve as the imperial capital. Following the proclamation of the first republic in 1889, this municipality was renamed the Federal District and administered separately from the other states. Rio retained the function of national capital until 1960, when President Juscelino Kubitscheck inaugurated the new capital in Brasilia. Rio de Janeiro then became the state of Guanabara, and maintained that status until 1975 when it once again fused with the state of Rio de Janeiro.

A review of nomenclature is insufficient to locate the city of Rio de Janeiro. A definition is required that takes into account geoeconomic areas as well as political and juridical boundaries. For the sake of discussion the urban areas of modern Rio may be divided into three parts. *Centro* (the downtown section) corresponds roughly to the areas of settlement during the colonial and imperial periods. In 1960 Centro housed a decrepit industrial base and highly dispersed artisan activity, but still monopolized city services. The rich and the middle class had long since abandoned the downtown district, and most of the remaining inhabitants were of modest means. A majority of the city's working class residents lived in *Zona Norte* (the north), where older industries were still located. *Zona Sul* (the south), containing the neighborhoods of Copacabana, Leblon, and Ipanema, was the favored place of residence of the Carioca middle class. Beyond the three urban zones lay metropolitan Rio de Janeiro, covering all the territory that furnished the city with foodstuffs, raw materials, and migrant labor for industry. Metropolitan Rio encompassed all of urban Rio, suburban satellite cities such as Nova Iguaçu, and its geoeconomic pull stretched into substantial parts of the states of Rio de Janeiro, Espírito Santo and Minas Gerais.[4]

RIO DE JANEIRO 1565–1930: PATTERNS OF PRODUCTION

The economic history of Rio de Janeiro offers fine proof of Napoleon's dictum that "geography is destiny." No factor has been more influential in determining the course of the city's growth than its position as an entry point for imported goods from Europe and a funnel for raw materials from the Brazilian interior.[5] Guanabara Bay served for three centuries as a docking station for Portuguese ships going to and from the New World. Shortly after the founding of Rio in 1565, the first sugar plantations were established on the outskirts of the city. Present-day reminders of the early sugar industry are neighborhood names like Engenho Novo and Engenho Velho. The plantations naturally needed manpower, which was soon supplied from Africa. To protect these prosperous holdings, the Crown erected a fort, called Castelo de Morro, near the town to defend Portuguese America from further attacks by the French and Spanish. Thus almost from the moment of birth, Rio de Janeiro attained certain advantages it has not lost to this day: a military garrison to protect Brazil, cash crops, a modicum of industry, and a locus for human settlement.

During the early colonial era most of the population lived next to the Castelo de Morro. Early inhabitants also occupied the area along the beach close to the hill later called Pão de Açúcar (Sugar Loaf). The geographic growth of the city during the first century of settlement followed a spider-web pattern, curving around the hills. (As late as 1960, one-fifth of Rio de Janeiro was classified as "mountainous.") After 1700 the population slowly spread from the Castelo to the valleys as the development of the sugar industry and the influx of African slaves meant that the area around Castelo de Morro could no longer contain the population. During the eighteenth century the backland of Rio de Janeiro was opened to human occupation and city limits were extended to Zona Norte. But Rio still lacked adequate transportation, paved streets, and lighting. Epidemics of malaria and yellow fever took a toll of hundreds each year.[6]

The mining boom of the early eighteenth century, situated in Minas Gerais, transformed Rio from a sleepy "city-cape" into one of Latin America's largest metropolises. The city served as a port of exit for gold and diamonds from Minas and as a port of entry for foodstuffs, clothing, and tools from Europe, and, most important, slaves from Africa. The Crown registered the shift in the economic axis of Brazil from the decadent Northeast to the vibrant Southeast when it designated Rio de Janeiro as the new vice-regal capital in 1763.

The collapse of the mining surge after 1760 caused a return to agricultural activity in Rio de Janeiro province, this time concentrated on coffee, and numerous plantations soon sprang up in the highlands region surrounding the city, the Planalto Fluminense.[7] Coffee cultivation drew thousands of Brazilians to the Southeast in the next decades, and Rio overtook Salvador de Bahia as Brazil's largest urban center in 1800. After the arrival of the Portuguese royal family, fleeing Bonaparte's troops, in 1808, all Brazilian ports were thrown open to foreign commerce, a gesture bound to benefit the new capital above all rivals. Most imports now passed through Guanabara Bay first.

The presence of the royal family made Rio Brazil's gateway to the world. Portuguese, French, and British merchants set up commercial houses, and new homes were built for João VI's courtiers. The Braganças promoted newspapers, schools, libraries, the Botanical Gardens, museums, and theaters. Rio became the imperial capital following the proclamation of independence by Dom Pedro I in 1822, and the city enjoyed another golden age. It was now both the leading port and the leading commercial center of the new empire; 422 ships called at Guanabara Bay that year.

Dom Pedro's heir, Pedro II, ordered a facelift for his capital, starting with a public cleaning campaign in 1852. Gas lighting replaced the old street lights, and the sewage system was renovated. Telegraph, submarine cable, and telephone linked Rio to Paris and Washington, D.C., by the end of the century. The commercial district located in Centro gained new roads—Ruas Direita, Ouvidor, Gonçalves Dias, and Assembleia. The building of the Dom Pedro II railroad (1854) was another sign of new times.[8]

Dom Pedro II may have been the emperor in politics, but coffee was still monarch of the economy. King Coffee needed machines to secure his reign. By the 1870s numerous small railroads linked Rio to the food-growing area of Campos in the backlands of the city, the Fluminense coffee cultivation zone, and the southern part of the state of Espírito Santo. In later decades the expansion of major lines like the Estrada de Ferro Dom Pedro II and the creation of dozens of minor ones joined Rio de Janeiro to Minas Gerais and São Paulo. Rio's stranglehold reached all the way north to Paraíba, where the sugar industry became a satellite of the Fluminense coffee interests. At the proclamation of the republic in 1889, Rio de Janeiro was not only Brazil's largest city but also boasted the nation's biggest port, the largest commercial, financial, and industrial center, and the most coveted consumer market, and remained crowned as the national capital.

One item from this impressive list is evident by omission. While Rio still led the nation in population in 1889, it did not posses Brazil's largest labor force. That distinction went to São Paulo, which housed the vast majority of European immigrants coming to Brazil after 1850. Migrants also flocked to São Paulo from Minas Gerais and the Northeast states, and many of them found work in the coffee lands, textile factories, and workshops of the "locomotive" of the Brazilian economy. Rio de Janeiro could not replicate this feat. The capital could promise migrants beauty, sophistication, and scenery but not a large number of industrial jobs. As late as 1893 the Federal District led the nation in the number of industrial firms—some 300 were counted that year, compared with 121 in São Paulo. But by 1920 São Paulo had captured first place in industrial production, and twenty years later it had twice the output of Rio de Janeiro. Manufacturing workers made up only 30 percent of Rio's labor force in 1920, and factory laborers just 10 percent. Rather than becoming part of the proletariat, migrants who came to Rio found unsteady jobs in day labor—chiefly construction, domestic service, and commerce.[9]

There is no doubt that internal migration was the biggest contributing factor to the city's growth. The first half of the twentieth century saw a pattern of population growth that was steady if unspectacular. Rio contained a population of 811,443 residents in 1906, and grew to 1,157,800 by 1920. At the peak of industrialization in 1940, the city's population rose to 1,764,100, and it stood at 2,377,400 in 1950. The influx of the rural poor was responsible for the constant increase of population. In 1950, 929,000 residents (48 percent of the population) of urban Rio had been born outside the city.[10]

SLUGGISH INDUSTRIALIZATION: 1930–1960

One of the foremost ironies of Brazilian history is that while the nation's productive forces expanded, the importance of the capital city within the national economy declined, completely the opposite of what occurred in Mexico and Argentina. What accounts for this? In one word, coffee. Cultivation in the Planalto Fluminense went into a tailspin at the end of the nineteenth century while coffee planting reached record heights in São Paulo state. The first Paulista industries were built with profits from coffee; the same class alliance of planters and industrialists could not be forged in Rio for lack of a viable cash crop. In the 1920s many coffee producers in the Planalto Fluminense shifted to citrus fruits to save their farms.[11]

But the state of Rio de Janeiro still supplied the city with coffee revenues, and when prices plummeted after the Great Depression of 1929, Rio de Janeiro's productive capacity was cut in half. The city faced a balance of payments deficit of 36 million pounds, and the circulation of money dropped by 17.5 percent. Government revenue fell by 20 percent in 1929. By 1930 there were a reported 40,000 jobless in the Federal District. Wages had fallen by 15 percent, and an estimated 35,000 persons a month left the city in search of jobs elsewhere.[12] Since exports were the lifeblood of the country, the federal government's first priority during the crisis was to rescue the coffee planters of São Paulo. Rio's industrialists did not oppose the policy of support for coffee prices begun by the Vargas regime after 1930, but pointed out that industrial recovery was equally necessary if Brazil was to solve its balance of payments deficit. Brazil now had to produce many consumer items previously imported by the middle and upper classes. Their demands were fulfilled by the Provisional Government (1930–1934) which channeled additional credit to Carioca industry through the Bank of Brazil.

By 1940 the effects of ISI on the economy of Rio de Janeiro were plain to see. Capital investment was concentrated primarily in electricity, gas, and refrigeration rather than textiles, which had dominated industry in the nineteenth century. Yet textiles still consumed the greatest amount of horsepower of all Rio industries, illustrating the backward nature of industrial technology even in the late 1930s.[13] Production of textiles, foodstuffs, leather items, and furniture was carried out only in part by organized industry; the majority of industrial work in the city was still done by artisans and small-scale manufacturers. During the early stage of ISI, which stressed production of light consumer goods, high growth rates were found both in the modern industrial sector—mechanical industry and chemicals—and in the more traditional branches of industry, such as textiles, bottling, and furniture.

The prevalence of backward technology did not prevent industry in Rio from acquiring certain traits associated with the economies of the advanced capitalist countries. While productive techniques remained bound in an earlier time, there was an important shift in property relations. As a consequence of economic growth, capital became concentrated in fewer hands. A study by the Instituto Brasileiro de Geografia e Estatística conducted during 1944–1945 revealed that the number of firms in key areas of industrial life in Rio was beginning to shrink. In the food industry the number of establishments fell from from 775 to 479 in the years

1940–1944, and a similar decline occurred in bottling, chemicals, and furniture.[14]

But contrary to the experience of the developed countries, industrialization and monopolization in Rio de Janeiro failed to produce a significant increase in the size of the labor force. The number of industries in Rio grew from 4,169 in 1939 to 5,693 in 1950, and the value of industrial production rose by 1.3 times. But the number of industrial workers did not increase in proportion to industrial growth. Rio had an industrial workforce of 123,459 in 1939, but just 171,463 in 1950, and only a small fraction of industries employed 100 workers or more.[15]

The prospects for industrial employment did not brighten with time. Due to the lack of sufficient financial capital and industrial infrastructure, Rio de Janeiro was unable to make the leap into the second or "heavy" phase of ISI during the 1950s, when capital goods and durable consumer products replaced light industry in output. Industry made up one-fifth of the Federal District's gross product in 1955, compared with the tertiary sector's 80 percent share. (Agriculture had dropped to an insignificant 0.85 percent.)[16] Chemicals and pharmaceuticals were the most important industries, with 4,745,587 cruzeiros invested, and textiles ranked second. If industry is measured by the number of workers employed, a different picture emerges. Textiles led with 29,239 workers followed by clothing, transformation of nonmetallic minerals, and chemicals and pharmaceuticals.[17]

Industrialization, however stunted, changed the face of the city. Every year after 1930, industrial firms moved further from the core of Rio toward the periphery. The central area ceased to be an important zone of industrial activity by the end of the 1940s. Rents in Centro were too high, and little space was available to house modern factories. What industry remained in downtown consisted mainly of small-scale enterprises dedicated to sewing and shoemaking, furniture manufacturing, publishing and graphics, and metallurgy establishments dating to before World War I.[18] The suburbs were the growth area for industry in Rio during this decade. The areas of heaviest activity were found along the Avenida Brasil, Avenida das Bandeiras, and the Rio d'Ouro railroad, which ran alongside the recently constructed Presidente Dutra Highway.

Physical relocation could not obscure the fact that industry in Rio de Janeiro had become stagnant. The 1960 census showed that the number of industrial establishments, 5,306, was virtually unchanged since 1950. The value of industrial production was 114.4 billion cruzeiros, of which 56.2 billion was concentrated in the transformation industry. The number of industrial workers had declined to 140,711. Salaries in the city totaled 17.5 billion cruzeiros, but only 11.8 billion went to industrial workers. The movement of industry toward the suburbs picked up pace during the 1950s. The district of Engenho Novo in Zona Norte had the largest number of industrial establishments in 1960, 461, with a production value of 12.9 billion cruzeiros; São Cristóvão held second place, with 385 establishments and a production value of 20.9 billion cruzeiros. Just over 16,000 workers were employed in each district. New industries emerged by 1960 in the peripheral satellite cities of Niterói, São Gonçalo, Duque de Caxias, and Nova Iguaçu.[19]

Brazil enjoyed one of the highest industrial growth rates in the world after World War II, registering an increase of 162 percent from 1948 to 1962.[20] The two main factors that made this possible were the huge influx of foreign investment into Brazil to promote the second stage of ISI, and the migration of laborers from the Northeast of the country to the Southeast. São Paulo benefited from both these developments, but Rio could gain only from the latter. Comparing Rio and São Paulo in their degree of participation in the Brazilian gross national product, the Federal District accounted for 15.48 percent of the GNP in 1948, compared with 45.40 percent for the state of São Paulo. (For statistical purposes the city and state of São Paulo were indistinguishable when measuring industry during this period.) But by 1960 only 9.66 percent of Brazil's GNP came from Rio, whereas São Paulo contributed 54.29 percent.[21]

UNEQUAL DEVELOPMENT: COMMERCE AND SERVICES, 1930–1960

Rio de Janeiro remained Brazil's commercial capital until the end of World War II and from 1939 to 1949 the total value of commerce—wholesale and retail —rose by 5.2 times. From 1950 to 1955, Rio was responsible for an estimated 16 to 20 percent of all commercial activity in Brazil. The number of commercial establishments at the start of the 1950s was 2,510, employing a total of 134,000 people.[22] Rio still led São Paulo in important sectors of wholesale commerce, such as electrical appliances, paper, and general merchandise, while São Paulo had pulled away in the sale of foodstuffs. But by 1957 Rio de Janeiro's participation in national commerce dropped to 15 percent, less than half of São Paulo's share.[23]

The process of monopolization that occurred in agriculture and industry also took place in commercial activity. In retail trade the number of establishments jumped from 11,500 to 15,612 and the value of sales increased by 6.3 times. Yet most retail firms remained small-scale, with capital invested averaging between 5,000 to 25,000 cruzeiros. In wholesale commerce the number of enterprises rose by 2.6 times while sales value went up by 5.8 times. Meanwhile, the medium-size firm was nearly driven out of existence.[24]

Rio's participation in the national service sector also declined steadily after World War II. In 1939 the tertiary sector in the Federal District claimed 23.68 percent of the total for Brazil, but this fell to 19.25 percent by 1960.[25] The single most important reason for this decline was the contraction of industry in Rio and the flow of investments to São Paulo, but other factors also came into play, among them competition for services from the states of Rio de Janeiro and Minas Gerais and new trade routes linking previously detached areas of the Southeast, allowing other cities to bypass Rio. Finally, the relocation of the nation's capital to Brasília on April 21, 1960, deprived Rio of the status of Federal District, causing it to lose personnel and money.

DYNAMICS OF CAPITAL, 1930–1960

The uneven development of the productive forces in Rio de Janeiro is evident from a review of the economic history of the city from 1930 to 1960; what fate provided with one hand, she took away with the other. The virtual disappearance of the coffee crop was mitigated by the successful transition to citrus products, but at the expense of the small farmer still mired in poverty. Industry made a healthy recovery from the depression of 1929 and took advantage of the first stage of ISI, only to stagnate after World War II. Commerce took a sharp drop following the war, but at the same time services expanded to fill new consumer needs. Yet Rio's place in the national service sector was eventually undermined by São Paulo and new rivals like Belo Horizonte. The removal of the federal capital to Brasília in 1960 was, if not a death knell for the city, a warning buzzer reminding Cariocas that Rio's best days lay far behind.

The combined features of economic growth in Rio are equally apparent. As one observer noted in the early 1960s, "besides churches and houses from the eighteenth and nineteenth centuries we are likely to find the great buildings of the twentieth century and, around the backyard gardens and small commercial houses that recall old Rio, we behold the great shops and firms all adopting the most modern methods of work."[26] This is an excellent metaphor for the complex web of Rio's economic life. In agriculture, outmoded methods of production were put to service for the benefit of the few large landowners. The backcountry and the surrounding region of Rio de Janeiro state fed the city's workers and thereby helped drive down the costs of reproducing the urban labor force. Thus a backward agricultural sector complemented a modern industrial sector. Industry in Rio was closely intertwined with the tertiary sector, and one of the advantages the city could still offer investors was its location as an administrative, military, and cultural center. The contraction of industry following World War II, and Rio's loss of status as Federal District, therefore had harmful but not fatal consequences for both industrial and service sectors.

RURAL EXODUS AND THE FORMATION OF THE SUBPROLETARIAT

The greatest gift Rio de Janeiro could offer Brazilian capitalists after 1930 was its impoverished masses desperate for work. A new Carioca working class was formed in the years following the Great Depression, as a consequence of the migration of hundreds of thousands of farm laborers from the interior of Brazil and the stupendous population growth in both countryside and cities throughout the nation (see Table 2.1). The state of Rio de Janeiro was the single largest source of laborers for the Federal District, and its economy demonstrated the decadence of the old agrarian regime and the causes of the flight of labor to the metropolises. The total land area cultivated in Rio de Janeiro dropped from 696,294 hectares in 1938 to 345,612 in 1947, a decline of 48.65 percent. Productivity by hectare suffered as rice cultivation fell from 1,386 to 1,303 kilos between 1945 and 1947, and sugarcane production declined from 58 to 52 tons. The crisis of agriculture in Rio de Janeiro state was attributable to a number of factors, ranging from the low degree of mechanization and labor-intensive methods of harvest to intolerable health conditions and physical exhaustion of the field hands, low prices for farm products, an inadequate transport system for agricultural goods, and the flow of laborers to the city, which acted as both cause and effect of rural decadence. Few of those who came to the city of Rio de Janeiro had owned land at home. *Lavrador* (agricultural worker) was the most common occupation stamped on their identity documents.[27]

Relocation to the city did not result in the complete incorporation of the landless laborers into the urban working class. Only a small number became full-time salaried workers with a signed labor card. Most earned only the minimum monthly salary or less. Their usual occupations were construction jobs for males and domestic service for females. The best way to describe them is to call them a subproletariat. The surge of industry in Rio de Janeiro under the Vargas regime, actually enlarged their ranks, and subsequent periods of economic growth that exaggerated income divisions between rural and urban areas of Brazil brought new recruits.

Table 2.1

Natural and Migratory Increase in Population of the Federal District and the Seven Major State Capitals, 1940–1950

Capital	Increase in Population	
	Natural	Migratory
Rio de Janeiro (F.D.)	175,764	437,546
São Paulo	239,553	632,282
Recife	42,551	133,707
Salvador	37,121	89,671
Belo Horizonte	41,867	99,480
Porto Alegre	34,088	87,831
Fortaleza	33,080	56,904
Belém	34,575	14,043

Source: Mortara, "O Aumento da população das grandes cidades do Brasil entre 1940 e 1950."

The distinction among the proletariat, the lumpen proletariat, and the subproletariat is crucial for understanding urban poverty in Rio de Janeiro and the growth of the favelas. The formal economy in Rio de Janeiro grew just enough from the 1930s onward to attract migrants to the city and offer a portion of them permanent employment. These laborers composed the urban proletariat of Rio de Janeiro: textile workers, stevedores, bottlers, and others who enjoyed permanent employment, steady wages, and after 1940 a guaranteed monthly minimum salary. The lumpen proletariat, men and women engaged in criminal activity like gambling and prostitution, flourished far from the favelas in the core of the metropolis, where tourists and workers with disposable income could sustain them. Although newspaper accounts of the period made it seem that Rio was infested with criminals, the lumpen proletariat did not become a significant segment of the shantytown population until the 1970s.

Subproletarians were workers obliged to sell their labor as a commodity to survive, but they lacked job security, steady wages, and union organization. They were found in both the formal and the informal economies. These workers held a strategic position in the accumulation of capital in Rio de Janeiro by indirectly lowering the costs of the reproduction of the wage force to the bourgeoisie through holding salaries down for the entire working class. Subproletarian females performed a direct service to the middle class through domestic services, freeing their female employers to seek work. The men often worked at construction jobs that did not require social security or insurance payments by their bosses. The combination of transience of employment and rising inflation led the subproletariat to erect the first large favelas in Rio de Janeiro.

THE LABOR FORCE IN RIO DE JANEIRO 1930–1960:
THE UNMAKING OF A WORKING CLASS

The economic growth of Rio de Janeiro from 1930 to 1960 produced radical and unexpected shifts in the structure of the labor force. Industrialization failed to create a large working class of permanent laborers, as it had in the developed world. During these three decades the rate of absorption of the potentially active population into the economically active population (EAP) declined. From 1940 to 1960 at least 40 percent of all persons over the age of ten in Rio de Janeiro were economically inactive in any given year. In 1940, 100 economically active inhabitants over the age of ten were responsible for 155 inactive ones; the number climbed to 179 in 1960. Industry, services, and commerce accounted for 64 percent of Rio's EAP in 1940 but only 52 percent by 1960. Industrial employment grew by only 2 percent from 1940 to 1960. Commerce and merchandising showed only moderate annual growth in employment, averaging 1.83 percent a year in the same period.

The informal economy of Rio de Janeiro provided most of the new jobs after 1940. The three branches of the EAP with the highest rates of annual growth in employment from 1940 to 1960, besides national defense, were "rendering of services" at 2.35 percent, "social activities" at 6 percent, and "other activities" at 6.8 percent. While in 1940 only 10 percent of the EAP were engaged in "social activities" or "other activities," this figure doubled by 1960. The informal labor force was a result of the deindustrialization of the city and the impoverishment of many working-class families. In order to meet the consumer demands of a growing low-income population, a fairly sizable goods and services industry arose in Rio de Janeiro that churned out locally produced consumer products. The *biscate* (informal labor sector) was nonproletarian and noncapitalist. Its participants did not own the means of production but also did not sell their labor power on a daily basis. The *biscateiros* were small-scale producers who worked at everything from merchandising to repair services, and their remuneration usually was payment in kind. The tiny purchasing power of their clientele ensured that they could never get rich. But they did not leave the labor force. Most biscateiros combined irregular part-time work with small business activities on the side.

The sexual division of labor in Rio de Janeiro also showed some interesting variations compared with the advanced capitalist countries. Industry employed one-fifth of the male EAP between 1940 and 1960. When commerce and services are added to industry, by 1960 over half of the male EAP in Rio was employed in these sectors. But in 1940 over 60 percent of the female EAP was employed in "rendering services"; and although the figure declined to 50 percent in 1960, when "social activities" are added to industry and services, three-quarters of all females were employed in these three sectors that year. Thus, while women were concentrated mainly in the tertiary sector, the variety of jobs in that sector made the female labor force more heterogeneous than the male.

Fewer Cariocas were entering the ranks of the working class during this generation. Participation in the EAP declined for both sexes from 1940 to 1960. In 1940, 60.5 percent of the male population of Rio was economically active, but this figure dropped to 54.7 percent in 1960. Female participation stood at 17.8 percent in 1940, rose to 20 percent in 1950, and dropped to 18.5 percent by 1960. Increased opportunities for schooling may have played a part by removing young men and women from the labor force, but the biggest cause for the drop in economic activity was the inability of the city to absorb new workers of either sex—hurling them toward the subproletariat.

The decline in participation in the EAP by both sexes must be qualified by the factor of age. Many male migrants from the countryside were joining the ranks of the unemployed and underemployed. Among those fifteen to nineteen years old, 55 percent were economically active in 1940 but only 39 percent in 1960. But those aged twenty to twenty-four, with more time in Rio de Janeiro, registered an increase in participation from 77.5 percent in 1940 to 80.5 percent in 1960 and the twenty to thirty-four age group went from 94.1 percent to 96.25 percent participation. The female EAP saw a decline in economic activity among ages of ten to nineteen as more young women entered school. But except for a brief surge in the 1950s, there was virtually no change in economic activity in the twenty-to-twenty-four age category; 34.5 percent of all females in this age group were economically active in 1940 and 35.5 percent in 1960. Among those aged twenty-five to thirty-four, there was an increase from 25 percent in 1940 to 30 percent in 1960. Rising male unemployment and the drop in real wages due to inflation, discussed below, apparently led many older married women to join the labor force. The percentage of women aged forty-five to sixty-four who were economically active in Rio de Janeiro grew from 17.9 percent in 1940 to 22.1 percent in 1960. Still, women never held a majority of jobs in any employment sector, and five men joined the work force for every two women.

The economically active life (EAL) of the working population—the amount of time one generation remained active in the labor force—furnishes further proof of the failure of the city economy to incorporate new workers. The gross EAL of men in Rio de Janeiro was 46.8 years in 1940, dropped slightly to 46.4 in 1950, and plunged to 43.3 years in 1960. But the EAL of females in Rio increased during these twenty years. Starting at 11.6 years in 1940, it rose to 12.6 by 1950, and stabilized at 12.5 in 1960. When the mortality rate is considered, Carioca men averaged 32.7 years of net EAL in 1940, registered a slight rise to 36.1 in 1950 then declined to 35.7 years in 1960. The increase in net EAL for women held fairly steady from 9.5 years in 1940 to 11.1 in 1950 and 11.6 in 1960. Men in Rio de

Janeiro spent less time in the labor force than their counterparts in the rest of the country, while Carioca women were economically active for a longer period than other Brazilian females.

The most important factor contributing to the growth of the Economically Active Population in Rio de Janeiro after 1940 was migration. From 1940 to 1950 two migrants entered the EAP for every native. (Immigration was no longer a significant factor in population growth.) Twice as many male migrants joined the city's work force as female newcomers. During the 1950s migration to Rio slowed down, corresponding to the capital's loss of attraction as a center of investment to São Paulo. Yet the ratio of migrants to Cariocas in the labor force rose to three to one, due to lower birth rates after World War II.[28]

Rio de Janeiro's working population in 1960 shared some traits with those of the advanced capitalist nations. Very little of the EAP was engaged in agriculture, and industry had declined in importance relative to the service sector. But the similarities are superficial. More men sought work in Rio de Janeiro during these years than ever before, but they found fewer employment opportunities. More women were employed than ever before, but in service jobs that paid very little. The result was the growth of the subproletariat that has remained a permanent feature of the economy of the city until the present day.[29]

THE LABOR FORCE IN RIO DE JANEIRO 1930–1960: QUALITY OF LIFE

An examination of the condition of the working class in Rio de Janeiro should begin with a survey of the minimum wage—the amount of salary estimated by the federal government as necessary to cover the costs of the bare necessities of life. But calculating the monthly minimum salary in Rio de Janeiro from 1930 to 1960 is an extremely venturesome enterprise, since few economists agree on the exact number of workers to whom it applied or how well it held up against inflation. Despite these difficulties, the evolution of the minimum salary is an important measure of the quality of life of the laboring classes. Placed into law by President Vargas on May 2, 1938, to take effect on May 1, 1940, the minimum salary covered all the employed who worked 200 hours per month, and assumed the wage earner spent half of his or her salary on food, 20 percent on rent, 8 percent on clothing, 12 percent on hygiene, and 10 percent on transportation. The first minimum salary was set at 202.50 cruzeiros per month and rose to 380 by 1943, with 410 cruzeiros for industrial workers.[30]

Inflation soon ate away at this modest gain. The real minimum salary in the Federal District fell by 53 percent from 1940 to 1951 when measured against the rising cost of living.[31] Increases in the minimum salary during the second Vargas administration (1951–1954), including the controversial 100 percent raise decreed by Minister of Labor João Goulart in 1954, helped ease the pain of inflation but still kept many workers below the poverty line. The one recent period in Brazilian history when the minimum salary kept up reasonably well with inflation was during the presidency of Juscelino Kubitscheck (1955–1960), when it was readjusted three times. In fact, 1957 the peak year for the minimum salary in Rio. Allowing for inflation, it stood at 159.8, compared with 100 in 1944.[32] A steady decline came thereafter until the installation of Goulart as president in 1961, in the midst of political turmoil.

Rising food costs were chiefly responsible for the deterioration of real wages in Rio de Janeiro. The diet of the Carioca worker of the 1930–1960 generation can be considered privileged only when compared with other parts of Brazil. In 1936 the National Health Department surveyed 12,106 families with 60,149 members living in the Federal District for a study of nutrition. Fifteen percent of the families lived in the middle-class residential areas of Rio (zone A); 21 percent in the commercial area (zone B); 16 percent in industrial areas (zone C); and 47.5 percent in poor residential areas (zone D). The entire survey group reported spending 54 percent of their monthly income on food and 25 percent on housing. Broken down by residential zone, the inhabitants of zone A spent 47 percent on food and the residents zone C, 50 percent. But the poorer occupants of zone D spent 57 percent of their earnings on groceries.[33]

Exactly how long could the typical laborer expect to survive on such meager rations? The most reliable figures on mortality, death rates, and life expectancy for the Federal District for 1939–1941 put life expectancy for males in Rio de Janeiro at 39.8 years and at 45.2 for females. This compared unfavorably with the city of São Paulo, where the respective figures were 46.7 and 51.8, but was still above the national average of 35 years for males and 38 for females.[34] The population of Rio de Janeiro in 1950 was estimated at 2,413,152. The death rate was 12.8 per 1,000 population, slightly higher than that of São Paulo (11.1) but much lower than that of Recife (23.1) in the Northeast and considerably lower than the national average of 17 to 21 per 1,000 population.[35]

Most deaths in Rio de Janeiro during the 1940s were the result of preventable diseases. In 1940, when the population of the city stood at 1,781,567, the leading causes of death were malaria, diphtheria, typhoid, dysentery, and tuberculosis.[36] These statistics were not broken down by residential area or income, but some idea of the link between the spread of contagious diseases and social class can be gleamed from the 1950 and 1960 censuses, when the city was supposedly undergoing an economic boom. In 1950, 83 percent of permanent private residences in the wealthy nucleus area had access to the metropolitan water supply; only 71 percent of homes in the immediate periphery of Rio, where the working class and favelados lived, shared this benefit, and just 36 percent in the intermediate periphery. Ten years later the figures were 82 percent for the nucleus, 79 percent for the immediate periphery, and 40 percent for the intermediate periphery. At the same time, 80 percent of the private residences in the nucleus were connected to the sewer system; only 39 percent in the immediate periphery were connected, and a mere 10 percent in the intermediate periphery.[37]

If living conditions for the working class had in many ways worsened after 1930, the next generation of laborers was illequipped to improve their lives. Lack of education was the biggest obstacle to success. To be sure, the literacy level in the Federal District for 1940–1960 far surpassed that of Brazil as a whole. The percentage of literates among the Carioca population ten years of age and older was estimated at 86.7 percent in 1940, with little difference between males and females. Brazil claimed a 43 percent literacy rate that year, with women holding a slight edge.[38] But the Rio de Janeiro school system was inadequate to prepare young people for a better future. A class-conscious educational system was bound to produce different levels of success for rich and poor. The middle and upper classes sent their children to private schools, while the poor were stuck in the underfunded public institutions. In 1940 a total of 13,473 students finished primary school in Rio de Janeiro; of these, 9,265 graduated from public schools and 4,208 from private institutions. By 1950 the number of students completing their courses was 17,482, but now the balance favored the private schools, with 9,102 graduates to 8,380 for the public schools. What was truly shocking was the failure of the public and private schools to retain students. Comparing effective enrollment with successful completion, as late as 1957 only 11 percent of primary school students in Rio managed to graduate—11.5 percent in the public schools and 9 percent in private units; a sad achievement for a city that claimed to be the cultural capital of Brazil.[39]

CONCLUSION

The best label for the evolution of the labor force in Rio de Janeiro from 1930 to 1960 is "incomplete proletarianization." The needs of capital in the city prevented the full integration of the migrant laborers from the countryside. An archaic agricultural sector, stagnant industry, and a tertiary sector that could not successfully compete with São Paulo conspired to keep hundreds of thousands of capable men and women out of the job market. The 1950s were the crucial decade in this bleak picture. Rio lost whatever chance it had of catching up to São Paulo in industry, but migrants continued to pour in from the nearby states and the Northeast.

The miserable condition of the Rio de Janeiro workforce can be explained only by the type of industrialization the city underwent and the occupational structure it engendered. The greatest priority of capital was to bring wages down. Large sections of the proletariat were unable to find steady jobs and were shunted into the service sector. Those workers who remained part of the economically active population were prized for their brawn and not their brains. The low standard of living of Carioca workers made them unsuitable for employment in the advanced capitalist countries but perfect for a nation undergoing peripheral industrialization. The subproletariat of Rio de Janeiro—men and women and children drifting in and out of the workforce, largely shut out of the consumer market, and denied access to health care, education, and housing—flocked to the favelas as their last chance for survival.

3

The Shanty

In the open-air markets of Rio de Janeiro customers can purchase paintings, postcards, and bric-a-brac with the favela as theme. Favelas—settlements erected by the poor on illegally occupied lands—have become indelibly associated in the public mind with the urban scene. Since World War II they have attracted considerable attention from both domestic and foreign students of Brazil. Most Brazilian observers at first concurred with the official government line pronounced by the Rio de Janeiro chief of police in the 1950s: he called the favelas an "evil threatening the security of the entire community."[1] Foreigners who examined the favela from sociological, political, and even criminological perspectives warned of the dangers squatters posed to economic development. For one American author favelas "violate legal regulations, deprive legal owners of their rights, and pose a political threat since they are often concentrated in [metropolitan] cities."[2]

Less alarmist but no less misleading was the definition of the favela as a "rural slum within the city," the prevalent in view in the early 1960s. According to this judgment, living conditions in the favelas supposedly resembled those of the residents in their home states. The cultural values of the favelados were said to be more in tune with those of rural folk than with the urban working class, making integration into the city very difficult.[3] The Fundação Leão XIII, a Catholic relief organization operating under the auspices of the city of Rio de Janeiro, also assigned culture a leading role in the predicament of the favelados, and damned the squatter settlement as a sewer of "promiscuity, disease, poor hygiene, family disorganization, high infant mortality and criminality."[4]

Starting in the late 1960s, however, anthropologists and sociologists took a second look at the favelas. Noting the resiliency of the squatter settlements, even under the threat of military repression following the coup of 1964, they questioned the notion that shantytowns were a marginal element of the Rio de Janeiro metropolis. Some academics stressed the dialectical connection between dependent capitalist development and the rise of shantytowns in Brazil.[5] Others, particularly the American sociologist Janice Perlman, carefully documented how favelas fit the standard definition of an urban community. The squatters valued work, family life, and responsibility toward their neighbors. They participated in the legal economic life of the city, paid taxes, built and improved their homes, and mobilized to put pressure on politicians to deliver goods and services to the urban periphery.[6]

The first large favela in Rio de Janeiro was located close to downtown on Morro de Providência, overlooking the city. It was founded in 1898 by veterans of the military campaign against the messianic rebel Antônio Conselheiro. "Favela" refers to a flower common in Bahia, and had designated one of the battlefields in the war. But it was not until the 1940s, following the mass migration of rural laborers from the interior of Brazil to Rio de Janeiro, that favelas overtook slums as the principal form of housing for the urban poor. This chapter analyzes the process of favela growth in the city of Rio de Janeiro from 1948, the year of the first favela census, to 1960, when Rio ceased to be the Federal District of Brazil and became the state of Guanabara. It seeks to delineate why the postwar years saw a tremendous explosion in the number of favelas and favelados. The historical reasons why favelas flourished first and foremost in Rio de Janeiro are examined, followed by a portrait of the favelado during this generation and look at how the squatment functioned.

Defining the favela is a complex task. How does one treat a part of the urban landscape that officially does not exist yet has consumed so much time and energy of city administrators, journalists, policemen, politicians and academics? The national census bureau of Brazil gave it a try in 1950 by grouping the more than one hundred favelas of Rio de Janeiro under five criteria.

1.   Minimum size—group of buildings or residences formed by fifty or more units.
2.   Type of habitation—predominance in the group of shacks or shanties of a rustic type, constructed principally of tin strips, zinc plates, planks, or similar materials.
3.   Juridical condition of occupation—construction without license or inspection, on land belonging to third parties or unknown owner.
4.   Public improvements—absence, in total or in part, of sewer network, electricity, telephones and/or indoor plumbing.
5.   Urbanization—nonurbanized area without streets, house numbers and/ or street signs.[7]

The census defined the favela primarily by what it lacked. It could therefore be considered as quantitatively different from the rest of the city. If only the favela had more and better of everything, this reasoning suggested, it would disappear from sight. But would a favela cease to exist if residents used cement blocks instead of tin strips to build their homes? Could the city eradicate the favela simply by moving its inhabitants from illegally owned properties to housing projects? This classification also erred in seeing favela dwellers as unable or unwilling to improve themselves, thereby placing their fate in the hands of "urban experts" and politicians.

Government authorities and hostile journalists who treated the squatter settlements as a threat to public safety or a marginal element of the city failed to grasp the function of favela formation. Whether located on abandoned factories, on construction sites, dumps, the back lots of upper-class buildings, military facilities, beachfront areas, or swamplands, favelas were a form of habitation in conflict with the law but serving the social, economic, and political purposes of both the residents and city authorities. To understand the birth and growth of the favelas, it is necesary to search for a historical definition.

The rise of an urban working class in Rio de Janeiro, as traced in the previous chapter, which owed fealty to neither party nor political boss posed a threat to the rural oligarchy that dominated Brazilian politics until 1930. The removal by persuasion or force of low-income groups from *Centro* (downtown) to the periphery marked the start of the twentieth century. The modernization of the city under the administration of Mayor Francisco Pereira Passos (1902–1906), involving the broadening of boulevards, expansion of port facilities, and sanitation campaigns, was designed to attract foreign investment to the "Paris of South America" and effectively disenfranchise the poor, many of whom were physically relocated to the suburbs. Widespread demolition in Centro, to make way for Avenida Central (later Avenida Rio Branco), displaced thousands of low-income residents. Financial pressures likewise played a part in the expulsion of the urban masses. The coffee boom of the first years of the new century, accompanied by wild speculation in real estate and high deficits from the cost of imports, made space in the center of Rio more valuable than ever before, and many workers could no longer afford to live in apartments that had housed their grandparents.[8]

The population shift from core to periphery accelerated in the next decades. Due to the widespread use of the automobile and the extension of railroad service, one-quarter of the population of Rio lived in the suburbs by 1950. The suburbs increased their population by 326.14 percent from 1906 to 1950, and the urban core grew by 283.15 percent.[9] The suburbs experiencing the largest growth after 1906 were the industrial neighborhoods of São Cristóvão, Tijuca, Vila Isabel, and Engenho Velho in the northern zone, of the city and the middle-class residential areas of Lapa, Glória, Flamengo, Botafogo, and Santa Teresa in southern zone. Both zones offered residents cheaper rents than in downtown, but lacked a sufficient number of hospitals, schools, and other city services.

The posh neighborhoods of Copacabana, Leblon, and Ipanema in Zona Sul were the favored residential areas of urban professionals in the 1920s and the municipal government went out of its way to accommodate them. President Washington Luis (1926–1930) declared, "To govern is to open roads," as the city witnessed a burst of tunnel construction and street paving. The Plano Agache of 1930, Rio's first official urban plan, foresaw the expansion of the rapid transport system in the southern zone, extension of port and railroad facilities further to the northwest, and the relocation of squatters to government-built housing in the suburbs. President Getúlio Vargas officially canceled the plan that same year, but its guiding principles remained operational.[10]

Vargas came to power in 1930 faced with the herculean task of strengthening the industrial bourgeoisie, winning the allegiance of the urban proletariat, and subordinating the rural oligarchy politically while leaving agrarian structures intact. In the Federal District, Vargas and his Carioca cohorts had to find jobs for the rural migrant population without endangering the city's economic recovery, a step made difficult by the lack of public transportation for the masses. The working class of Rio did not reside near areas of employment. As industry, especially civil construction, moved to Zona Sul and the suburbs, the city failed to provide adequate means of transport. Only one railroad, the Central do Brasil, linked the suburbs to the center of Rio de Janeiro, and the system of mule-driven *bondes* and *gôndola* streetcars was decrepit.

The housing available to migrants who wished to reside near their place of work were not attractive. Exact figures are not available, but perhaps as many as one-quarter of the city's population lived in one of the following types of collective units by 1930:

- *Cortiços*; famous from fictional accounts by Machado de Assis, Lima Barreto, and other writers of the turn of the century, the cortiços were nineteenth-century buildings run by slumlords; beehive like dwellings, usually consisting of two stories and rented to dozens of families. Most were located in downtown and Zona Norte. *Casas de cômodo, estalagens*, and *cabeças de porco* were smaller but similar structures.
- *Casas de dormidas*; cramped residences rented for a night's sleep.
- *Avenidas*; alleys of working-class houses.
- *Vilas operárias*; grossly overcrowded housing projects financed by the municipal government, really a racket for the real estate companies.
- *Loteamentos*; small houses built by the government in the 1920s and located in the rural suburbs far from Centro; they alleviated unemployment by putting residents to work in agriculture and cattle-raising.[11]

None of these dwellings provided a permanent solution to the housing crisis. Families newly arrived in Rio could not afford to live in the cortiços and the casas de cômodo (rent in 1930 averaged forty dollars a month). Vilas operárias and loteamentos were usually located too far from the workplace of the family head. The cramped rooms made it impossible to raise a large family or invite relatives to reside, and the Municipal Code gave the landlord extensive powers of eviction.

The only alternative left for many of the poor was to construct their own homes above the city. The Plano Agache of 1930 had referred to a "semi-nomadic population" living in the hills. The 1933 survey of housing in Rio de Janeiro, *Estatística predial do Distrito Federal*, listed 57,889 "rustic habitations" within city limits and specified a number of *morro* (hillside) residences occupied by the poor, nearly all located between Centro and Zona Norte: 1,504 homes in the neighborhood of Salgueiro, 712 in Arrelia, 489 in São Carlos, 73 in Babilônia, 33 in São Antonio, and 61 in Chico.[12] The trek of the poor up the hills was an economic decision. The morros were unwanted by industry and the real estate companies, but hillside homes offered propinquity to the workplace. Other benefits that accrued from favela living included raising animals and growing crops to cut down on food expenses. In addition, the closer the residents stayed to the nucleus, the more likely they were to receive city services. There was a political advantage to hillside residency as well. The Rio de Janeiro Civil Code of Public Works forbade construction of unauthorized dwellings or improvement of old ones within city limits, so the high climb up the mountainsides kept the favelados safe from the police.

But the favelas were never far from the public spotlight. Largely out of concern for internal security, Vargas ordered his man in Rio de Janeiro, Mayor Henrique Dodsworth, to look into the matter. At the end of his term (1937–1945) Dodsworth produced a brief essay analyzing the growth of favelas and the efforts of his administration to deal with the dilemma:

More than forty years have gone by and the problem persists, and now its urban and medico-social aspects have been aggravated. This in turn complicates other problems such as hospital care and nourishment. Without a frontier police to impede the flow of the poor, without the prohibition of migration from the interior of the sick and the homeless, the problem will worsen, to the detriment of the good and humble people who live in the favelas, exploited, as they are already, by some sinister figures who constitute the most despicable and paradoxical of all those classes involved in this tragedy: the "absentee landlords" and rich private parties who make profits from public lands. All of them are responsible, by guilt or omission, for the existence of the favela.[13]

Contrary to the thinking of Dodsworth and other city officials, the favela was not a problem that could be resolved through more extensive use of police powers. The shantytown was qualitatively different from slums, tenements, and other types of low-income housing prevalent in Rio de Janeiro prior to 1930 because of who lived there. The favela was the home of the urban subproletariat. Industry, large and small, acted as a centripetal force for the Carioca poor after 1930, and the squatter settlements were the result of the contradiction between urbanization and industrialization in Rio de Janeiro. No amount of repression could impede the spread of shantytowns; only decent jobs and housing near the place of work could do that.

THE FAVELA EXPLOSION AFTER WORLD WAR II

The censuses for 1940 and 1950 rang the alarm bell. In 1940 the Federal District had an occupancy rate of 6.84 persons per building and 2.57 per bedroom (690,844 bedrooms; thus an estimated population of 1,774,693). If two persons per bedroom is normal for comfortable residence, then Rio de Janeiro should have possessed 887,347 bedrooms. Instead, it suffered a shortage of 196,503. A decade later the situation had deteriorated. The number of persons per building reached 7.54 with 2.83 persons per bedroom. Rio had an estimated population of 2,470,784 in 1950, and the number of existing bedrooms was 873,069. At two persons per bedroom the. city should have had 1,235,392 units; hence it suffered a deficiency of 362,323. Low salaries, inflation, and high rents—in 1950–1960 the average Carioca spent one-quarter of the monthly minimum salary on rent—made the move to the squatments a matter of necessity for the poor.[14]

The housing crunch forced many workers to flee to the suburbs because, to paraphrase Willie Sutton, "that's where the jobs were." The most important new industrial growth district in the 1940s was Méier in Zona Norte, particularly the area along Avenida Suburbana. The giant favela of Jacarézinho, which still stands today, arose near this spot in the mid-1930s. Next in importance came the neighborhood of São Cristóvão, ideally close to the port and located halfway between the two major concentrations of population in the city, Zona Sul and the area along the Central do Brasil Railroad. Barreira do Vasco, still one of the best-known favelas in Rio, flourished there.[15]

New transportation routes likewise stimulated favela development. The completion of three more railroad lines in the 1940s—the Leopoldina, Rio d'Ouro and Linha Auxiliar of the Central do Brasil railroad—created more jobs in Zona Norte. The opening of Avenida Brasil in 1946 generated a host of small industries, along with garages and warehouses, providing occupants for new favelas like Brás de Pina. In Zona Sul street construction gave birth to more favelas and expanded old ones such as Praia do Pinto, located on the border of Leblon and Gávea. Thanks to the railroads and expanded bus service, squatters no longer had to cling to the hillsides, but the relatively high cost of transport for the urban poor meant that many still found it necessary to reside close to their place of work. In Zona Norte and the suburbs, half of the favela residents worked in the same zone where they lived, and this also this applied to three-quarters of favelados in Centro and Zona Sul. Others were willing to commute if it meant higher wages. Less than 14 percent of favelados lived in Centro but 37 percent of those economically active worked there. Figures for Zona Norte were 64 percent residence and 40 percent employment; Zona Sul had 20.9 percent of all favelados and employed 21.1 percent.[16]

Sanitation campaigns launched by the Vargas regime and its civilian successors during the 1940s and 1950s, particularly in the Acari and Menti valley regions, facilitated the movement of the poor toward the periphery. The fear that the growing migrant population might contaminate the middle class with tuberculosis was primarily responsible for motivating government action, which unquestionably saved many lives, but the sanitation drive did little to arrest the diseases common to favela children, such as diphtheria, diarrhea, influenza, and polio.

The city of Rio de Janeiro took a long time to officially acknowledge the existence of the favelados. Significantly, the first reliable census of Carioca squatter settlements was carried out in 1947–1948 by the secretary-general of interior and security affairs, reflecting the city's fear of the squatters as troublemakers. Using a vague definition of "disordered nuclei of impoverished persons," it counted 105 favelas housing 138,837 persons, 68,953 male and 69,884 female, living in 34,528 shanties—an average of four inhabitants per shack. Favelados made up 7 percent of the total population of Rio de Janeiro in 1948, but of the 437,546 migrants who arrived in the Federal District from 1940 to 1950, only 12 percent moved to the favelas[17] (see Map 3.1).

The census registered a growing geographic shift of shantytowns since the 1930s away from the hills and toward the suburbs in response to the availability of

Map 3.1
Favelas of the City of Rio de Janeiro in 1948

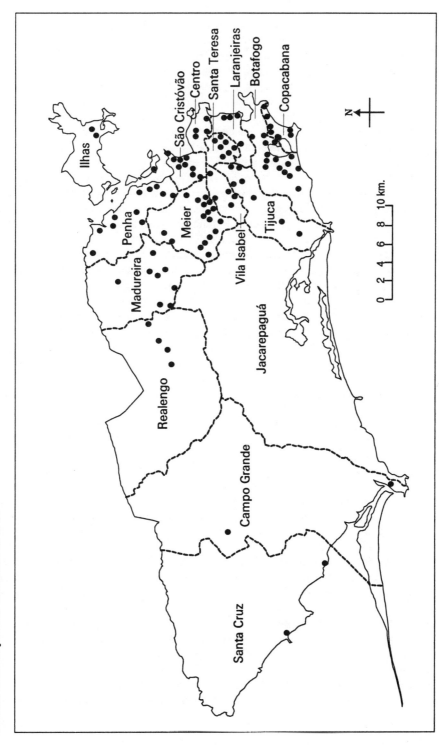

employment. Centro contained four favelas, and the middle-class neighborhoods of Estácio de Sá, Laranjeiras, Botafogo, and Copacabana had a total of thirty-two. The industrial quarters of São Cristóvão, Tijuca, Vila Isabel, Méier, Madureira, and Penha had fifty-eight. The eleven remaining favelas were found in the rural areas of the Federal District and Ilhas. The favela of Jacarézinho in the district of Méier had the greatest number of inhabitants, 15,510, crowded into 3,325 shanties.

The national government gave statistical recognition to the favelas for the first time in the census of 1950. Squatter settlements of less than fifty units were eliminated from the federal count, and a strict demarcation line was drawn between a favela and its surrounding area. By these methods the 1950 census listed 58 favelas rather than the 105 found in 1948, but with more inhabitants. The population stood at 169,305 (50.05 percent male and 49.95 percent female) living in 45,236 domiciles for an occupancy rate of 3.7. Favelados composed only 7.12 percent of the total city population, but the growth in absolute numbers meant that only ten Brazilian cities had more residents than the favelas of Rio.

The location of the favelas in 1950 confirmed the continued flight of the poor away from the city nucleus. Centro had just two squatments now; Estácio de Sá, five; Laranjeiras, eight; Botafogo, twelve; Copacabana, eight; São Cristóvão, five; Tijuca, three; Vila Isabel, six; Méier, three; Madureira, three; and Penha, three. Seven neighborhoods contained more than 10,000 favelados each: Engenho Novo, Gávea, São Cristóvão, Copacabana, Rio Comprido, Tijuca, and Penha. The suburban zones housed the largest number of favelados (64,590), followed by Zona Sul with 43,098. But Zona Sul led the way in the number of favelas, twenty-five; just thirteen in suburbia. Suburban favelas tended to form around industrial establishments, while those in Copacabana and the rest of Zona Sul were scattered next to construction sites[18] (see Map 3.2).

During the presidency of Juscelino Kubitsheck (1955–60), marked by high inflation and the development of industry at the expense of agriculture, a human tidal wave inundated Rio de Janeiro. The number of favelas rose to 147 with a population 335,063 by 1960 (167,189 males and 167,874 females), a growth of 168,000 inhabitants since the previous census. Thirty-nine percent of the increase was due to the growth of old favelas and 61 percent to the birth of new ones. Rio de Janeiro's total population reached 3,307,000 persons, which meant that roughly one in ten Cariocas lived as a squatter. The average number of inhabitants per shanty was 4.8. One-third of all favelas and favelados were in the northern suburb of Leopoldina near Avenida Brasil. Zona Sul housed 20 percent of the favelas and 18 percent of favelados (see Map 3.3). The inflationary spiral of the late 1950s encouraged landlords to hold on to properties in Copacabana and Leblon and build high rises that competed with favelas for space. Highway construction and government subsidies for busing were largely responsible for the spread of squatter settlements at long distances from urban Rio de Janeiro after 1960. New metropolitan suburbs like Nova Iguaçu, Duque de Caxias, and São João de Meriti, peopled mainly by the poor, blossomed in the Baixada Fluminense region north of Rio de Janeiro.[19]

Squatter settlements were, of course, not unique to Rio de Janeiro. *Mocambos*

Map 3.2
Growth of the Favela Population, 1950–1960

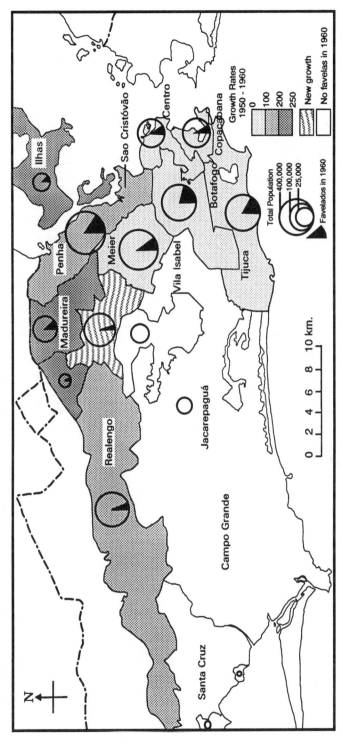

Note: Based on censo de 1o-VII–1950 and Brasil, VII recenseamento geral do Brasil. Data reproduced in Guanabara, Comissão Executiva para Desenvolvimento
Urbano. *Guanabara: a plan for urban development*. Athens, n.p., 1965.

Map 3.3
Favelas of the City of Rio de Janeiro in 1960

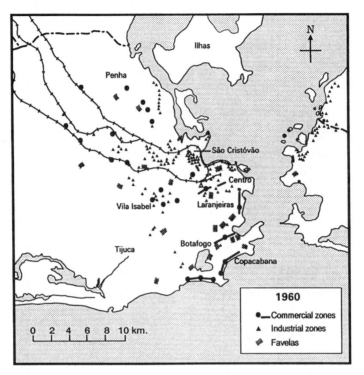

in Recife, *malocas* in Porto Alegre, and shantytowns in Belo Horizonte and São Paulo housed hundreds of thousands by 1960.[20] The rural exodus assured the cities of the Southeast a constant supply of human beasts of burden. High rents, inflation, and housing shortages had always been the curse of the working class throughout Brazil. What was new about the years after World War II, and what made Rio de Janeiro the squatter capital of the country, were the predominant elements of the city economy and politics. This generation witnessed a great leap in favela construction due to a combination of new factors. The relocation of industry to the periphery, especially in Zona Norte, combined with the shortage of space in old favelas, forced the urban poor to build hundreds of new shantytowns far from the nucleus, a step made possible by improvements in transportation. The postwar building boom in Zona Sul destroyed many working class-lodgings but also gave job opportunities to migrants, and the chance to build new homes next to their work place. The two populist administrations of Getúlio Vargas (1930–1945, 1951–1954), aiming to court working-class support, extended bus and railroad transportation to poor areas, combated disease through health campaigns, and looked the other way while squatters erected their shacks. A symbiotic relationship among the state, industry, and the subproletariat ensured the continual expansion of the favelas.

A PORTRAIT OF THE FAVELADOS, 1948–1960

Disease is the most frequent metaphor found in nearly every description of the favelados published prior to 1960, as demonstrated in this passage from the novel *Parias da cidade maravilhosa*:

The "favela" triumphant, with its sinister court of miseries. The social cancer that annihilates human lives without pity, infecting all souls that slither within it. Home to honest workers, small entrepreneurs, maids and laundresses. Secure refuge of bums, pimps, thieves, assassins, gamblers, pederasts, prostitutes, and, also, victims of cancer, leprosy, tuberculosis, syphilis and other ills generated by the dry belly of black misery. In this Dantesque laboratory, where necessity manipulates all diseases, the preferred guinea pigs are the legion of the malnourished. . . . The inhabitants of the "favela" don't live—they vegetate.[21]

Few outsiders could grasp the profound changes going on inside the favelas and in the lives of the favelados during this generation. If on the surface continuity prevailed, underneath, the squatter settlements were bubbling with activity. Surveys conducted from 1948 to 1960 shattered many stereotypes about the favelados. They prove that squatters took advantage of urban institutions and networks to ease their integration into the city. Favelados forged links with politicians, clergymen, and employers that could never be shattered, no matter how painful the transition from migrant to resident. The favela of 1960 was quite a different entity than the shantytown of the 1940s.

Sixty percent of the 138,837 favelados registered in 1948 hailed from the states of Rio de Janeiro, Minas Gerais, Espírito Santo, and elsewhere in Brazil. In the favela of Rocinha, second largest in the city at the start of the 1950s, Fluminenses (born in the state of Rio de Janeiro) made up 52 percent of the population of 1,011 families; Cariocas, 20 percent and Northeasterners, 14 percent.[22] But the squatter population had begun to reproduce itself. In 1948, 52,956 shanty dwellers counted were native-born, and 60 percent of them were under thirteen years of age.[23] By 1960 nearly half the favelados had been born in Guanabara, and of these more than one-third were under four years old.[24] This development was significant, because as Rio de Janeiro lost out to São Paulo and Belo Horizonte in generating new jobs after 1960, migrants made up a smaller proportion of the squatter population. Nevertheless, the favelas continued to grow as a result of the impoverishment of larger numbers of Cariocas.

The composition of the squatter population also changed by gender. The 1948 census, as previously noted, registered a slightly higher number of women in the 105 favelas surveyed. In 1950 the percentage of males was 50.05 percent, versus the females' 49.95 percent, but these figures allow for a margin of error. In addition, the growth of favelas in the suburbs was bound to shift the balance toward males, because Rio's outer areas always had a greater proportion of men than the city center. Ten years later an important trend emerged. Females were more numerous overall, but particularly in the category of ages fifteen to twenty-four, the years of highest economic activity. This was a mark of what sociologists dubbed "the feminization of poverty'' in Rio de Janeiro. Starting around 1960, more women than men migrated from one favela to another, a sign of the desperation of the female poor in a city that had little use for them except as domestics.

Many misperceptions about the favela arose from failure to consider the factor of age. In 1948 children and adolescents up to the age of twenty made up 48 percent of the favela population. Over one-third of the population was no older than seven, and only 15 percent was over age forty. The high proportion of youth along with low life expectancy, especially among males, meant favelas gained many economically inactive persons and lost potential producers. The 1950 census showed 45.7 percent of the population no older than nineteen, and 16.3 percent aged over forty. As the favela population began to reproduce itself, the average age of the favelados dropped. In 1960, of 335,063 favelados counted, those under twenty years old totaled 176,131 (52.5 percent). These figures challenged the theory of favela marginality. The high ratio of economically inactive persons in the squatter settlements was due above all to the overwhelming number of youth who lived there, not to any unwillingness to work on the part of the inhabitants.[25]

Most of these young people were the offspring of stable, long-term unions between their parents. The first favela census, without indicating the exact age groups surveyed, found 47.5 percent of favelados single; 22.9 percent married, and 22.4 percent living in consensual unions. The rest were widowed or separated. Counting only persons over fifteen years of age, the 1950 census found 48.8 percent of the population single, 41.9 percent married, and 9 percent widowed. The figure for single persons was a bit higher than for the Federal District population as a whole (42.6 percent) and that for married persons was lower (48 percent) but this is explained by the large number of teenagers in the favela and the tendency of many Brazilians to marry after age twenty-five. The 1950 national census of Brazil found singles constituted 48.8 percent of the favela population of Rio de Janeiro over age fifteen while 41.9 percent were married, and the rest were widowed or separated.[26] A study of fifty households in the favela of Esqueléto conducted by a nun in 1955 found 36 percent of the couples linked by civil and religious vows, 16 percent by religious vows only, and 16 percent by civil vows only. The rest were living in "natural unions," or consensual arrangements.[27]

No question is more inflammatory in Brazil than race, and most students of the favelas have done their best to avoid this combustible topic. Listing favela residents as white, black, *pardo* (mulatto), and Asian, the 1948 census found blacks and pardos made up 70.9 percent of the population. Since "people of color" made up 29 percent of Rio's population but more than 70 percent of the favela population, there was a distinct connection between race, social class, and residency, despite Brazilian claims to "racial democracy." The situation did not improve with time. The 1950 national census registered 61.6 percent blacks and pardos living in the favelas, and the 1960 census of Guanabara listed 68.6 percent (see Table 3.1).

The spread of favelas did, however, rearrange the patterns of segregation in Rio de Janeiro, moving many blacks and pardos closer to the white population. Squatter settlements, especially those built after World War II, were likely to spring up

Table 3.1
Favela Population of Rio de Janeiro by Race and Sex in 1950

		Ratio	Percent of Total Population
Whites			
Men	30,959	48.14	18.28
Women	33,348	51.86	19.69
Total	64,307	100.00	
Blacks			
Men	29,003	52.31	17.13
Women	26,433	47.69	15.61
Total	55,436	100.00	
Yellows			
Men	9	60.00	
Women	6	40.00	
Total	15	100.00	
Pardos			
Men	24,465	50.01	14.45
Women	24,446	49.99	14.43
Total	48,911	100.00	
Race Undeclared			
Men	303	47.64	.0017
Women	333	52.36	.0019
Total	636	100.00	
Total	169,305	100.00	

Based on Censo de 1o-VII-1950 and data reproduced in José Alipio Goulart, *Favelas do Distrito Federal.* Rio de Janeiro: Ministerio de Cultura, Serviço de Informação Agricola, 1957, Appendix.

where well-off whites built their homes and managed their factories. The district of Rio de Janeiro with the highest proportion of "colored" in 1948 was Gávea with 19 percent; it was the site of Praia do Pinto and other large favelas, but also home to many of the Carioca rich. The north-northeast section of the city had the highest percentage of colored, 48.1 percent, but the fewest favelados: 9,982. In the south-southeast people of color made up 23.4 percent of the total and the favela population came to 39,596.[28] The need of industry for low-cost labor had unintentionally redistributed the colored population of the city.

The surveys of favelado economic activity during these years shattered the notion that the squatment was peopled by marginals. Excluding residents under thirteen years of age (a controversial decision, since child labor has always been commonplace throughout Brazil), the 1948 census found 31.5 percent of favelados without any declared profession. But if sex is considered, a different picture emerges. Among those who declared no profession, 75 percent were women; and since housework was not counted as an "economic activity," it stands to reason that most adult favelados who could work, did so. Among the economically active population, half were employed in industry, 25 percent in services, and 10 percent in commerce. Salaried workers, those with a signed labor card, numbered 50,342, and of these over one-quarter earned less than the minimum monthly salary. Two years later the national census carried a separate category for "unremunerated domestic work," and by factoring out this element, the economically inactive population of the favelas, counting those ten years and older, came to a mere 8.9 percent. The economically active population, counting residents of all ages, stood at 52.3 percent, which compared favorably with that of the Federal District as a whole (50.2 percent economically active) (see Table 3.2).

Table 3.2

Economic Activity of Rio de Janeiro Favela Residents, Aged Ten Years or More, in 1950

Branch of Activity	No	%
Agriculture, livestock, and forestry	190	.15
Extractive industries	1,179	.94
Transformation industries	28,292	22.79
Merchant commerce	5,559	4.47
Commerce in real estate, credit, insurance and capital	190	.15
Rendering of services	17,886	14.40
Transportation, communication, and warehousing	5,890	4.74
Liberal professions	116	.09
Social activities	2,133	1.71
Public administration, legislature, justice	876	.70
National defense and public security	1,997	1.60
Nonremunerated domestic activities and learning	48,103	38.75
Other activities	594	.47
Inactive	11,130	8.96
Total	124,135	100.00

Total rounded off to 100.0%

Based on Censo de 1o-VII-1950 reproduced in José Alipio Goùlart, *Favelas do Distrito Federal.* Rio de Janeiro: Ministerio de Cultura, Serviço de Informação Agrícola, 1957, Appendix.

Many favela workers were still stuck in the subproletariat. In the settlement of Cantagalo in Zona Sul, almost 70 percent of the 887 male heads of household worked in unsteady professions: civil construction employed 24.9 percent; *biscate* (informal work) 9.4 percent, and 35.2 percent were undeclared. Women workers were largely consigned to domestic service. The Cantagalo survey found 344 female heads of households; close to half were employed as maids.[29] But a working class did emerge in the favelas during these years as squatters built homes close to their workplaces, formed families, and acquired a rudimentary education. A survey carried out by students of the Pontifical Catholic University of Rio de Janeiro in the early 1960s in the populous favelas of Babilônia in Zona Sul and Cachoeirinha in

Zona Norte, found that 80 percent of the sample group in each favela was employed in remunerated work; over 50 percent had never changed jobs, and over one-third worked at specialized labor.[30]

The contradiction of work versus school has always been one of the chief obstacles to a favelado's advancement. The 1950 and 1960 censuses showed that of the total number of squatters five years and older, only half were literate. But the younger generation had some hope. In 1950, 67 percent of the children ages ten to fourteen could read and write, and by 1960, 78 percent of this group were literate.[31] Though these last figures were impressive, they could also be deceiving. The education of many favela children was sporadic at best. A study conducted in the favela of Vila Isabel in Zona Norte during the school year of 1956 revealed 60 percent of the neighborhood children began school at seven years of age, but only 30 percent of the favela's children did so. There were 314 youngsters enrolled in first grade that year, but only 181 were beginners; the rest were repeating, perhaps not for the first time. In fifth grade a mere 13 percent of the pupils were favela residents, the rest had been retained or had dropped out.[32]

School and church were the most important institutions forming the favelados' view of the outside world. Though statistics for 1948–60 show over 95 percent of favela residents proclaiming themselves Roman Catholic, the most important feature of religious life in the favelas was syncretism. The census takers noted the presence of Protestants, spiritualists, Jews, Muslims, and Buddhists. Favelados simply saw no reason why they should not take Communion at the Catholic Church in the morning and attend a *candomblé* ceremony at night. Many chapels hastily constructed by the residents for the local priest doubled as centers of Afro-Brazilian cults.[33] By 1960, however, a distinct new presence could be found in favela religious life—evangelical Protestantism. French researcher Jean Pierre Bombart encountered Presbyterian, Methodist, Congregational, Baptist, and Assembly of God churches operating in the huge favela of Jacarézinho, competing with the Catholic Church for members and with local authorities for the political loyalty of the poor.[34]

Favela politics has always been personal, and party affiliation and electoral allegiance depend largely on whom the mayor or governor appoints as his representative in the community. Still, it would be unwise to see the favelados as clay in the hands of manipulating political operators. Analysts who recorded the political views of squatters in the 1950s got some startling answers. A survey of a thousand adult residents of the favelas in 1958 discovered that 77.5 percent had a definite political opinion: 28 percent called themselves "progovernment"; 24 percent were Communists; 19.5 percent were "populists" or followers of São Paulo Governor Adhemar de Barros; 3.8 percent referred to themselves as "opponents of the government"; and 2.2 percent expressed a preference for the fascist Integralist Party. Nearly seventy percent were opposed to foreign participation in the Brazilian petroleum industry. Forty-two percent were voters but less than 20 percent had new voting cards.[35]

Favelados were active players in city and even national politics from the 1930s onward. Vargas's first appointed administrator in Rio de Janeiro, Pedro Ernesto

(1931–1936), fearing that the existence of the favelas was "an invitation to revolution," persuaded the president to revoke the Plano Agache as a threat to poor people's housing and instead treat the favelados as outcasts who should be reintegrated into the city through education, health programs, and social assistance. In return, the squatters would give their political loyalty only to Getúlio. This populist perspective on the favelas was later embraced by Henrique Dodsworth (1937–1945), who aimed to capture the allegiance of favelados by them resettling them in housing projects that he dubbed "provisional proletarian parks." The postwar mayors, Filadelfo de Barros Azevedo, Hildebrando de Gois, and General Angelo de Moraes, tried to repress favelado political activity after Vargas was removed from the presidency in 1945, and delegated social service work in the favelas to the Catholic Church. The victory of Vargas in the 1950 presidential election was due in no small part to the support of the urban poor in Rio de Janeiro, who clamored for his return. His political allies, mayors João Carlos Vital (1951–1952) and Francisco Negrão de Lima (1956–1958), attempted to revive the populist tradition by personally intervening to stop the eviction of squatters from some of the largest favelas in Rio, including Jacarézinho. After 1960 many local, state, and national politicians counted on the favelados of Rio de Janeiro to supply them with a large number of votes in return for social services.[36]

The typical favela family in 1960 was likely to be composed of a young black couple and their two children, living in a shanty located somewhere in the suburbs. The male had probably migrated directly from the interior of Rio de Janeiro state and the female from another favela, but their children had been born in the shack. The father was employed a few months per year at a construction site while his mate found more steady but less rewarding work as a maid. One of the spouses was literate and the youngsters had a few years of primary schooling. Outside the shanty the family's social contacts were limited to the bar and community store, along with weekly visits to church. The parish priest and local politicians kept the head of the household informed about events in the rest of the city. The outside world was hostile to the favelados, judging by the pronouncements of politicians, churchmen, and journalists, but they had striven successfully to hold home and hearth together and made it impossible for the city to demolish their dwellings.

HOW THE FAVELA FUNCTIONED

The favelados had to reinvent themselves and devise survival strategies to keep their hard-won homes. Strangers in a strange land, they used heads and hands to fashion a home with only the basic elements of earth, water, and fire. The squatters beat dirt into a square formation and called it a floor. Molding clay or mud with bare fingers, they pasted pieces of bamboo together and erected walls, using string or cloth to hold the four intersections. Overhead they raised roofs made of tin cans, zinc, cardboard, and, for the lucky ones, tile.

Big stakes driven into the ground sustained the house. If located on the hillside, the shack was surrounded with stones to serve as a dam during the rainy season. Students of topology might do well to explore the *barraco* (shanty); its shape, height, width and length depended on the terrain, the elements, the availability of raw material, and, most important, the financial status of the owner. Beams overlapped, angles failed to meet, and the structure seemed to have been built by a blind person or an architect with a malicious sense of humor. The shanty was never finished—its construction was a constant chore, and its features changed from one week to the next.

Space was the most valuable commodity in any squatter settlement. Walking through was difficult enough for a newcomer making his or her way without the guide of numbered streets, down alleys filled with mud, garbage, and sewage. But movement inside the shanty was equally restricted. Every room in the barraco served myriad purposes. Within six to nine square meters as many as six people might huddle. Washing, cleaning, and cooking were done in the cramped kitchen area. A stove was a luxury, one for which favelados saved for months to acquire. The bedroom was utilized for sewing, repairs, and wood-working, and often doubled as bathroom. A simple crate functioned as a table one day and a bed the next. On the walls hung plants, utensils, plates, and pictures of saints. Yet however rustic the habitat, a claim on the land dedicated the favelado to the city. In 1960, 70 percent of the 69,690 favela residences counted by the census were privately owned.[37]

Squatters of the generation of 1948 were determined to claim a permanent place in Rio de Janeiro by converting their shacks into houses. Store-bought furniture and modern conveniences were more than creature comforts—they represented the successful attempt of the favelados to become Cariocas and make their eviction by city authorities extremely difficult. In 1960, 26,118 favela domiciles had access to gas, 39,049 possessed indoor sanitation, and 54,821 had electricity. Favelados owned 43,135 radios, 4,830 refrigerators, and 958 television sets.

Squatters improvised city services easily available to the middle and upper classes. The humid climate of Rio de Janeiro and the sparse foliage in most favelas made water as precious a resource to the favelados as to an Arab sheik. Few wells existed, and excavation was out of the question because hardly anyone could afford tools. Cleaning, bathing, and cooking required daily trips to the spigot, located far from the barraco. There residents waited in line for hours to fill their cans and carry them back up the hillside, a ritual repeated every few days. Yet favelados were not kept from pressing for urban services. Through political pressure they won water for their communities. By 1960, 15,589 of their crude homes were connected to the city water supply.[38]

Water could also be a mortal enemy. Contaminated water, usually stored in cans and buckets at home, was the perfect breeding ground for mosquitos carrying yellow fever and malaria, and still among of the biggest killers of children in Brazil even at the end of the twentieth century. Of more pressing concern, however, was the danger posed by rain. Floods were an annual occurrence in Rio de Janeiro, and mud slides took a toll of hundreds each year in the 1940s and 1950s. Indeed, the disappearance of an entire favela was a perfectly imaginable catastrophe, as the following verse composed by the inhabitants of Rocinha testifies:

How I cried, I cried of sorrow,
seeing such pain
caused by the storm.
The stones rolled down from the hilltop,
it looked like the end of the world.
All of Rocinha cried.[39]

The other natural elements proved equally perverse. Foreigners who visited Rio de Janeiro were struck by the inordinate use of fire in nearly every favela. The shantytown was kept lighted day and night as a warning to criminals and the police that the inhabitants could defend themselves. Inside the homes crude devices provided for cooking and ironing. Women and children were more likely to work with fire than were men, in a fascinating offshoot of the sexual division of labor. Wood, coal, and kerosene were highly priced commodities bought and sold by petty entrepreneurs. But fire could also eradicate a squatment, as almost happened in the Zona Sul favela of Praia do Pinto in 1956 and again shortly before its official extinction in 1969.

Like his relatives in the interior of the country, the favelado had to make use of nature to survive. The flora and fauna of the favela served highly utilitarian purposes. Plants and fruits grown for consumption and sale included manioc, corn, sugarcane, sweet potatoes, onions, garlic, and bananas. Flowers were grown for ornaments but also lent themselves to medicinal purposes. Denied health care by the city, the squatter turned to *curandeiras*—female practitioners of popular medicine—who conjured up exotic recipes of herbs and spices to aid women in childbirth, induce abortion, or lift curses. It would be informative to compare poor people's medicine in the favelas with similar practices in Haiti and other Afro-American societies. Animal husbandry turned into a lucrative venture in some shanties. Families sometimes kept dogs for protection, despite the health hazard they posed to children. Pigs roamed the landscape, eating garbage while being fed for slaughter. Favelados kept goats and sometimes even cattle for milk, meat, and skins. Roosters crowed the start of the day, and hens provided eggs for breakfast and a tasty treat for dinner.

Ask anyone who saw a favela only from the outside for his or her most memorable impression, and the likely reply is "garbage." Alleys, streets, trenches, and ditches filled up with bottles, cans, excrement, newspapers, toys, and almost every other imaginable object. The reason for this was not a predilection for uncleanliness on the part of the inhabitants but the fact that the garbage dump the city provided was usually too far away to be of use. The sanitation problems caused by the piling up of garbage in the favela presented a tremendous health hazard. Uncollected refuse undermined the foundations of many houses by contributing to soil erosion, which caused landslides during the rainy season. The passivity of the city of Rio de Janeiro before this catastrophe threatened all inhabitants.

The fight for refuse removal and adequate sewage systems has been a stirring chapter in the history of many favelas. Residents of Brás de Pina in Zona Norte fought tenaciously in the early 1960s to get the city to eliminate the hazardous conditions cited in a government report:

The favela of Brás de Pina did not possess even those minimal sanitary conditions indispensable to human life. The air, highly polluted, showed the existence of gases provoked by the digestion of organic material accumulated in the flood areas. The presence of high bacteriological content denounced the flagrant presence of human waste in the water. The existence of great quantities of mineral and organic solids justified, without the slightest doubt, the interdiction of this area.[40]

The right to adequate sanitation became a rallying point of the poor. Residents used the threat posed to children by cesspools and dumps to shock and mobilize public opinion to do something about the favelas.

Garbage had another dimension, one of benefit to the favelado. Cans, bottles, and especially newspapers could be sold to recyclers. A number of women and children earned the greatest part of their daily income by carefully going through dumps and picking out the best commodities to take to the local dealer in scrap iron or paper. In her diary of favela life in São Paulo in the 1960s, which contains many observations pertinent to Rio de Janeiro, Carolina Mária de Jesús recounts her life as a scavenger and how she provided a living for her children through selling junk.[41]

The favelados were far from being urban hunter-gatherers. They fought for the modern conveniences, too. Ironically, it was usually far easier for squatters to gain access to electricity than to water. What made it possible was the hookup system to a single fusebox used collectively by several families. Naturally, this service did not come free, and the owner of the fusebox charged far higher rates than those billed to customers in the rest of the city. Since favelas often lacked numbered streets, the city government sometimes detected the presence of a new squatter settlement through unusual electricity usage.

The use of electricity divided the favelados along lines of class, sex, and age. Men used electrical energy for domestic artisanal production such as wood-working and forging of crude tools for sale. Women needed it for sewing. Children were usually excluded from electricity usage, in contrast to the use of water and fire. Access to electricity was always an explosive political issue in the favelas. The supplier often abused his position to extract political loyalty from his customers, and the demand that electrical service be extended to the favelas became the battle cry of squatters pitted against the municipal government.

No tour of the favela would be complete without mention of two institutions that acted as socializing agents and simultaneously linked the inhabitants to the rest of the city: the *botequim* (community store) and the lottery game known as *jogo do bicho*. A favelado wishing to go into business could simply convert his or her shanty into a commercial establishment for a few hours a day. The botequim sold food, drink, cigarettes, lamps, spare parts, furniture, clothing, and other items at higher prices than in the rest of the city; the cost, the owners claimed, of operating without a license in a dangerous neighborhood. Though these establishments were usually male-owned, women sometimes operated restaurants, doing the cooking themselves.

As significant as the commercial activity in the botequim was the store's function as a source of credit. Customers bought food and drink on weekly or monthly installments and the owner, if trustful, would also extend loans. The botequim was a fascinating phenomenon: a case of the poor employing the poor and selling to the poor. Hence it acquired a deep social and political significance in the community. Newcomers went there to learn the ways of the favela. Men congregated to drink and escape their families, for this was a male preserve *par excellence*. Local bigshots showed up to talk politics and gather votes. Often, the only radio or television set in the community perched on a stool in the botequim. If the favelado wished to find out about national and international news, he'd have to step outside of his hovel and head for the nearest botequim.[42]

The *jogo do bicho* shared many qualities with the community store. It flourished in that twilight world between prohibition and toleration that marks so many public activities in Brazil. The *bicheiro* (numbers man) was an important political personality, a loan shark, and a capitalist all in one. Quite frequently the money to purchase a shanty or store came from credit extended by the lottery runner. His "office," which might be on a street corner, was an obligatory stop for politicians hustling votes, a meeting place for men, and a school for children in the conduct of the street. The lottery exploited the favelados' dreams, yes, but it also gave gamblers a sense of shared identity—a common trust in fate—they could not acquire at home or work. It also provided hope.

The favela was neither a nest of marginals nor a self-contained world but a mirror image of the metropolis. Just about anything to be found in Rio de Janeiro could be seen inside the squatter settlement, from schools to movie theaters to gambling joints. The favelados built a parallel city, operated and run by the poor and striving to imitate the working and middle classes.

CONCLUSION

The favela explosion of the 1940s and 1950s continued the process of peripheralization of the Rio de Janeiro proletariat begun at the start of the century. The new working class forged from rural migrants was expelled from the core to the suburbs by high rents and then kept there by the promise of employment. In this way the poor could be housed without upsetting the geographical distribution of social classes and races in the city. The existence of the favelas relieved the city fathers from doing anything about the housing shortage. Poor people were tacitly, if not legally, allowed to build their own homes on government property and disputed lands. Favelas were a dark mirror of modernization; an inevitable product of the economic model Brazil follows, which sacrifices distribution of wealth and decent living standards to the Moloch of growth.

The poor made a compromise with the city by erecting shantytowns. Favelas offered a way to keep the family together in one place and send for relatives from the interior, an impossibility in the housing projects, which forbade unregistered tenants. Favelados prized family life, and most succeeded in holding their households together against daunting odds. Shantytowns provided residence close to the workplace, and some were erected literally in the shadow of construction projects. The ability to own one's home without paying rent appealed to the favelado. It was up to the favelado and his family to decide what improvements to make on the place, and if he joined with other squatters, they could pressure the city for services like water, electricity, and sewers. After 1960 few could picture Rio de Janeiro without the favelas—a measure of both the desperate poverty of the inhabitants and their resilience in carving out a section of the city for themselves.

4

One Generation

Following John F. Kennedy's inauguration as president of the United States in January 1961, *Esquire* magazine proclaimed, "The Twentieth Century Begins Today." The editors explained to those who might be puzzled that Kennedy was the first of the generation born after 1900 to become president, and therefore had missed many of the formative events of his fellow statesmen around the globe, such as World War I and the Russian Revolution. A generation is not simply a slice of time, though in everyday usage many take it to mean a cycle of twenty-five to thirty years. To the historian one generation is a collection of shared experiences, whether of a private or public nature. John Stuart Mill wrote of generations as "intervals of history, during which a new set of human beings have been educated, have grown from childhood, and taken possession of society." To José Ortega y Gasset they marked "a new integration of the social body."[1] What men and women remember, and cry, laugh, and argue about, is what makes them part of the same generation.

The second part of this volume centers on the shared experience of poverty in three favelas of Rio de Janeiro from the early 1940s to the late 1960s. The beginning and the end of this generation were set by four considerations. First, the formation of family households: the typical age for marrying and starting a family in the shantytowns was twenty to twenty-five and, as we shall see, many favela marriages and consensual unions remained stable for decades. The second factor was the length of stay in the labor force, which for most favelados ranged from age fifteen to twenty until their sixties. The third consideration was the physical state of the favela itself: the transition from the age of wooden shacks to brick-and-mortar housing and the rise of a favela middle class. Finally, this generation witnessed the political awakening of the favelados—from passive observers of the political scene to organizing the first shantytown social movements.

The favelas chosen for analysis symbolize major characteristics of the squatter settlements of Rio de Janeiro. Six factors were considered to encompass the greatest possible varieties of favela living.

1. Population in 1960. The favelas had to be small enough for survey but large enough to be considered typical.
2. Location. The problem here involved finding three favelas that together traced the evolution of the shanties from Zona Sul to Zona Norte and then to the suburbs along Avenida Brasil.
3. Topography. Favelas built on hillsides and on level ground served as test cases.
4. Economic activity. The importance of temporary work to the favela family—civil construction for men and domestic work for women—has been noted. The favelas fit for study had to have a large number of residents employed in these tasks as well as in industry.
5. Age of the favela, which is always a cloudy issue. A study of one generation should encompass favelas formed after 1930, as a result of the rural exodus, but before 1960, when the squatter settlements spread beyond the boundaries of the city of Rio de Janeiro and into the metropolitan periphery.
6. Current status. The possible fates of a favela are extinction, planned growth, and the transformation of the shantytown into a "community" recognized by the city, or an unplanned population explosion.

By these criteria three favelas were chosen: Praia do Pinto, Brás de Pina, and Jacarézinho.

PRAIA DO PINTO

Ordinarily, the exact location of a residence should not be a point of dispute, but there is nothing ordinary about the favela. Where was Praia do Pinto? In the early 1940s Praia do Pinto was mapped in Zona Sul, facing *Lagoa* (Lagoon) Rodrigo de Freitas, with access via Rua Humberto de Campos. It was contiguous to two other favelas, Cidade Maravilhosa and Largo da Memória, both of which were destroyed in 1942. The residents of these two favelas were removed to housing units built by the city especially for the squatters called *parques proletários provisionais* (provisional proletarian parks), located nearby in Leblon and Gávea. The 1950 federal census placed Praia do Pinto in Gávea, and counted 7,142 residents. The census of 1960 located it in Leblon and listed 6,976 inhabitants. But both these counts drew an arbitrary line between Praia do Pinto and the surrounding favelas of Ilha das Dragas, Favela Jockey Clube, and Parque Proletário do Leblon.

It appears that Praia do Pinto, Largo da Memória, and Cidade Maravilhosa always constituted a single favela subdivided into three units, and that the parques proletários built in 1943 soon became satellites of this larger unit because members of some families lived in both places and the parques overlapped in construction with Praia do Pinto. What matters most, obviously, is how the favelados viewed the matter, and there is no doubt they considered the three favelas and the parques as one settlement. Ilha das Dragas, though touching on Praia do Pinto, did not fall into the same category, nor did the Favela Jockey Clube[2] (see Map 4.1).

Map 4.1
Praia do Pinto and Surrounding Neighborhood in 1969

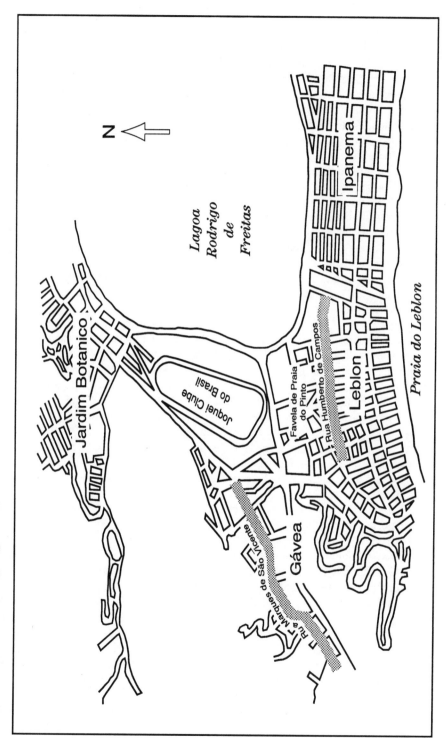

The origins of Praia do Pinto are mysterious and controversial. One source dates the first occupation as far back as 1918. Some former inhabitants claim that migrants began arriving between 1927 and 1928 but were quickly expelled by the mayor's office. By another account the favela was not formed until 1935, through the expulsion of residents from another shantytown, Chaćara do Céu. Evidently Praia do Pinto had its own story of genesis, followed by exodus and rebirth. The extension of the bus line Jardim-Leblon to Lagoa Rodrigo de Freitas, which allowed the poor to travel to work almost anywhere in Zona Sul, along with construction of the Jockey Clube and the real estate boom in Leblon during the 1920s, creating coveted jobs in the construction industry, were the principal reasons why Praia do Pinto became one of Rio's biggest squatter settlements by 1940.[3]

Praia do Pinto arose, prospered, and ultimately died as a result of the symbiotic relationship between itself and the rich neighborhoods of Leblon, Gávea, Ipanema, and Copacabana, where the subproletariat worked for the superrich. The construction industry, department stores, domestic services, and businesses catering to tourists in Zona Sul employed most of the adult inhabitants of Praia do Pinto on a temporary basis. The favelados had only seasonal security in their jobs, and were permitted to keep their homes only as long as the land under their feet was unwanted by their wealthy neighbors.

Praia do Pinto also suffered from an image problem. The inhabitants themselves admitted to the press that they had a reputation as vagabonds and drunks. For this reason, in the 1940s the city tried to cover up this eyesore through the construction of the proletarian parks. Eight hundred shanties in Cidade Maravilhosa and Largo da Memória, and some in Praia do Pinto, were demolished in 1942–1943 to make way for Proletarian Parks Numbers 1, 2, and 3. Park No. 1 was located in Gávea and was entered through Rua São Vicente 147. The property had belonged to the Instituto Nacional de Previdência Social (INPS, the National Social Welfare Institute) and also to a private party, Marieta Pires Ferreira. The Federal District bought the land in 1941, when Zona Sul land values had driven the price sky high, but apparently, as far as INPS was concerned, the deal was never finalized.

By 1943, Park No.1 held a population of 3,912 persons, drawn from Largo da Memória and Cidade Maravilhosa, housed in 892 barracks. Park No. 2, located on Rua Bonfim, died at inception, never growing beyond 322 houses. Park No. 3 was located in Leblon and was contiguous to the favela of Praia do Pinto. Built in April 1943, it initially housed 800 settlers in 162 houses. The land had been purchased from the Merchants' Institute of Rio de Janeiro, and most of the families removed from the subunit of Praia do Pinto were settled there. City authorities neglected Park No. 3 in favor of the showpiece of the project, Park No. 1, and construction of new homes was abandoned a few months after inauguration. A fourth park was built in 1947 in Praia Pequeno, giving homes to favelados displaced from the favela Jockey Clube to make way for the construction of Maracanã Stadium, but it must have had a short life. It was not counted in any of the city censuses of the favelas taken after 1948.[4]

The Catholic Church also tried its hand at doing away with Praia do Pinto, first by establishing a local outpost of the Fundação Leão XIII in 1948, and then by launching the ill-fated Cruzada São Sebastião, an apartment complex built inside Praia do Pinto, in 1956. Due in part to these experiments, by the 1960s Praia do Pinto had lost most of its population to other favelas, and when the city government decided on complete eradication in 1969 in order to open up space for the real estate interests in Leblon, the remaining residents were helpless to protest.[5]

BRÁS DE PINA

Driving down Avenida Brasil in Zona Norte, it is easy to lose sight of Brás de Pina. But even if the vehicle slowed down, it would be hard to recognize, since the favela is completely urbanized today and blends easily with the surrounding neighborhood of the same name. Located close to Rua Ourique and facing Avenida Brasil, Rio de Janeiro's busiest highway, the community bears little resemblance to its former self. Once a tiny squatter settlement housing 906 souls in 1960, today it is home to over 10,000 people. Two geographical factors have determined the favela's destiny—proximity to Avenida Brasil and the quality of the soil.

Access to Avenida Brasil gave the inhabitants quick transportation to jobs throughout the city. At first this factor worked more to the benefit of the women of the favela, who commuted to work in Leblon, Ipanema, and Copacabana, while their husbands sought employment in the vicinity. The avenue itself had dozens of automobile repair shops, restaurants, and department stores that offered employment to favelados. The flow of traffic through Avenida Brasil also brought customers to local street vendors who offered everything from trinkets to candy. By the late 1940s migrants from Minas Gerais, Rio de Janeiro state, and the Federal District flocked to Brás de Pina, hoping to cash in on the prosperity associated with Avenida Brasil.

But the attraction of Brás de Pina was balanced by another consideration. Until recent times most of the favela was covered by swamps. All the original shanties built in the 1930s and 1940s stood on stilts. Most were constructed next to the main streets of Brás de Pina—Toborapi, Alquindar, and Japegua. In an interesting geographical twist, Brás de Pina grew from the geographical periphery towards the core. The most distinctive feature of the favela in its early years was the existence of a large mud pool close to the entrance. The original settler families built their homes as far as possible from this health hazard; later arrivals had no choice but to camp nearer the pool. Flooding perpetually troubled all the inhabitants and motivated the campaign begun in the mid-1960s to renovate the community (see Map 4.2).

The first shanties in Brás de Pina may have been built in 1934, but effective occupation did not begin until 1946 with the opening of Avenida Brasil. The land originally belonged to the Brazilian navy, but except for brief skirmishes with the police during 1942–43, no one questioned the settlers' right of residency until the 1960s. In 1964 Carlos Lacerda, the governor of Guanabara, decided to evict the inhabitants, ostensibly to move them to Vila Kennedy and Vila Aliança, two housing projects on the outskirts of Rio de Janeiro built under the auspices of the

Map 4.2
Brás de Pina and Surrounding Neighborhood in 1967

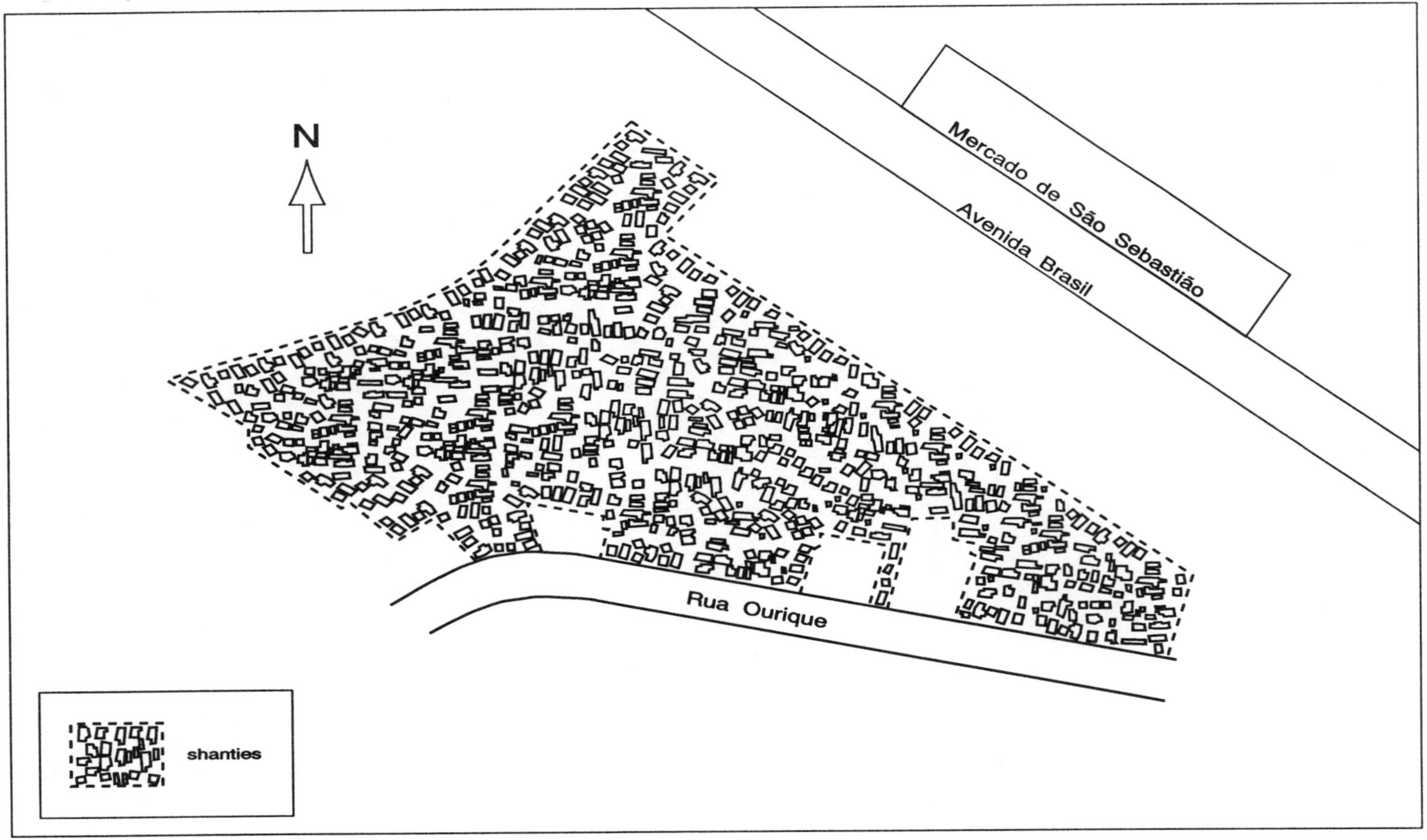

N

Mercado de São Sebastião

Avenida Brasil

Rua Ourique

shanties

Alliance for Progress. Lacerda's real motivation was to put the land of Brás de Pina up for sale and raise money to eradicate other favelas in the city, a seeming obsession since his journalist days. After a fierce personal confrontation with the squatters in December 1964, the governor withdrew his threat, and the favelados promised to make improvements in Brás de Pina if they could receive city help. A public company, Companhia de Desenvolvimento de Comunidades (CODESCO), was started for this purpose in 1966. The "urbanization" program launched in 1967, in conjunction with the local residents' association, lasted eight years and brought Brás de Pina cement housing, electricity, clean water, and paved streets, but also split the community between collaborators and opponents of CODESCO, a division that remains bitter to this day.[6]

JACARÉZINHO

Jacarézinho never had any trouble being overlooked on the map; on the contrary, many people mistook it for a mini-city. It was the largest favela in the state of Guanabara in 1960, with a population of 22,714. Today, with its numbers swollen to over 100,000, it occupies a humble second place behind the favela of Rocinha. Jacarézinho overlaps two neighborhoods, Maria da Graça and Jacaré, both located in the district of Méier in Zona Norte. It is bounded by Avenida Suburbana, Vieira Fazenda station of the auxiliary line of the Central do Brasil railroad, and the Jacaré river. The favela has three major subdivisions: riverside, where the poorest migrants have always settled; the main area, also called Vieira Fazenda, which touches on the Central do Brasil; and the hillside, *Morro Azul*, (Blue Hill), where the first inhabitants set up home. An important unofficial boundary marker between the favela and the rest of the city is the General Electric factory, north of Vieira Fazenda and next to the railroad[7] (see Map 4.3).

While it may have been predestined that a favela would arise in Jacarézinho, given the availability of factory jobs, there was nothing inevitable about its staying power and expansion. They were due primarily to the strong presence of industry in the area and the political savvy of the inhabitants. A few scattered shacks may have been built in the 1920s, but residents insist that occupation did not begin until 1932. The central feature of Jacarézinho back then was a large country house owned by a Portuguese family. Fruits, vegetables, and sugarcane grew in the fields. In the first decade of occupation, ten courageous migrant families staked out a claim on the hill overlooking Jacarézinho, Blue Hill, so called because it brought them happiness. The occupation of Jacarézinho occurred from the top of the hill downward. Curiously, today this process is reversing itself, with space on the plain running out, many newcomers are forced to climb the hillside to build their homes, just like the founders of the favela.

Jacarézinho's conquest of the title of the number one favela in Rio de Janeiro in the 1950s can be attributed to three factors. The improvement and extension of the Central do Brasil railroad allowed local residents to commute to jobs in Centro and Zona Sul. The favela was infused with new blood when the construction of Avenida Presidente Vargas in Centro displaced many of the downtown poor toward Zona

Map 4.3
Jacarézinho and Surrounding Neighborhood in 1965

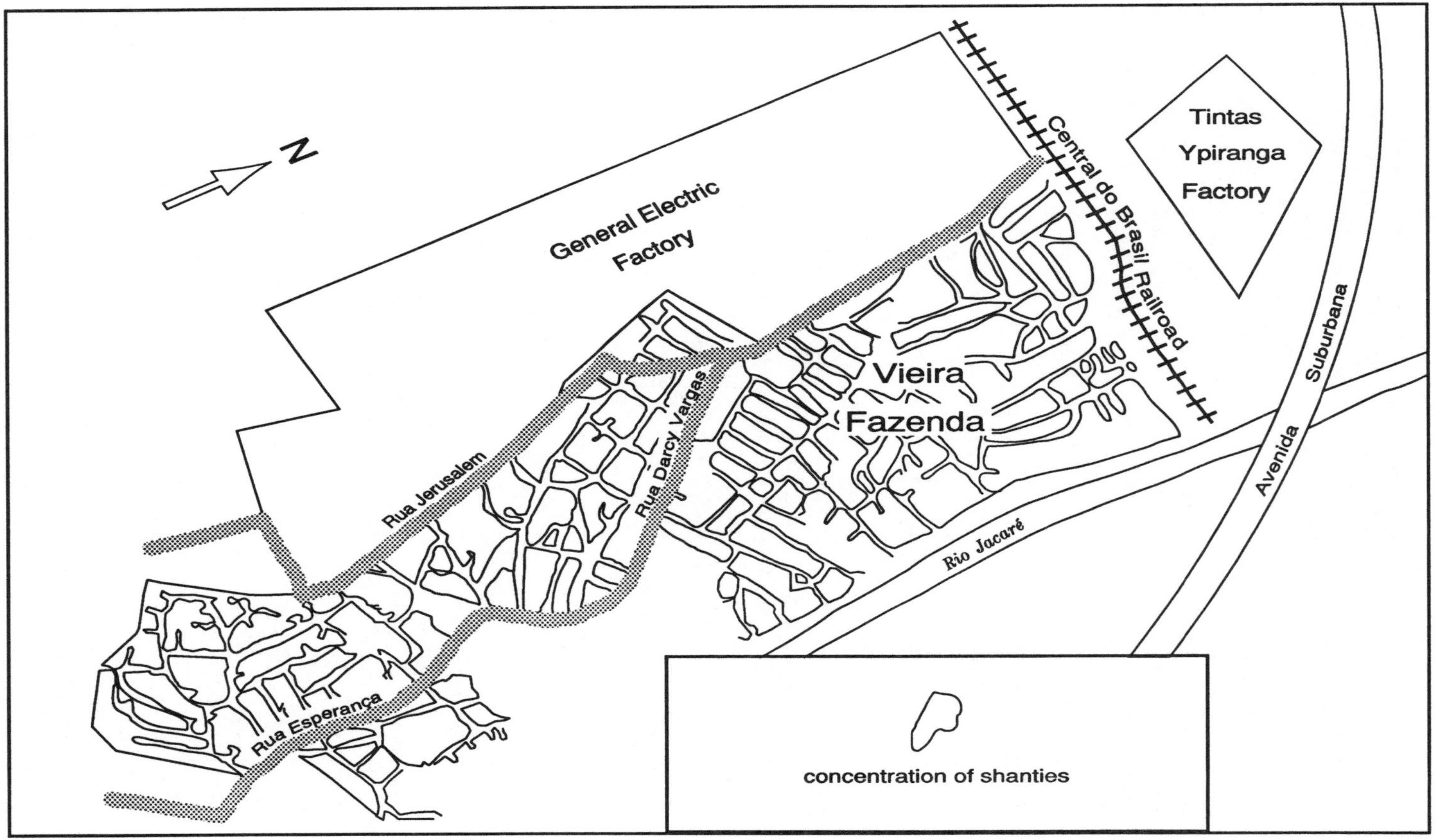

N

Tintas
Ypiranga
Factory

Central do Brasil Railroad

Avenida Suburbana

General Electric
Factory

Vieira
Fazenda

Rio Jacaré

Rua Darcy Vargas

Rua Jerusalem

Rua Esperança

concentration of shanties

Norte. But the crucial element in the spectacular growth of Jacarézinho was the expansion of industry in the district of Méier following World War II. Some local factories like General Electric dated from the 1920s, but it was not until the late 1940s and 1950s that industrial jobs beckoned large numbers of the homeless to Jacarézinho. In 1950 some 40 percent of the workforce in Jacarézinho was employed in factory work.[8]

Industry had a stake in the survival of Jacarézinho, as shown by the willingness of local entrepreneurs to come to the aid of the residents when the favela was threatened with extinction. The first such incident occurred in 1945, when one of the original owners of the area, Mario de Almeida, who realized just how valuable his domain had become thanks to local industry, demanded his land back. After the police repeatedly invaded the favela with vans and armored vehicles, the residents organized a march on the Presidential Palace at Catête, and extracted a promise from Getúlio Vargas to put an end to evictions. In the late 1940s the Companhia Concórdia Imobiliárial, a real estate firm, pressured the city government to evict the thirty thousand squatters living in Jacarézinho, but the bosses of the GE factory, along with other industrialists, came to the defense of the favela and the effort failed. A more serious melee ensued in the 1950s when the Companhia Administradora São Paulo petitioned the city to expel the inhabitants and hand the land of Jacarézinho over to it. The company won its case in court but lost the sympathy of city officials, who moved to buy the land and grant it to the favelados. By 1960 Jacarézinho had become too large to eradicate but impossible to urbanize, according to city planners. The result was uncontrolled growth and the renovation of the favela by the residents themselves, a pattern followed since then in many other shantytowns.[9]

CONCLUSION

Praia do Pinto, Brás de Pina, and Jacarézinho are a motley collection of squatter settlements. Each had its own identity and suffered a different fate. The first was destroyed and the second was integrated with Rio de Janeiro, while the third came to resemble and function as a miniature city. Nevertheless, there are unifying factors the historian can detect that allow for a comparative analysis. In all three settlements the inhabitants married, made love, and raised families; attached themselves to any job they could find; invested time, money, and effort to build homes and businesses; and pressured the city to recognize their right to live as a separate community.

The next four chapters analyze the dialectic of the reproduction of poverty and the resistance of the poor in three favelas of Rio de Janeiro as seen in patterns of household life, economic activity, living standards, and the political activity of the squatters.

5

Organization

The hypothesis that family disorganization was responsible for consigning the favelados to a lifetime of poverty, even before they were born, was widely shared by urban analysts in Brazil from the 1940s to the 1960s. In a typical assessment, the Social Planning Center of the Pontifical Catholic University of Rio de Janeiro, an institution supposedly friendly toward the favelados, referred to the favela household as "fragile, precarious, open, and variable; people come and go, to the point that the family is reduced to blood ties between mother and children."[1] Prejudicial views such as these served the political purposes of the city fathers of Rio de Janeiro, who wanted to eradicate the favelas without analyzing the material factors that produced and reproduced them. Official assertions of the incompatibility of the institution of the family with living in the favelas have thus far gone largely unchallenged, and even contemporary students of the squatter population of Rio de Janeiro, while exploding the myth of favela marginality, have cast no more than a cursory glance at household life among the Carioca poor.[2]

This chapter focuses on the squatter household in Praia do Pinto, Brás de Pina, and Jacarézinho from 1942 to 1969. It explores the survival and reproduction of the household in poverty, the role of women in the favela, and the social and economic reasons for various household compositions. Judged by size and structure, the households of this generation had a great deal in common with many working-class homes in Rio de Janeiro. The male-headed nuclear household prevailed in all three settlements, despite substantial differences in economic activity and living standards. Female-headed households seem to have formed a minority of the total, but their importance grew toward the end of the 1960s. Overcrowding, a lack of steady jobs, and the absence of adequate education and health care put severe stress on households in the favelas, but a great many survived nevertheless.

PRAIA DO PINTO

Most of the evidence for the early history of the household in Praia do Pinto comes from city officials associated with the construction of the proletarian parks. Largo da Memória, one of the subunits of Praia do Pinto, was surveyed by the city shortly before its destruction in 1942. Figures compiled by social worker Maria Hortencia do Nascimento Silva, based on several trips to the favela in October 1941, show a population of 1,619, with an average of 9 households per 7 shacks. Of the inhabitants, 820 were under 20 years of age, leaving 799 adults. Females outnumbered males 832 to 787, due mainly, said health workers, to the high mortality rate among male children induced by tuberculosis. There were 360 whites living in Largo da Memória, 561 blacks, 6 "yellows," 480 mixed-race (pardo), and 212 of undeclared race. Rio de Janeiro state supplied the largest number of settlers, 663, followed by the city of Rio de Janeiro (then the Federal District of Brazil) and Minas Gerais. The single largest group of migrants (667) had arrived in the favela during 1939–1941, which means Largo da Memória was inhabited mainly by newcomers and that earlier squatters had found local living conditions so appalling they had fled.

Even in such terrifying surroundings family life survived: 949 residents, including children and adolescents, were listed as single, 392 were married; 102 were widowed; 1 was separated; and 119 lived in consensual unions (56 residents remained uncounted in the marital survey). In light of the fact that only 170 men and women fell in the age category of 20 to 25, the most likely age to marry, the percentage of marriages among those over age 20 was a surprisingly high 49 percent. Equally impressive, the number of legal marriages was more than three times the figure for consensual unions.

The nuclear family was most common among the early settlers. Under the heading "relationship to those responsible for the shanty," 373 listed themselves as head of household, 817 as son/daughter of the head, and 245 as "companion," meaning by marriage or consensual union. The extended family was barely represented: only seven grandsons/daughters, two grandparents, eleven nephews/ nieces, ten brothers, and six fathers-in-law/mothers-in-law lived with the owner of the shanty. There is some indirect evidence for the presence of female-headed households in this early stage of the life of the favela. One-quarter of all households were said to lack a head, "either because he is absent or financially incapable of supporting the family."[3] Silva did not obtain information on whether these were headed by a woman or by a male relative of the head, but the large number of females in Largo da Memória makes the former more probable.

Further information on household structure in Praia do Pinto during its formative years is available from the papers of the city commissioner charged with overseeing the construction of the proletarian parks, Dr. Vitor Tavares de Moura. Table 5.1 shows the comparative populations of the subunits of Largo da Memória, Praia do Pinto, and Cidade Maravilhosa in 1942. The subunit of Praia do Pinto contained 1,779 shanties housing 3,987 persons. More than half the population was under 15 years of age, but the number of children per household, 1.14, was not very high. Cidade Maravilhosa, the largest and to the news media the most notorious of the three subunits, had a huge population of 4,737 cramped into 1,344 shacks, an average of 3.5 persons per household. The favelados here were much older than their neighbors in Praia do Pinto; over 60 percent were aged 15 years and above. But the average number of minors under age 15 per household came to 1.4, significantly higher than in Praia do Pinto. The provenance of the populations could not have been a factor in the discrepancies between the average age of the occupants of the two settlements. Half of the household heads in both Cidade Maravilhosa and Praia do Pinto had migrated from Rio de Janeiro state, a quarter from Minas Gerais, and the remaining quarter from elsewhere in the city of Rio de Janeiro and from other states. It is possible, however, that Cidade Maravilhosa was settled earlier than Praia do Pinto and Largo da Memória, accounting for both the older population and the greater number of children per household.

Table 5.1a
Population of Largo da Memória in 1942 by Age

Age	N	%
0 to 2 years	177	8.73
2 to 15 years	662	32.64
Above 15	1,187	58.58
Total	2,026	100.00

Total rounded off to 100.0%

Total number of shanties 450
Average of inhabitans per shanty 4.5
Average number of occupants above age 15 per shanty 2.6
Average number of occupants below age 15 per shanty 1.9
Source: Moura, "Apuração do censo realisado na favela Largo da Memória," Moura Family Papers.

Table 5.1b
Population of Praia do Pinto in 1942 by Age

Age	N	%
0 to 2 years	454	11.38
2 to 15 years	1,584	39.72
Above Age 15	1,949	48.88
Total	3,987	100.00

Total rounded off to 100.0%

Total number of shanties 1,779
Average of inhabitants per shanty 2.3
Average number of occupants above age 15 per shanty 1.09
Average number of occupants below age 15 per shanty 1.14
Source: Moura, "Apuração do censo realisado na favela Praia do Pinto," Moura Family Papers.

Table 5.1c
Population of Cidade Maravilhosa in 1942 by Age

Age	N	%
0 to 2 years	382	8.06
2 to 15 years	1,507	31.81
Above Age 15	2,848	60.12
Total	4,737	100.00

Total rounded off to 100.0%

Total number of shanties 1,344
Average of inhabitants per shanty 3.5
Average number of occupants above age 15 per shanty 2.1
Average number of occupants below age 15 per shanty 1.4
Source: Moura, "Apuração do censo realizado na favela Cidade Maravilhosa," Moura Family Papers.

Writing for the press in the early 1940s, Dr. Moura concluded that the high number of occupants per shanty in all three subunits of Praia do Pinto proved the existence of "illicit unions, social maladjustment and an inadequate preoccupation about stable family organization" on the part of the inhabitants.[4] That was an overstatement, as proved by the statistics on household size and structure that he and others had compiled, but more to the point, Moura failed to consider how the economy of the area surrounding the favela influenced family organization. The fate of the laboring population of Praia do Pinto in the 1930s and 1940s was linked largely to the construction business in Zona Sul. Although the inhabitants were wretchedly poor, the favela was located on the borders of two of the richest neighborhoods in the city. The industrialization of Rio de Janeiro under Vargas contributed to the growth of Praia do Pinto by spurring real estate development in Gávea and Leblon.

Favelados living in the area surrounding Lagoa Rodrigo de Freitas depended on the continued prosperity of their neighbors for jobs, and the city tolerated the shantytown as the price to be paid for cheap menial labor. Nearly all the adult men in Praia do Pinto worked as bricklayers in construction and the vast majority of women took temporary jobs as domestics.

The Mayor's Office was persuaded by Moura that relocation to a better environment would force the squatters of Praia do Pinto to reform themselves and become better citizens; the doctor was convinced that the success of the proletarian parks would one day make the favelas a distant memory. During the Christmas season of 1942, Largo da Memória, Cidade Maravilhosa, and a large section of Praia do Pinto were razed on orders of Mayor Henrique Dodsworth and the inhabitants were removed to the proletarian parks. The families resettled in the parks were a guinea pig population chosen to prove the efficacy of eradication as a solution to the favela "problem." The city authorities carefully chose those residents of the favela they felt could reproduce the ideal nuclear family. Park No. 1, located on Rua São Vicente in Gávea, just a few blocks from Praia do Pinto, began with a population of 3,673. Forty percent of the inhabitants were under 15 years old, and the single largest age group among them was infants up to one year old. There were 860 houses for these proletarian pioneers, which resulted in an occupancy average of 4.26 inhabitants per household: 2.55 adults and 1.71 children (see Table 5.2).

Table 5.2
Population of Provisional Proletarian Park No. 1 in 1943 by Age

Age	N	%
0 to 2 years	225	6.1
2 to 7 years	514	13.9
7 to 15 years	736	20.1
Above Age 15	2,198	59.9
Total	3,673	100.0

Total Rounded off to 100.0%

Total number of shanties 862
Average of inhabitants per shanty 4.2
Average number of occupants above age 15 per shanty 2.5
Average number of occupants below age 15 per shanty 1.7
Source: Moura, "Estatística do Parque Proletário Provisório No. 1," Moura Family Papers.

The optimism of Moura and the other planners as to the success of the proletarian parks was not borne out by events. By the early 1950s no one could pretend that Proletarian Park No. 1, the showpiece of the project, was anything but a rebaptized favela. The population in 1952 had swollen considerably beyond original estimates for maximum capacity, reaching 5,262. Females outnumbered males 2,809 to 2,453. A new generation had come of age with only vague memories of life in the favelas. The number of inhabitants between the ages of 8 and 21 came to 1,749—a core of youth desperate for work and education and finding neither. The park also re-created Brazil's much-publicized "racial democracy," which in fact consigned blacks and mulattoes to the bottom of the social ladder. On the basis of self-classification, 2,295 residents listed themselves as pardos, along with 1,749 whites and 1,228 blacks. (For unknown reasons another ten persons appeared in the racial count of the park population.) But the real number of pardos was probably higher, said social workers due to the tendency of some members of this group to classify themselves as white.[5]

The dedication of the park planners to maintaining a "Christian" environment where the nuclear family could reproduce denies the historian a full knowledge of the constitution of the household because couples living in consensual unions were not officially recognized by the authorities. Nearly 40 percent of the population over age 16 was listed as single, and only 22.4 percent were legally married. But the compiler of the census noted that many of those over age 16 who were listed as single or widowed were probably living with a companion of the opposite sex. Despite the attempt by the planners to prevent a population explosion in the park, household size had increased in comparison with the favelas whence the residents had been removed. The 1952 count registered 955 households, with nearly half (45.1 percent) made up of 4 to 6 members.[6]

The number of *agregados* in the park provides clues to the survival of the extended family among favelados. This category included parents, older children who had not been living at home, grandparents, grandsons, nephews, nieces, in-laws, and others who now lived in the same shack as a recognized head of household. Only a seemingly small number of agregados (383) lived in Park No. 1 in 1952. But another survey of 249 households in the park that same year found that 38 lived in their own homes but were related to the heads of the remaining 211 households and made some sort of financial contribution to their relatives.[7] The construction of the park apparently attracted poorer relatives to come and live alongside those lucky enough to have been granted shelter by the city. Instead of preserving the nuclear family, the park experiment helped to undermine it.

Accounts of family life in the park provided by health volunteers who served there in the 1940s and 1950s allow us to dig underneath these statistics and grasp the enormous failure of this experiment to remold the favelados. Though the names of their charges had to be disguised, the wrenching stories recorded in the notebooks of the volunteers bear witness to their travails. Apparently the strain of living in these collapsing, cramped quarters, with little prospect for work or social mobility, took its toll on the patriarchal family. The interviews emphasize the irresponsibility of men and the endurance of women. A typical case of an ex-favelada now living in the park was the woman identified as "B," found bleeding one day by a social worker.

The doctor counseled immediate admission to the nearest hospital, telling her she might need three transfusions of blood. One of B's sister's came to keep her company and then her husband came, which allowed to her to go to the hospital. The sister took her nephews home to take care of them while their mother was hospitalized.

A few days later B returned home weakened, but she still had to do all the domestic chores. . . . B's husband is an electrician who, according to her, leaves home early and returns late. He faces many financial difficulties and seems not to care about her health or that of her seven children. All are of a weak constitution and four of them, although of school age, are still not enrolled in school. Despite poverty, B's home shows order and group solidarity. Family disadjustment is due to several factors [including] economic misery, conditions of habitation, and a lack of interest by the family head.[8]

The patriarchal household did survive in the park, but according to social workers, many males were torn between their duties as workers, residents, and family heads. The case of "J," an elderly Portuguese male with a Brazilian family, was somewhat extreme but perhaps not all that unusual. Suspected of carrying leprosy, he was visited one day in his home by an assistant social worker.

The assistant observed a malconstituted family. The head had separated from his first wife and formed this illegitimate family over 20 years ago. From this union he had 3 children: 2 boys; the eldest, 19 years old, the second, 17; and a girl, 12. The 17-year-old boy and the girl suffer from "attacks." The woman of the house told us her companion was interned at the leprosy ward of Curupaiti hospital; the two sick children were under treatment and the eldest at work. In fact "J" had left the hospital without informing the staff, and when asked to explain, he said he had, "business to take care of, from which I maintain the family." His companion feared "J" might be interned permanently, depriving the household of its bread winner. Fortunately, he was persuaded to go in for an examination, and the results proved negative.[9]

Other interviews illustrate the growing importance of wives and companions to the sustenance of the home and the rise of the female-headed household.

Family X
A young pardo couple, husband white and wife mixed race, with two girls ages 12 and 15. The head had contracted pulmonary tuberculosis. The youngest girl was skinny, pallid, and of poor eyesight. As to their economic situation, Mr. X was a driver with the Electric Company, and received medical treatment almost free of charge. But his wages had been reduced on account of illness and the family budget was considerably curtailed. Mrs. X's salary as an unskilled worker and his pension were not enough to cover the family's essential expenses.

Family Y
An illegally constituted union, since the male was already married before in Portugal. In fact, this couple had already separated due to "many fights." They had eight children, all white like their parents. Despite their difficulties, "Mrs." Y as well as her children, all under 15, seemed healthy and happy. The family was sustained by her work as a laundry woman, along with occasional gifts from private parties. Their two-room house had no running water, lacked a water closet and was located in one of the worst areas of the park, next to one of the ditches. The interior of the house was a complete mess.

Family Z
The case of Mrs. Z was typical of the tenant families, that is, those persons who without permission from the administration, occupy one of the houses in the park. The family was composed of Mrs. Z, a somewhat elderly widow, and her son M. Mrs. Z, somewhat Negro in complexion, was small and skinny, well groomed and clean. Her son was a boy of 19, tall, skinny and also slightly Negro in color. Mrs. Z belonged to a Baptist sect organized inside the park. It was a member of the sect who gave her shelter, since her married sons had neither the space nor the means in their homes to care for her and her son. They were sustained these past few years by M's salary, though he was currently unemployed, and by donations from poor friends. Mrs. Z and M were staying with two women who worked outside the park.[10]

The proletarian parks experiment, intended to re-create "ideal Christian families," had merely added one more shantytown to Rio de Janeiro, complete with the same horror stories. By forcing young men and women to abide by the ideal of the nuclear family, without providing the economic infrastructure to make such an arrangement functional, the park organizers wound up undermining patriarchy and fostering female independence.

The patriarchal nuclear household in Praia do Pinto was also under siege from the profound changes in the city's economy and the geographical distribution of industry after 1950. The deindustrialization of Rio de Janeiro and the shift of industries to the northern suburbs and metropolitan periphery during this decade virtually eliminated factory work as a source of income for male residents of Praia do Pinto. Previously men in the favela had been able to travel by bus or bicycle to industrial jobs in the Zona Sul and Centro. Now those jobs had been displaced to the further reaches of Zona Norte and beyond. At the same time women were finding it easier to obtain local employment thanks to the construction of more housing for the middle class in Leblon, Gávea, and Ipanema.

During the 1960s the proletarian parks were rechristened conjuntos habitacionais sociais (CHS) (social housing combinations) and by 1967 some city authorities considered Praia do Pinto, the nearby favela of Ilha das Dragas, CHS-1 (Gávea), and CHS-3 (Leblon) as *de facto* a single huge favela because their populations intermingled and, with the exception of CHS-1, shared contiguous physical space. A survey carried out on behalf of the city by the Comissão Executiva de Projetos Específicos in 1967 counted 1,107 households in Praia do Pinto with a total population of 4,459. Household size remained relatively small, averaging 4 persons per shanty. Of these households, 210 had 3 members, 195 had 4 members, and 135 had 5. Only 43 households had 9 members or more (see Table 5.3).

Table 5.3
Praia do Pinto: Household Size in 1967

No. of Persons	No. of Households	%
1	122	2.7
2	194	8.7
3	210	14.1
4	195	17.5
5	135	15.1
6	88	11.8
7	65	10.2
8	55	9.9
9	16	3.2
≥10	27	6.8
Total	1,107	100.0

Source: Comissão Executiva de Projectos Específicos, Serviço de Estatística, "Dados estatísticos referentes à favela Praia do Pinto, Ilha das Dragas, CHS-1, CHS-3."

CHS-1 in Gávea contained 6,736 residents and 1,271 households, an average of 5.2 occupants per shanty. Most households fell in the range of 4 to 7 members. CHS-1 also had 253 agregado households containing 719 members living apart from their relatives. CHS-3 in Leblon, which had once been a poor relation to No. 1 in Gávea, was little more than an appendage to Praia do Pinto at the close of the 1960s. The population was small and overcrowded. In 1967, 506 households were counted with a total population of 2,703, an average of 5.34 per shack. The number of large households was much higher: 38 households, (15.5 percent of the total) had

10 members or more. CHS-3 had 138 agregado households with a total of 397 members (2.94 per shanty). Since one aim of the original proletarian parks project had been to reproduce small nuclear families, the conjuntos had failed on this score. Couples here tended to have more children than their neighbors in Praia do Pinto, and it is not too fanciful to suggest that the higher costs of living there may have been responsible. In this instance, expanding the family might have seemed a useful survival strategy to bring in more wage earners.[11]

As twilight set on the favela in 1969 and city authorities came to conduct one last census, they were confronted with the perennial problem of locating Praia do Pinto. The 1967 survey had distinguished between Praia do Pinto, Ilha das Dragas, CHS-1, and CHS-3, but this time the four subunits were treated as one complex. The total population was 15,184, grouped in 3,335 households, making it one of the largest favelas in Zona Sul. Over half the population was under 20 years of age. Females outnumbered males 7,949 to 7,235 (see Table 5.4).

Table 5.4
Praia do Pinto: Distribution of Population by Age in 1969

Age	N	%
0 to 1	444	2.90
1 to 5	2,024	13.60
6 to 10	1,804	12.10
11 to 15	1,702	11.40
16 to 20	1,523	10.20
21 to 25	1,538	10.30
26 to 30	1,421	9.50
31 to 35	1,055	7.10
36 to 40	1,031	6.90
41 to 45	678	4.50
46 to 50	514	3.40
51 to 55	378	2.50
56 to 60	307	2.10
61 to 65	163	1.10
66 to 70	154	1.00
Over 70	132	.89
Total	14,868	100.00

(316 individuals did not declare their age)
Total rounded off to 100%

Source: Estado da Guanabara. Secretaria de Serviços Sociais, "Praia do Pinto," 30.

Despite the huge increase in the number of residents, the formation of stable families continued to be important to the favelados: 40 percent of household heads in Praia do Pinto were married and 23.7 percent were living in consensual unions. Singles made up 25.4 percent of the adult population above age 20 but census officials noted the possibility that this category actually included many persons living with a partner (see Table 5.5). Nuclear households were still in the majority, but half the shanties housed at least one elderly relative. Most households remained small. Even counting the Conjuntos Habitacionais Socias and Ilha das Dragas, the average household size was 4.5. Although government and church authorities blamed the tendency of the poor to have too many offspring as a major cause of poverty, couples in Praia do Pinto tended to have fewer children at the end of the 1960s than in earlier decades. The largest percentage of households (28.4 percent) had no children, followed by those with one child (21 percent).[12]

Table 5.5
Praia do Pinto: Marital Status of Household Heads in 1969

Marital Status	N	%
Married	1,333	40.3
Single	841	25.4
Consensual union	784	23.7
Legally separated	13	0.3
Separated	28	0.8
Widowed	308	9.3
Total	3,307	100.0

Total rounded off to 100.0%

Source: Estado da Guanabara. Secretaria de Serviços Sociais, "Praia do Pinto," 34.

One feature of family life in Praia do Pinto that received special attention in this last survey was the marital status of women. Just over half (52 percent) of the female companions of the male household heads were married and 48 percent were linked to their spouses by consensual unions. The 1969 survey also found a relatively high percentage of female household heads (31.2 percent), compared with male (68.7 percent).[13] The matrifocality of households among the urban poor in Brazil during the 1960s has been put on prominent display through anecdotes in the popular literature, but so far very little statistical information has been gathered. As the sections dealing with Brás de Pina and Jacarézinho below reveal, it does not appear that female-headed households were common in the favelas of Rio de Janeiro during this generation. How, then, can their larger presence in Praia do Pinto at the end of of the favela's life be explained?

The occupational structure of Praia do Pinto in 1969 may provide some answers. The economy of Zona Sul, built around the service sector, encouraged females to experiment with living arrangements. The women of Praia do Pinto did not need many skills to find employment. Leblon, Copacabana, and Gávea thrived on tourism and leisure activities requiring temporary labor. By 1969 Praia do Pinto was surrounded by apartment buildings, restaurants, supermarkets, and other institutions of middle-class life. Bourgeois matrons needed female laborers from Praia do Pinto to scrub floors, cook and clean, and watch their children while they were at work. Favela women were enticed by their employers to forgo marriage by the promise of unsteady but relatively high-paying jobs. The high degree of matrifocality in Praia do Pinto can be therefore seen as a personal response by women to changing economic conditions. Favela women carefully weighed the benefits and drawbacks of marriage, consensual unions and single motherhood, often practicing all three in a lifetime.

Praia do Pinto underwent many reincarnations in its history, from squatter camp to the proletarian parks experiment to superfavela, but the household did not expand significantly beyond the nuclear core. Few lone individuals, male or female, lived in the favela for any lengthy period of time. Marriage or long-term cohabitation made sense to many men on economic as well as social grounds. But the old rules regarding male-female partnerships changed as the economy of the area boomed while male favelados were often the last to be hired. The most significant transformation in household structure from the 1940s to the 1960s was the emerging economic importance of women and the decision by many of them to form temporary unions with men, based on their own degree of financial independence. In this regard Praia do Pinto foreshadowed the "feminization of poverty" in Rio de Janeiro in the 1970s. When the favela was set aflame in 1969, the city lost an important monument to family and women's history.

BRÁS DE PINA

Like Praia do Pinto, Brás de Pina was settled largely by migrants from the interior of the states of Rio de Janeiro and Minas Gerais. Apparently one of the first occupants was Geraldina de Paula Monteiro, who still lived in the favela as of 1990. Born in Vicas in Minas Gerais, she migrated first to the small city of Ramos in the state of Rio de Janeiro and then to Brás de Pina at the invitation of her female boss in 1934. Having no children of her own, she raised three adopted ones. Another early migrant was Eloysa da Conceição Pereira. Born in Petrópolis in Rio de Janeiro state, she settled in Brás de Pina in 1947. Already married when she arrived, she and her husband brought along two children. While she worked as a maid by day, the couple built a shanty at night.

The second wave of migrants included both single people and large families. Rute Costa Moreira was asked by her sister to come and live in Brás de Pina in 1955. She recalls that at that time a shack could be constructed for 6 cruzeiros worth of building materials. Another newcomer that decade was Sebastião Vitor Campos. Born in Leopoldina in the state of Minas Gerais, he moved first to Caranjolas, in the same state, and then to Duque de Caxias in Rio de Janeiro, and finally settled down in Brás de Pina in 1956 at the invitation of his daughter. Married at the time of his arrival, he raised five children in the favela. José Fernandes, born in the state of Rio de Janeiro, had a similar experience. He came to Brás de Pina in 1958 and fathered seven children. Diocilia de Souza was born in Espírito Santo, and came to Rio de Janeiro to work as a domestic. Her first home was in Maracanã. In Brás de Pina she and her first husband reared eight children. Around the same time Hilda Pereira Rocha, who had been born in Laijinha, Minas Gerais, came to Brás de Pina, at the request of her mother. She soon found a husband and gave birth to five children.[14]

A few families may have trickled in during the 1930s and 1940s but as late as 1950 the favela was a still tiny blip on the map of Rio de Janeiro. In the national census of that year it was not listed as a separate settlement but was linked to the nearby favela of Lucas. Their combined population came to 5,100: 2,542 men and 2,558 women. The growing traffic along Avenida Brasil and the large number of commercial establishments there after the avenue's opening in 1946 lured enough settlers to earn Brás de Pina recognition from the city as a separate favela. The 1960 Guanabara census registered a population of 906 persons divided between 425 men and 481 women.[15]

The political turmoil of the mid-1960s caused by Guanabara Governor Carlos Lacerda's plan to eradicate Brás de Pina and remove the favelados to housing projects on the outskirts of the city focused attention on the favela and left historians with valuable information on household life. At Lacerda's urging, the state housing agency, the Companhia de Habitação Popular do Estado da Guanabara (COHAB) conducted a quick survey of Brás de Pina in 1964. It counted 323 households, but this figure covered only squatters residing in the part of the favela declared "uninhabitable" by COHAB, where demolition was scheduled to begin. Carlos Nelson Ferreira dos Santos, an architecture student who later went on to command the transformation of Brás de Pina from squatter settlement to urban community, claimed the entire favela contained 980 households when Lacerda made his offer to relocate the inhabitants to the projects and that only 180 accepted his proposal.[16] But even if the COHAB census is based on a small sample, it still provides interesting clues to household structure.

The founding generation had not been able to escape poverty but instead passed on the favela to its offspring. Children and adolescents under 20 years of age accounted for over half (55 percent) of the 1964 survey group. Brás de Pina was also more densely settled than most shantytowns: 1,777 persons were grouped in 323 households (5.5 per shack). Households including one to three members comprised 37 percent of the total, and those with four to six members comprised 42.2 percent. The extended household was gradually disappearing. Seven to nine members made up only 17.6 percent, and those numbering ten were virtually extinct at 2.8 percent (see Table 5.6).

By the late 1960s Brás de Pina had been recognized as one of the poorest but also one of the most vibrant squatter settlements in Zona Norte, continuously drawing in new people. In 1967 the Companhia de Desenvolvimento de Comunidades (CODESCO), created by the city to urbanize Brás de Pina, conducted one of the most thorough surveys of favela life ever undertaken in Rio de Janeiro: 812 shanties, including those housing only one person, housed a population of 4,416 (2,231 males and 2,185 females), for an occupancy rate of 5.43 persons (see Table 5.7). But poverty had not caused a significant expansion of household size. The 892 households in Brás de Pina averaged 4.95 members, and over half (55 percent) had 3 to 4 members.

The adult population gathered in households—meaning heads, housewives, and economically active dependents—numbered 2,084. It contained a high percentage of married persons, 48.5 percent; only 12.6 percent lived in consensual unions; 28.5 percent remained single; 3.3 percent were separated; and 6.3 percent were widowed. Most households (83.5 percent) were formed by men and women 26

Table 5.6
Brás de Pina: Household Size in 1964

N. of Persons	No. of Households	%
1	20	6.2
2	48	14.8
3	52	16.0
4	45	13.9
5	52	16.0
6	40	12.3
7	30	9.3
8	16	4.9
9	11	3.4
≥10	9	2.8
Total	323	100.0

Total rounded off to 100.0%

Source: Companhia de Habitação Popular do Estado da Guanabara, "A COHAB através de números e imagens."

Table 5.7
Brás de Pina: Distribution of Population by Age in 1967

Age	N	%
Under 1	114	2.6
1 to 3	398	9.1
4 to 5	280	6.3
6 to 8	398	9.1
9 to 14	732	16.6
15 to 18	373	8.4
19 to 21	196	4.4
22 to 25	273	6.1
26 to 30	355	8.0
31 to 35	270	6.1
35 to 40	331	7.5
41 to 45	189	4.3
45 to 50	153	3.5
51 to 55	107	2.4
56 to 60	86	1.9
61 to 65	67	1.5
66 to 70	37	0.8
Above 70	50	1.1
No Response	7	0.2
Total	4,416	100.0

Total rounded off to 100.0%

Source: Pontifica Universidade Católica, Escola de Sociologia e Política, "Tres favelas cariocas: Mata Machado, Morro União, Brás de Pina-Levantamento sócioeconômico," 95, Table 9.

years old and above, so at least in Brás de Pina few youngsters dared early marriage. Patriarchy was firmly entrenched; 81.7 percent of households were headed by males and only 18.3 percent by females. The CODESCO team attributed the existence of matrifocal homes to the intolerable economic situation in Brás de Pina and the lack of government assistance to the families settling in the favela before 1967.

CODESCO gave special attention to the role of women in the favela. The 1967 survey distinguished between "household heads," male and female, and "housewives"—female companions of the male household heads or any female in charge of domestic chores. Contrary to the experience of Praia do Pinto, almost all adult females in Brás de Pina were attached to a partner. Among 892 household heads, 107 were single, 504 were married, 133 lived in a consensual union, 47 were separated, and 101 widowed (see Table 5.8). The number of housewives was 648, of whom 13 were single, 499 were married, 128 were living in a consensual union, 1 was separated, and 7 were widowed.[17]

Table 5.8
Brás de Pina: Marital Status of Household Heads in 1967

Marital Status	N	%
Married	504	56.5
Single	107	11.9
Consensual union	133	14.9
Separated	47	5.2
Widowed	101	11.3
Total	892	100.0

Total rounded off to 100.0%

Source: Pontifica Universidade Católica, Escola de Sociologia e Política, "Tres favelas cariocas: Mata Machado, Morro União, Brás de Pina-Levantamento sócioeconômico," 100, Table 11.

The extended family does not appear ever to have formed a large segment of the population of Brás de Pina. Unlike many previous censuses of the favelas, the 1967 survey divided the household into head, companion of the head, sons and daughters, agregados living with the head, and tenants who resided in the same shack but were not related to the owner. By this criteria 81 percent of household members living with the head and his/her companion were sons or daughters, 15.3 percent were agregados and 3.6 percent were tenants.[18]

Brás de Pina at the end of the 1960s had only half as many female-headed households as Praia do Pinto, fewer consensual unions, and a much smaller number of extended families. The economic fortunes of the generation that founded the favela may provide a clue as to why. Brás de Pina residents could claim some advantages over other squatters. The location of the settlement offered special employment opportunities for both sexes: 1,509 residents were economically active in 1967, including 845 male household heads, 121 housewives, and 543 dependents with their own income. Three-quarters of the economically active population had jobs and one-quarter were unemployed. Women formed an important component of the labor force; 70 percent of the females worked as domestics, 10 percent held jobs with textile firms, and the rest earned a living as street vendors.[19] The extension of the railroad network into Zona Norte in the 1940s and the improvement of the bus system in the 1950s undoubtedly allowed many residents to commute to Zona Sul for work in the high-rises of Leblon and Copacabana. But it was the opening of Avenida Brasil in 1946 that transformed the economic life of the favela. The working-class community surrounding Brás de Pina thrived as bars, restaurants, and retail shops went up on both sides of the new highway. Many in the favela augmented their meager incomes through the sale of cheap homemade or second-hand goods to their neighbors, an option not available to the poorer squatters of Praia do Pinto, who were surrounded by the middle- and upper–class inhabitants of Leblon and Ipanema. The participation of so many men and women in the informal economy of the area seems to have reinforced marriage and the patriarchal household while discouraging matrifocality and extended households.

Brás de Pina shared many features with the older and more populous squatter settlements of the city—genesis from the rural exodus, precarious employment opportunities for the inhabitants, constant battles with the city government over the right of occupation—but had more stability and better prospects for the next generation. The nuclear household was the bedrock of the community. Indeed, one could argue that this was a factor in saving the favela from destruction. It was difficult for the city authorities to convince wealthier Cariocas that residents of Brás de Pina were marginals or troublemakers when the majority had succeeded in forming stable homes.

JACARÉZINHO

First settled during the mid-1930s, Jacarézinho blossomed with the shift of industries to the suburbs that began under Vargas. After 1940 small and medium-sized Brazilian firms as well as larger industries backed by foreign capital moved to the northern suburbs of Rio de Janeiro to take advantage of the low rents and cheap labor supplied from the shantytowns of the area. The region of Méier, of which Jacarézinho formed a substantial part, boasted the second largest industrial concentration in Rio de Janeiro in the 1950s. Unlike Praia do Pinto and Brás de Pina, the growth of Jacarézinho depended on the steady work available to the inhabitants—more factories meant more jobs for favela residents. It was this factor that kept families intact through decades of economic and political upheaval. The proletarianization of the workforce provided the material conditions whereby the nuclear household could thrive.

The city fathers watched the growth of Jacarézinho with concern. The first official census of the favelas in 1948 did not break down population figures per settlement, but some information regarding the larger ones was made available to the press. Brazil's largest-selling newspaper of the 1940s, *O Globo*, reported that Jacarézinho had the largest population of all the favelas of Rio, and in fact the number of inhabitants surpassed that of many Brazilian cities. The population of

Jacarézinho in 1948 stood at 15,510 persons, of whom one half were under age 20.[20] That same year authorities from the Fundação Leão XIII counted 17,979 persons living in Jacarézinho, housed in 4,109 dwelling for an occupancy rate of 4.3.[21]

The 1950 national census declared Jacarézinho the most populous squatter settlement in Rio de Janeiro, with a population of 18,424 inhabitants, including 9,302 males and 9,122 females.[22] By 1960 Jacarézinho had grown so large that it was the only favela in Rio de Janeiro listed separately in the census. The population numbered 22,714 at the start of the decade, including 11,273 males and 11,441 females (see Table 5.9).

Table 5.9
Jacarézinho: Distribution of Population by Age in 1960

Age	N	%
Under 1	734	3.2
1 to 4	2,945	12.9
5 to 9	3,145	13.8
10 to 14	2,322	10.2
15 to 19	1,978	8.7
20 to 24	2,188	9.6
25 to 29	2,138	9.4
30 to 34	1,797	7.9
35 to 39	1,408	6.1
40 to 49	1,913	8.4
50 to 59	1,211	5.3
60 to 69	646	2.8
Over 70	246	1.0
No Response	43	0.2
Total	22,714	100.0

Total rounded off to 100.0%

Source: Brasil, Instituto Brasileiro de Geografia e Estatística, Serviço Nacional de Recenseamento, *VII rencenseamento geral do Brasil—Censo demográfico de 1960. Vol. 4, Favelas do Estado da Guanabara*, 29ff.

The adult population committed itself to matrimony to a much greater degree than in other favelas. Among the 13,568 persons over the age of 15 (6,724 men and 6,844 women) living in the favela, more than half were married: 3,802 of the males and 3,830 of the females (twenty-eight women were married to men outside the favela). Residents of Jacarézinho entered into consensual unions very infrequently—just 708 of the men and 719 of the women reported living in such arrangements. The number of singles among those over age 15 was not very high: 2,600 males and 1,788 females; this last number reflects the tendency of women in the favelas to marry at a much younger age than men (see Table 5.10).

The average household size was small. Jacarézinho's total population of 22,653 was grouped into 4,647 households, an average of 4.8 persons per household. The number of children living with a household head in Jacarézinho, including those from previous marriages, came to 10,769, 2.3 per household. Male-headed nuclear households predominated: 3,947 households were headed by males and only 700 by females. The extended household had shrunk to insignificance. Agregados, a category the census reserved for parents, in-laws, and grandchildren living in the same home as the head, accounted for less than 1,000 of the total population.[23]

The favela witnessed a population explosion in the first half of the 1960s as a result of migration, but observers were unsure of the extent. Officials of the Twelfth Administrative Region of Rio de Janeiro, of which Jacarézinho formed a large part, counted a population of twenty-five thousand in 1965. The Fundação Leão XIII came up with a figure of 176,000. The Guanabara housing agency (COHAB) proposed a more modest total of thirty-six thousand, but omitted any count of the shanties found along the banks of the Rio Jacaré. Aralá Moreira de Sá, an engineer who came to work in Jacarézinho, put the total population at fifty-two thousand, housed in twelve thousand to thirty-five thousand shanties. Residents themselves estimated the population at fifty thousand to sixty thousand. The discrepancies seem to lie in the refusal of some observers to count the primitive shacks being erected in Jacarézinho as permanent fixtures or their inhabitants as full-fledged residents of the squatment. As far as most authorities were concerned the title of "favelado" had to be earned.[24]

Table 5.10
Jacarézinho: Marital Status of Population over Age Fifteen in 1960

Marital Status	N	%
Married	7,632	56.2
(Including 1,427 consensual unions)		
Single	4,388	32.3
Legally separated/divorced	11	0.0
Separated	503	3.7
Widowed	1,018	7.5
No response	16	0.1
Total	13,568	100.0

Total rounded off to 100.0%

Source: Brasil, Instituto Brasileiro de Geografia e Estatística, Serviço Nacional de Recenseamento, *VII. Rencenseamento geral do Brasil—Censo demográfico de 1960. Vol. 4, Favelas do Estado da Guanabara*, 36-37.

Household size also seems to have increased during the 1960s. The census conducted from January through February 1965 by the Medical Health Center of Jacarézinho confirmed the trend toward larger households. A sample survey of 66 households showed an average size of 5.9 members, including 3.8 children.[25] Yet according to investigators, favelados felt a strong sense of family obligations. One engineering survey of Jacarézinho in April 1962 found "most families are legally constituted with an average number of five children. While offspring are numerous, the number of abandoned children is small."[26]

Despite tremendous population growth in the 1960s, family life in Jacarézinho remained centered on the male-headed household. The dominance of patriarchal households must be considered against the backdrop of the profound changes under way in Jacarézinho after 1950. In this decade Jacarézinho acquired the most important proletarian population of any favela in Rio de Janeiro. A landmark study published in the newspaper *Estado de São Paulo* in April 1960, "Aspectos humanos da favela carioca," (Human Aspects of the Carioca Favela) estimated that 40 percent of the economically active population in Jacarézinho worked at the General Electric plant and other nearby factories, such as Fábrica Jumbo, Fábrica de Tinta Superior, Tintas Ypiranga, Cisper, Laboratório Silva Araujo, and Café Predileto. Jacarézinho also featured a growing merchandising sector: 458 stores operated inside the favela, and many others were just beyond the gates. The typical worker in Jacarézinho was as likely to put on a factory suit as a bartender's uniform. Steady jobs with a regular income, no matter how minuscule, laid the basis for patriarchy.[27]

The large number of marriages, infrequency of consensual unions, and the small percentage of female-headed households in Jacarézinho testified to the persistence of the squatters' quest for the security of a home. Full-time work in nearby factories allowed mothers and fathers to pass on their shanties and houses to a new generation that maintained the favela intact, turning Jacarézinho into a permanent fixture in Zona Norte.

COMPARISONS

How typical were the favela households of Praia do Pinto, Brás de Pina, and Jacarézinho? The survey of Rio de Janeiro favelas published in the *Estado de São Paulo* in 1960 estimated that 49 percent of the squatters in Rio de Janeiro over age fifteen were unmarried, a figure not much higher than for the rest of the city. Interestingly, the survey found that the percentage of married women in the favelas actually surpassed that of the rest Rio. Migration patterns may explain the difference. Single men were apparently more likely to migrate directly to the favelas than single women, but married women were more likely to stay put in the shantytowns.[28]

Sample surveys from other squatter settlements confirm the stability of the favela family. The American sociologist Andrew Pearse, judging from his own visits to the favela of Esquéleto in the early 1960s, concluded that "the nuclear family is the norm in the favela, i.e., man and woman living together with children, but without grandchildren or other members of the family of origin or any other person. . . . the nuclear family is threatened by unemployment, abandonment, death of the family head (or spouse) and when this happens the remaining able members call on members of the family of origin to help reconstitute the nuclear family."[29]

Studying two Carioca favelas in 1964, Babilônia in Zona Sul (population five thousand) and Cachoeirinha in Zona Norte (population thirty thousand), a survey team from the Pontifical Catholic University observed "the greater part of the population (of both favelas) lives quite normally from the standpoint of marital status. In Babilônia 60 percent of the adults are married compared to 16 percent who live in consensual unions. In Cachoeirinha 41 percent are married and 28 percent living in consensual unions." Small households were common in both favelas. In Babilônia 27 percent of the households with children had one or two, and 26 percent had three or four. In Cachoeirinha 37 percent of households had one or two children, and 25 percent had three or four.[30] Janice Perlman in her study of two favelas and one poor neighborhood at the end of the 1960s concluded: "As for family life in the favela, it is relatively stable by any standard. Ninety percent of those we interviewed are members of a nuclear family (37 percent heads of household, 38 percent their spouses and 15 percent their children). About 80 percent of households are headed by males, and two thirds of residents are married or (joined in informal but stable unions)."[31]

A 1966 survey of all 79 favelas in the city of Belo Horizonte, capital of the state of Minas Gerais, counted 119,799 persons living in 25,076 shanties, 4.7 per shack. The favelado population was 48.3 percent males and 51.6 percent females. Youngsters up to fourteen years of age made up 47.6 percent of the population; 65.5 percent of the total population was single and 27.3 percent was married while only 0.14 percent was living in consensual unions.[32] Daniel Cavalcanti Bezerra conducted a study of squatter families who had invaded unoccupied land in Recife, in the state of Pernambuco, in 1965. On one site he found 1,874 households containing 8,844 persons for an average of 4.7 per shanty. Of the squatters, 53.1 percent were below nineteen years of age. No statistics on marital status were provided.[33]

The family life of favelados in Rio de Janeiro from 1942 to 1969 can be usefully compared with the experience of other urban poor groups in Latin America in this same generation. Helen Safa's study of the Los Peloteros shantytown in San Juan, Puerto Rico, conducted in 1959 found half the households gathered into nuclear families, 20 percent comprised of extended families, and another 20 percent headed by females. She attributed the relatively high degree of matrifocality to lack of job opportunities that prevented many males from assuming the rights and duties of household leadership.[34] Safa's more recent research on female-headed households in Puerto Rico and the Dominican Republic suggests this trend accelerated in the 1970s and 1980s with the rise of export-led industrialization and the growth of female employment in the Caribbean.[35]

Larissa Adler Lomnitz's 1969-1971 survey of the Cerrada del Cóndor shantytown of Mexico City found extended households that joined two or more nuclear families along with unmarried kin to be the norm. These made up the majority of households in Cerrada del Cóndor, whereas single nuclear households were in the minority. Limited space in the shantytown forced nuclear families to live together, but another key factor was the economic position of women. Unlike their favela counterparts, who usually worked as maids, most of the Mexican shantytown women earned a living as vendors in the informal economy, working together with other family members or neighbors. Coresidence of several families therefore made economic sense.[36] The male-headed nuclear family could also be produced by economic conditions very different from those of Brazil. Peter Lloyd, in his 1979 book *Slums of Hope?* reported a survey of a *barriada* (shantytown) in

Lima, Peru where four-fifths of the households came under the classification of nuclear families.[37] Bryan Roberts's fieldwork in one Guatemala City shantytown from 1966 to 1968 found a large majority of male-headed households, with the percentage of female-headed households decreasing over time. He concluded that shantytown life did not expand family size, rather the growth in family size was one factor motivating people to move to the shantytown in the first place.[38]

CONCLUSION

The true representative figures of the favelas were not the bums or scavengers but the father and mother who raised a family on starvation wages. Most favelados prized family life and entered into marriages and consensual unions in their early twenties. Nuclear families prevailed in the squatter settlements from the 1940s to the late 1960s. Commonly the shanty was home to the spouse, sons, daughters, and at times the elderly relatives of the head—seldom anyone else. The idea, so commonly pronounced in studies of the Latin American urban poor, that household size expands to allow the head to utilize more wage earners, must be be questioned on the basis of figures from the three settlements covered by this study. The extended family was an exception in the favela, and the coresidence of kin found in rural Brazil did not seem to flourish in the city, though further research is needed on interhousehold family connections. The extent of female-headed households among the city poor is still not well documented. Their number seems to have grown considerably at the end of this generation as squatter settlements in Rio de Janeiro grew more numerous and the inhabitants poorer.

6

Production

Nothing has damaged the squatters of Rio de Janeiro more in their quest for dignity than the popular image of their being vagabonds living off the sweat of other Cariocas. Popular notions of the favelado as street urchin, hustler, scavenger, and criminal have persisted for at least a half-century. The truth is more complicated but no less dramatic. Favelados have served Rio de Janeiro in virtually every imaginable capacity, but when their services are no longer required, they are discarded like rotten fruit. This chapter examines the working populations of Praia do Pinto, Brás de Pina, and Jacarézinho from the 1940s to the 1960s, focusing on economic activity, occupations, salaries, and class consciousness. The majority of squatters in this generation formed part of an urban subproletariat who maintained precarious connections to the job market but nevertheless performed economic functions necessary to the running of the city. At the end of the 1960s all three favelas also witnessed the growth of a proletariat—workers with year-round employment and decent salaries, who often acquired middle-class lifestyles and aspirations. The history of these three favelas teaches that the size and composition of the working population of each ultimately determined the fate of the settlement. It is the key to understanding why the first was destroyed, the second survived, and the third thrives to this day.

PRAIA DO PINTO

Favelas proliferated in Zona Sul after 1940 as a by-product of the building boom in Leblon and the expansion of bus service through the neighborhood of Gávea, which allowed the poor to seek jobs outside their immediate vicinity. During the 1940s, residents of Praia do Pinto worked as bricklayers and restaurant cooks in Zona Sul and rode to jobs in the textile industry or with the city government in Centro. These were the lucky few. Most adults in the favela were not integrated into the formal economy. The majority of jobs were unsteady, and the number of unemployed and underemployed was worrisome. Dr. Vitor Moura claimed that the favelados he studied in Praia do Pinto in 1942 could not be considered a true part of the working class:

I came across all sorts of professions [while talking to people in Praia do Pinto]. Yet the predominant cases were those individuals who told me: I am an assistant to this or that and who, nevertheless, had a signed work card. I had a chance to examine these cards and here's what I found: 94% of those who had a work card came under the following categories: only 17% had a signed card perfectly annotated, with the right date and salary posted. Another 30% or so had a job every few months, I call them "butterflies." I found many others whose cards had been signed but never used; apparently they were a kind of . . . protection against the police. When the police came to pick them up they flashed the card to defend themselves.[1]

In fact there were more full-time laborers in Praia do Pinto than Moura was willing to acknowledge. According to the survey of the favelas of Lagoa Rodrigo de Freitas conducted under his direction in October 1942, the subunit of Largo da Memória housed a population of 799 adults over the age of 20; 450 (56 percent) were economically active, which compared favorably with the rest of the city. But the economy of Zona Sul limited their options for employment: 160 residents of Largo da Memória worked in the service sector; 72 in domestic services; 24 as housewives; 30 in commerce; 6 in the textile industry; 33 were employed by the city, and 2 were federal employees; 5 served in the military; and 20 in transportation; 6 were disabled. Only forty-one residents of Largo da Memória were unemployed at the time of the survey, and fifty-one held unspecified jobs.[2]

Social worker Maria Hortencia do Nascimento Silva conducted her own survey of the labor force in Largo da Memória in 1942 and concluded that most inhabitants were members of the subproletariat. The largest job category was domestics, 182; the rest held temporary jobs such as plumber, carpenter, bricklayer, and shoemaker. A surprising number, 152, were factory workers, but there is no indication whether these jobs were located in Zona Sul. Only twenty favelados performed *biscate* (informal work) full-time (see Table 6.1).

Silva reported to her superiors:

The majority of men in Largo da Memória are manual workers, especially bricklayers. The women do not lag behind the men. Almost all of them work, and those who are not domestics wash clothes at home, which is not easy since they have to haul water for long distances, and they hardly have any space . . . to hang their clothes to dry. Few *malandros* [vagabonds] are to be found . . . those who are idle are usually so because infirmities make them incapable of working. They sincerely wish to return to work and will do so as soon as they feel better.[3]

Silva also commented on the social divisions among the poor. She found little sense of group solidarity among the squatters. "Almost all of them like to say that they

Table 6.1
Occupations in Largo da Memória in 1942

Occupations	N	%
Tailor	2	0.1
Children's nurse	1	0.1
Barber	3	0.2
Informal work	20	1.2
Plumber	5	0.3
Sales clerk	8	0.5
Carpenter	8	0.5
Debt collector	2	0.1
Porter	2	0.1
Commerce	28	1.7
Streetcar conductor	1	0.1
Seamstress	13	0.8
Domestic services	182	11.3
Waxmaker	2	0.1
Nurse	1	0.1
Blacksmith	1	0.1
Stoker	1	0.1
Municipal employee	18	1.1
Federal employee	1	0.1
Private clerk	2	0.1
Laundress	40	2.5
Mechanic	12	0.7
Soldier	7	0.4
Bus driver	7	0.4
Factory worker	152	9.4
Bricklayer	28	1.7
Baker	4	0.2
Fishmonger	1	0.1
House painter	9	0.6
Doorman	2	0.1
Shoemaker	4	0.2
Unskilled assistant worker	47	2.9
Dyer and cleaner	4	0.2
Fare collector (bus)	2	0.1
Guard, watchman	5	0.3
Retired	4	0.2
Undefined	73	4.5
No profession	5	0.3
Student	134	8.3
Other professions	33	2.0
Undeclared	270	16.7
Children	472	29.2
Total	1,616	100.0

Total rounded off to 100.0%
Three individuals chose not to respond.

Source: Maria Hortencia Silva, *Impressões de uma assistente sobre o trabalho na favela*, 56.

do not get along with any of the other inhabitants, unless it's a neighbor, and the better-educated ones elaborate on the need for the Mayor's Office to do away with the shantytown to make the city more beautiful." Geography also divided neighbors.

There is an extraordinary difference between the disposition of those who lived in the elevated area of the favela and those who live at ground level. And the odd thing is that contrary to other favelas, those on the hill are socially superior to those on the ground. The ones living on the hill are organized into families living in well-built, clean shacks. This may be because they were the first to arrive in the favela, and could find more stable employment. Those at ground level are ignorant and hostile; they gather together in their *biroscas* [stores] to get drunk, and constantly provoke fights.[4]

Praia do Pinto had been in existence for less than a decade, but residents were already split along lines of occupation, education, and location.

Cidade Maravilhosa, located next to Largo da Memória, had a very similar employment pattern. The population of 4,737 had 1,320 economically active members. The service sector employed 398 favelados, and domestic services 275. Only 84 squatters were unemployed at the time of the survey. Close to half worked in the same neighborhood where they lived (see Table 6.2).

Table 6.2
Occupations in Cidade Maravilhosa in 1942

Occupations	N	%
Service sector	398	30.1
Domestic services	275	20.8
Other	318	24.0
Retired	4	0.3
Commerce	106	8.0
Transport	41	3.1
Municipal employee	19	1.4
Federal employee	9	0.6
Unemployed	84	6.3
Undeclared	4	0.3
Electric co.	24	1.8
Disabled	8	0.6
Soldier	11	0.8
Textile worker	8	0.6
Dying and cleaning	11	0.8
Total	1,320	100.0

Total rounded off to 100.0%

Source: Moura, "Apuração do censo da favela 'Cidade Maravilhosa.'" Moura Family Papers.

The subunit of Praia do Pinto, which housed 3,987 persons in 1942, received special attention from Moura. In a note entitled "To the Secretary General," dashed off after the founding of Proletarian Park No. 1 in 1943, he claimed that of 1,547 individuals counted in Praia do Pinto, 430 refused to give him any information on employment; 118 said they were unemployed; 59 said they were unskilled manual workers; and 741 were bricklayers. Only 12 were factory workers and 23 street vendors.[5]

The full survey is reproduced in Table 6.3. Absence of stable work was the most salient characteristic of the labor force in Praia do Pinto. Few squatters held factory jobs, and many worked as an unskilled assistant to a more qualified worker. Females were concentrated in domestic services and dry cleaning. Only 67 favelados held full time jobs in the informal sector.

The migrant of the 1930s had left the backcountry of Brazil only to find work on a bigger but no less cruel plantation in the city, where daily rations were bought by wages. For a closer look at the connection between income, housing, and family life in the favelas, Moura examined living standards in all three subunits of Praia do Pinto before the construction of the proletarian parks. His main conclusion was that for the favelados, family formation made economic sense. The major reason migrants chose to move to the favela, he gathered from his talks with the inhabitants, was the high cost of residing almost anywhere else in the city, where a one-bedroom apartment rented for Cr$100. Self-construction of their own home was the best option for the families coming to Rio de Janeiro, leading to the formation of favelas close to the job sites of both husbands and wives. The subunit of Praia do Pinto had grown since the 1930s to contain 1,779 shanties in 1942. The average salary of 1,344 household heads came to Cr$280 per month and the average combined salary of the 1,779 households came to Cr$283.[6] Cidade Maravilhosa housed 4,737 residents in 1,344 shanties. A total of 1,196 household heads reported earning an income, an average of Cr$279 per capita; 1,900 shanties reported an average income of Cr$245 per household.[7]

One might conclude from these figures that women were not represented in the favela labor force, since the average salary for the heads nearly matched the average household income. Yet such a judgment would be premature. Largo da Memória, the first section of the favela scheduled for demolition, contained 450 shanties in 1942; 415 household heads reported an earned average salary of Cr$277 a month. The Moura survey leads us to believe that nearly all these family heads were males. But 400 shanties reported an average household income of Cr$433 per month, so the remainder had to come from females and perhaps children.[8]

The meager earnings recorded in Praia do Pinto denied the subproletarians full entry into the working class. But could this be accomplished by fiat? The proletarian parks experiment, which lasted from the early 1940s until the late 1960s, was a cruel joke in one sense—it failed to transform the favelados into proletarians. In 1950 the economically active population for all the favelas of Rio de Janeiro was 52.3 percent; and of the city, it was 50 percent.[9] In 1952 the population of Proletarian Park No. 1 in Gávea stood at 5,262, of whom 2,354 (44.7 percent) were

Table 6.3
Occupations in Praia do Pinto in 1942

Occupation	N	%
Electrician	3	0.19
Teacher	1	0.06
Barber	9	0.58
Soldier	14	0.90
Commerce	12	0.77
Agriculture	5	0.32
Electric company	23	1.48
House painter	7	0.45
Fare collector (bus)	4	0.25
Supplies	2	0.12
Shoemaker	10	0.64
Gardener	3	0.19
Informal work	67	4.33
Stonemason	4	0.25
Stableman	19	1.22
Bricklayer	741	47.89
Truckdriver	32	2.06
Factory worker	12	0.77
Carpenter	29	1.87
Dyer and cleaner (male)	1	0.06
Dyer and cleaner (female)	40	2.58
Domestic service	235	15.19
Other	1	0.06
Tailor	6	0.38
Fisherman	7	0.45
Municipal employee	26	1.68
Federal employee	10	0.64
Unskilled work	59	3.81
Plumber	5	0.32
Street vendor	23	1.48
Seamstress	10	0.64
Nurse	2	0.12
Textile worker	1	0.06
Bus driver	1	0.06
Retired	3	0.19
Disabled	2	0.12
Unemployed	118	7.62
Total	1,547	100.0

Total rounded off to 100.0%

Source: "Apuração do censo realisado na Favela Praia do Pinto," Moura Family Papers.

economically active. Since 2,202 residents were under 15 years of age and 44 female inhabitants worked exclusively as housewives, this left 652 residents of economically active age who were absent from the job market. Even this figure is somewhat misleading, since those counted as economically inactive included students, disabled persons, and residents older than 65.[10]

Almost all the able-bodied adults in the park worked, but the great majority of the working population continued to toil at jobs with slight guarantee of security. The twelve categories that employed the greatest number of inhabitants in Proletarian Park No. 1 in 1952 are listed in Table 6.4. Some items on this list merit explanation because they were peculiar to the economy of Zona Sul. The Jockey Club in Gávea hired many young men to clean the grounds, groom horses, and repair saddles; hence many male residents of the park called themselves "stablemen." Almost all the female residents held hobs connected to the service sector, working as maids, laundresses, and seamstresses. Out of a working population of 2,354 only 60, presumably male, residents were classified as factory workers. The absence of an industrial proletariat in the park was also confirmed by a sample survey of fourteen resident households that same year which showed that nearly three-quarters of the male economically active population worked in the service sector of Zona Sul, and women consigned to home production.[11]

Table 6.4
The Major Occupations in Proletarian Park No. 1 in 1952

Occupation	N
Laundress	185
Bricklayer	135
Domestic service	122
Textile worker	108
Seamstress	107
Washroom attendant	107
Dyer and cleaner	86
Driver (truck and bus)	83
Unskilled work (janitor, waiter, etc.)	82
Stableman	61
Operative	60
Plumber	57

Source: Adelaide Silva, "Estudo sobre um inquerito realizado no Parque Proletário Provisório No. 1," Appendix 3.

As the proletarian parks project collapsed in the 1950s from lack of government interest, the Catholic Church took over the task of trying to put an end to Praia do Pinto. Dom Helder Câmara, bishop of Recife, supervised the construction of a model apartment complex, the Cruzada São Sebastião, inside the favela. Since almost all the occupants were former residents of Praia do Pinto, employment statistics compiled by an assistant to the Cruzada afford an opportunity to ponder the changing lot of the favela worker in the late 1950s. Table 6.5 shows economic activities of a sample male working population of 360.

Construction jobs and factory work accounted for almost 60 percent of the economically active male population, but in neither case was much technical skill required. The "other" category included mostly unskilled work, such as elevator operator and watchman. Informal work employed only 1.4 percent of the adult male working population.

Table 6.5
Economic Activities of Males in Praia do Pinto in 1957

Activity	N	%
Factory worker	106	29.4
Construction	96	26.7
Commercial employees	64	17.8
Public employee	33	9.2
Other	28	7.8
Bus drivers	11	3.0
Industrial worker	8	2.2
Student	8	2.2
Informal work	5	1.4
Merchants	1	0.3
Total	360	100.0

Source: Coutinho, *Um ensaio de aplicação das técnicas de organização social de comunidade de um projeto piloto de conjunto residencial para ex-favelados,* 64.

Women in Praia do Pinto sometimes found it easier to obtain employment than men did because they specialized in short-term work, as Table 6.6 reveals. While her more affluent sisters worked as secretaries and teachers, the favela woman was stuck at the bottom of the job pyramid.

Table 6.6
Economic Activities of Females in Praia do Pinto in 1957

Activity	N	%
Domestic services	234	60.0
Laundress	40	10.3
Factory worker	22	5.6
Seamstress	17	4.4
Commerce worker	6	1.5
Industrial worker	2	0.5
Informal worker	1	0.3
Unemployed	68	17.4
Total	390	100.0

Source: Coutinho, *Um ensaio de aplicação das técnicas de organização social de comunidade de um projeto piloto de conjunto residencial para ex-favelados,* 66.

Praia do Pinto staggered into the 1960s by absorbing the proletarian parks and the adjacent favela of Ilha das Dragas. But the growth of the favela was matched by the appearance of more high-rises around Lagoa Rodrigo de Freitas. Because it stood in the way of new real estate ventures, Praia do Pinto became increasingly vulnerable to destruction. To discredit the inhabitants and make demolition possible, the city authorities revived the old stereotype of the favelados as marginals. The press soon entered the campaign. In 1964 one of Rio's largest daily newspapers, the *Correio da manhã*, published a story on the three favelas surrounding Lagoa Rodrigo de Freitas—Praia do Pinto, Catacumba, and Cantagalo. Significantly entitled "The Favelas of the Lagoa Are the Worst We Have," the article quoted the conclusions of an allegedly scientific survey carried out by the Instituto de Pesquisas de Mercado (IPEME).

According to the survey, while 74.5 percent of all adult males in all the favelas of Rio de Janeiro had steady work, only 65 percent of those in Zona Sul did so, and just 52.3 percent of those in the Lagoa favelas. Among women, 33.9 percent of all favela females held regular jobs; the figures for Zona Sul and the Lagoa were 27 percent and 16.9 percent, respectively. Households with children who worked accounted for 4.1 percent of all favela households but 9.2 percent of those in Zona Sul and 17.1 percent in the Lagoa favelas. The spokesman for IPEME, Walter Rocha, concluded that "the favelas of the Lagoa are schools of delinquency, nests of marginals and have the lowest index of local workers."[12] Were his findings accurate or just speculation on the part of one who wanted to eradicate the favelas? The last census conducted in Praia do Pinto provides some surprising answers.

In 1969, on the eve of destruction, the favela had a total population of 15,184. The potential economically active population was 10,044 (66.1 percent). This figure included all residents between the ages of 14 and 50 who could conceivably enter the work force. Of these, 7,867 (78.3 percent) were actually employed. Therefore the unemployment rate for Praia do Pinto was 21.6 percent. Praia do Pinto had 7,867 inhabitants who were both producers and consumers and 7,317 who were solely consumers, a ratio of virtually 1:1. This meant that a worker with an income of two minimum salaries at the most had to support at least one unemployed person.[13]

Examining the type of employment available to residents of Praia do Pinto in the late 1960s, as listed in Table 6.7, reveals that few of these occupations could provide the kind of long-term employment necessary for survival. Over half the employed population worked in construction and domestic services. Furthermore, among those who worked in domestic services, 82.3 percent were maids and servants, working in the bars, restaurants, hotels, residences, and office buildings of Zona Sul.

But a substantial segment of the working population of the favela was starting to enter the ranks of the working class. Those who toughed it out and stayed in Praia do Pinto long enough to acquire an education and on-the-job skills found some measure of security in their employment. Manually untrained occupations employed 4,327 workers (57.7 percent of the total economically active population) in 1969; trained occupations gave work to 2,006 favelados (26.7 percent). Despite the odds against them, favelados dedicated themselves to remaining at one place of employment as long as they could. Half of the household heads possessed signed work cards, indicating steady participation in the wage-labor force, and 2,050 workers had been with the same employer for one to five years.[14]

Table 6.7
Occupations in Praia do Pinto in 1969

Occupation	N	%
Agriculture	55	0.73
Informal work	431	5.75
Storage	19	0.25
Bar, hotel, restaurant	222	2.96
Commerce	633	8.44
Building maintenance	235	3.13
Construction	1,089	14.52
Military	216	2.88
Education, medicine, sports	79	1.05
Office, bank	135	1.79
Government employee	185	2.48
Mechanic	199	2.65
Metalworker	26	0.35
Other	46	0.61
Domestic services	3,107	41.41
Undefined, retired	315	4.20
Pharmacy	42	0.56
Textiles	67	0.89
Transportation	374	4.98
Total	7,503	100.00

Total rounded off to 100.0%

Source: Estado da Guanabara, Secretaria de Serviços Sociais, "Praia do Pinto," 62.

The peculiarities of the economy of Zona Sul had not doomed the working family in Praia do Pinto. The men, women, and children of the favela had few skills to offer and received meager wages, but they were still better off if they pooled their resources. Every member of the household in the favela had to be mobilized for the job market just to stay alive. The average salary for a household head in 1969 was NCr$261.38 (new cruzeiros), or two minimum salaries; the average salary for a couple came to NCr$318.79 (2.4 minimum salaries) and household income averaged NCr$434.79 (3.3 minimum salaries).[15]

Even though Praia do Pinto was located in an area with little industry and fleeting employment, only 5.7 percent of household heads were outside the job market in 1969, and the group of residents not engaged in remunerated economic activity was composed of housewives and companions to the household head, children, relatives and tenants living with the head.[16]

By working and combining their salaries, squatters saved their families from extinction. But not the favela itself. Workers with jobs tied to the economy of Zona Sul fought tenaciously against the threat of demolition, and in favor of urbanization of the community. "The only good thing about this place is the location," Antônio da Silva, a bricklayer, told the *Correio da manhã* in 1967. "I work in Copacabana, and when I don't have the money for bus fare, I am willing to walk. We have to resolve this problem of eradication."[17]

But his words went unheeded. The lack of factory jobs and the absence of a local demand for homemade goods in Zona Sul made Praia do Pinto residents reliant on part-time work in the commercial and service economy of the area. This dependency proved fatal to the survival of the favela because Praia do Pinto lacked any sort of organic tie to the surrounding community. Possessing few skills, the workers who lived there had little to offer as producers, and could easily be replaced in their jobs. At the same time, their low earnings denied them any political influence as a consumer force vital to the shops of the neighborhood. When the city of Rio de Janeiro moved to eradicate the favela in 1969 in order to provide more space for high-rise construction in Leblon, the squatters could only stand by and watch helplessly as their shanties went up in flames. Today, aside from ex-residents and experts on the squatter settlements, few remember that Praia do Pinto ever existed.

BRÁS DE PINA

Most of the older inhabitants of Brás de Pina fondly recall the first jobs they held after arriving in the favela in the late 1940s and 1950s. During an interview session in 1990, retired workers mentioned a wide variety of first-time occupations, including ditch digger, soap factory worker, security guard, railroad worker at Leopoldina Station, mechanic, seamstress, maid, and merchant. Almost all reported earning less than the minimum salary. Most men had carried work cards; few women did so. A few parents had sent their children to work in an office or factory to earn extra income, but on the whole, child labor was uncommon. One couple who settled in Brás de Pina in the 1950s is typical of the workforce of that era. Aristotelina Pimentel and her husband were born in Minas Gerais. In Rio de Janeiro she found work as a cook for the rich in Zona Sul, including for a time the family of Economic Minister Delfim Neto. Her husband had worked as a cattle driver in Minas Gerais, but after moving to Brás de Pina he took a job with the Costume Carioca clothing factory and joined the Sindicato de Trabalhadores de Artefatos—the textile workers' union. With their combined salaries the pair bought a small piece of land from the Brazilian navy and built their own shack.[18]

Female workers complained about having to switch employers frequently. Several of them spoke of combining part-time work as maids with odd jobs to supplement the family income. Maria de Lourdes Ferreira married in the city of Duque de Caxias and came to Brás de Pina with her mother and husband. In the favela she raised four children and supported the family by working as a maid and selling toys. Maria Nazare also came to Brás de Pina from the interior of Rio de Janeiro. Having nine kids to feed, she worked as a baby-sitter and washed clothes. One elderly resident born in Minas Gerais lived briefly in the favela of Barreira do Vasco and finally settled in Brás de Pina. A housewife with one child, she earned money by taking in laundry and selling wood. Judging by their testimony, women were more likely than men to participate in the informal economy of the favela; for this reason they were seldom eligible for the minimum wage.[19]

The first statistical evidence on how those who lived in Brás de Pina earned a living comes from the Guanabara Public Housing Agency (COHAB). The COHAB survey of Brás de Pina in 1964 revealed that the Central do Brasil and Leopoldina railroads employed close to 44 percent of the 366 economically active household heads that year; 10 percent worked in Zona Norte; and 17.4 percent held jobs in downtown and Zona Sul. Further, 5.4 percent of household heads made their living exclusively as local street vendors, a higher figure than in most favelas. The daily traffic along Avenida Brasil brought customers to the very entrance of Brás de Pina and gave sales opportunities to residents willing to offer homemade goods. Many inhabitants of the favela participated in the informal economy part of the time because salaries from regular jobs were not sufficient to sustain the family. Statistics on household income for 1964 confirm the weak earning power of Brás de Pina residents. One-third of the household heads earned less than the minimum salary. But earnings among favelados had begun to diverge. Over one-quarter of household heads took home two to three minimum salaries that year.[20]

A more thorough survey of employment and living conditions in Brás de Pina was conducted in 1967 by investigators working for the Companhia de Desenvolvimento de Comunidades (CODESCO), the agency in charge of urbanizing Brás de Pina. The large number of young people under 15 living in the favela put Brás de Pina at a disadvantage compared with the rest of the city workforce: 4,416 squatters lived in Brás de Pina that year, but only 2,402 were between the ages of 15 and 60; thus the potential economically active population came to 54.4 percent. By comparison, the figure for the state of Guanabara was 62.7 percent. The economically active population of 1,509 included 845 male household heads, 121 housewives, and 543 dependents with their own income. The unemployment rate stood at 22.6 percent, but the rate of employment—the economically active population divided by the total number of inhabitants—came to 34.2 percent. By way of comparison, the corresponding figure for Guanabara was 37.8 percent. Since Brás de Pina contained a much lower proportion of potentially active people than the city as a whole, the ability of favelados to find even temporary jobs was impressive.[21]

A significant number of Brás de Pina residents were self-employed. Over 12 percent of male workers were full-time *biscateiros* (informal laborers). Only 6 percent of women depended on street sales for income, but we can presume that many who worked as domestics (close to 70 percent) sold goods on the side.[22] The informal labor sector was an important source of income for workers in Brás de Pina. In addition to the small stands set up along Avenida Brasil, by the end of the 1960s the favela featured numerous establishments selling vegetables, fruits, and liquor. A shoe-repair shop, a bakery, and various little places offering plastic goods were open to the squatters and their neighbors (see Table 6.8).

Brás de Pina, like Praia do Pinto, saw the growth of a proletariat alongside the subproletariat in the late 1960s: 666 residents worked in semispecialized manual occupations in 1967, 762 were in either specialized manual occupations or nonmanual work, and another 33 worked in supervision and inspection. By type of

Table 6.8
Occupational Categories of Economically Active Population in Brás de Pina in 1967

Occupation	N	%
Construction	169	11.2
Transport, communications, storage	121	8.0
Electric co.	13	0.9
Domestic services	427	28.4
Public safety (police, military, private security)	51	3.4
Office work	48	3.2
Metallurgy	28	1.9
Mechanical work	84	5.6
Furniture	56	3.7
Glass, plastics, rubber	10	0.7
Leather industry	46	3.0
Clothing	75	5.0
Chemical products, pharmaceuticals	3	0.2
Textile industry	17	1.1
Foodstuffs	16	1.0
Graphics	12	0.8
Commerce	52	3.4
Street vendor, informal work	162	10.7
Owner of commercial establishment	33	2.2
Agriculture	4	0.3
Building maintenance	9	0.6
Education, recreation, medical care	11	0.7
Barber	11	0.7
Gasoline, petroleum refining	3	0.2
Other	40	2.6
No response	8	0.5
Total	1,509	100.0

Source: Pontífica Universidade Católica, Escola de Sociologia e Política, "Tres favelas cariocas: Mata Machado, Morro União, Brás de Pina-levantamento sócio-econômico," 127, Table 27.

employer, the economically active population likewise demonstrated the growing ranks of squatters who depended on steady salaried work: 772 (51.2 percent) of that group in Brás de Pina worked for private firms; 135 (8.9 percent) worked for the government; and 600 (39.8 percent) (this figure did not include domestics) were self-employed. Women dominated this last category. Three-quarters of those economically active had no full-time employer but worked at home or as maids, laundresses, and seamstresses.[23]

A good number of the squatters held steady jobs. Over half of the economically active residents reported working for the same employer for one to five years. Among dependents with their own income, the instability factor was somewhat higher: 45 percent had spent less than one year at their current employment and 64 percent less than five years.[24] Of the economically active, 79 percent had a signed work card, a percentage much greater than in most other favelas, but the figures for women (75.2 percent) and dependents with their own income (69.5 percent) were significantly lower than that for men (85.6 percent).[25]

The majority of the working population of Brás de Pina at the end of the 1960s fell under the broad category of a subproletariat. First, nearly one-quarter of the economically active population was unemployed. Second, a large portion of Brás de Pina workers was concentrated in the informal economy, and self-employment played a much bigger role in generating income than in most other squatments. But a third segment of the working population consisted of residents tied to the formal economy who usually could count on a few years of employment before being forced to move on to another post. They were more likely to have arrived in Brás de Pina first, to occupy better terrain, and to participate in the informal economy as a sideline to their formal jobs.

Brás de Pina was still mired in misery on the eve of urbanization. The average individual income for the economically active population in 1967 came to NCr$102.68, slightly below the minimum salary of NCr$105. One important reason for such depressed wages is that female participation in the labor force had increased since the start of the 1960s, but most women were still concentrated in low-paying occupations. Four-fifths of the females in Brás de Pina earned less than the minimum salary. Home production, rather than salaried work, was the more important female contribution to the family salary. Almost half of the women owned sewing machines, which they used to make clothes for sale outside the favela.[26]

Most households continued to rely on the male wage earner for survival. The average household income in Brás de Pina came to NCr$162.37, just NCr$60 above the average individual income. Over three-quarters of the households earned two minimum salaries or less. At the bottom of the poverty scale were the 18.7 percent of working families who earned just one minimum salary and the 41.4 percent who took home one and a half.[27]

Even among the poorest of the poor, class unity cannot be taken for granted. The predicaments of favela living produced contradictory strains of class consciousness among the squatters. Housing, salary, and self-identity were interrelated in their minds. Interviews conducted by CODESCO during the initial phase of the urbanization project in early 1967 make it abundantly clear that the favelados' sense of identity derived for the most part from location and not occupation. The shanty, not the factory, was the fulcrum of class consciousness for many of the poor, and the acquisition of a new home for each family took precedence over a collective struggle for better salaries. Brás de Pina's location on Avenida Brasil tended to reinforce this petit bourgeois outlook by permitting favelados to engage in small business activity to supplement their salaries. The experience of living in a favela did not *ipso facto* dispose the inhabitants toward collective action with other equally deprived workers.

The limits to class consciousness induced by living in the favela can be grasped by looking at the construction of the shantytown as an option reluctantly taken to improve one's lot in life individually rather than to unite with other workers. Relocating to a squatter settlement was an economic survival strategy for the poor, but one that many embraced only as a last resort. As one resident of Brás de Pina told the CODESCO interviewer, "No one really likes to live in a favela, but there's just no other way to survive." Another added, "We live here because we cannot afford the rent in the city." A third party defended the privilege of living so close to the work place: "A neighbor offered me his rights to live in the Jardim América housing project, but this place has the advantage of location."

Stratification based on salary also contributed to disharmony. The CODESCO interviewers noticed definite patterns of response based on financial status when they described to favelados the possible options for financing and building their new homes. Households in which the head earned two and a half minimum salaries or more opted for loans to allow them to purchase construction materials but did not ask for money to hire workmen, figuring they could use their own money to hire other favelados from the neighborhood for next to nothing. Households where the head earned between one and two and a half salaries asked for loans for both materials and labor, reasoning that what little money they had saved should be spent on food, clothing, health care, and education for their children. Some of the oldest families in the favela wanted loans for construction material only, because they could count on free labor donated by relatives and friends. They had apparently built up a solidarity network inside and outside the favela that they could mobilize in times of need.

The hopes and dreams of the favelados were also subject to class divisions. The poorest families told CODESCO they would save some of their money, make improvements on the shanty, and devote more time to raising their children. Favelados who owned shops and stores planned to make improvements on their establishments. Both workers and merchants thought that urbanization would lead to an infusion of money into Brás de Pina from the rest of the city.[28]

Despite these differences, it was the class composition of this community that allowed it to survive and become a candidate for urbanization. A favela on Avenida Brasil was not so easy to abolish as one in Leblon, where demolition plans had a vocal constituency of real estate developers. This shantytown was not considered an eyesore or an exotic element in Zona Norte, as Praia do Pinto was in Zona Sul, but merely an extension of the neighborhood of Brás de Pina. The squatters lived, worked, and shopped in the same places as the inhabitants of the surrounding community. The sizable informal economy benefited the favelados by tying their economic interests to their working-class neighbors who served as customers. When governor Carlos Lacerda clumsily attempted to expel its residents, the whole favela mobilized to stop him. The union of squatters and workers preserves Brás de Pina to this day.

JACARÉZINHO

The reasons behind the spectacular growth of this favela are complex, revealing much about the symbiotic relationship between industry and the squatter settlements of Rio de Janeiro. Since the 1930s Jacarézinho has formed the largest part of the industrial neighborhood of Jacaré. As noted in Chapter 3, the high rents and shortage of space in the downtown area had forced many factories to relocate to the suburbs of Zona Norte after World War I. But no establishment could afford to be located too far from the financial district and the wealthy customers of Centro. Jacaré had the advantage of being located close to the Rio d'Ouro railroad line, later supplemented by the Central do Brasil, giving industries access to Centro without paying the price of settling there. But a greater advantage to building factories in Jacaré was the availability of an ever-growing local labor force. It could hardly have escaped the notice of businessmen that many factories had moved to the northern neighborhoods of São Cristóvão, Benfica, and Engenho Novo during the 1920s in order to utilize the labor market of older shantytowns such as Barreira do Vasco.

The most important firm to move to Jacaré during the 1920s was General Electric (GE). The favela and the factory then grew in the shadow of each other. GE employed a considerable portion of the male working population of Jacarézinho and spawned a web of complementary commercial establishments, from bars to clothing stores, that catered to the needs of its employees. The reverse side, of course, is that when the factory floundered, the whole favela suffered from unemployment.

One worker from Jacarézinho remembered:

The first favela where I saw people putting up shanties was in Caju. That was in 1940 or '41. Around 1942 Barreira do Vasco was built. Then, from Barreira do Vasco, in the middle of 1942, they came to Jacarézinho. When I came here in 1943, there were already a handful of houses built. At that time only the Cisper and GE factories were here. Everything else was empty land ready to be used. I also remember the Rio d'Ouro railroad line passing through, with that little train and big smoke.[29]

Perhaps unique among the favelas of Rio de Janeiro, Jacarézinho began life with an industrial proletariat inside its gates and only later gave birth to a subproletariat. The very different class composition of this favela, compared with others in the city, was noted in the first official census of the squatter settlements of Rio de Janeiro. The newspaper *O Globo* printed partial results of the tally in 1948. In Jacarézinho the editors noted "an alarming number of unemployed." Out of a total of 15,510 inhabitants, including 7,854 women and 7,656 men, the census found 3,051 men and 6,513 women without work, although this figure included 1,494 boys and 1,565 girls under age 7. But the real revelation to emerge from the census was the high number of industrial laborers in Jacarézinho. Over half the employed population of 3,543 came under the category of "operatives" employed in the many factories within walking distance of Jacarézinho. A high percentage (12.6 percent) worked in commercial establishments, and only a small number were in the common professions for favelados—domestic services and construction work (see Table 6.9).

The formidable concentration of industrial laborers within its borders did not spare Jacarézinho from misery. In 1948 a high number of inhabitants, 10,575 (7,054 women and 3,521 men), earned no more than 200 cruzeiros per month, and almost half the work force (43.85 percent) earned less than 1,000 cruzeiros a month.

Females formed the most miserable segment of the working class in Jacarézinho. Thousands of women participated in the labor force—combining housework; domestic production in sewing, cooking, and laundry work; and work outside the favela—but they received only a fraction of the male's already meager salary. Most often they worked as maids or laundresses, or engaged in other low-paying activities. Just fifty-four of them earned a salary higher than the minimum.[30] Even when male and female salaries were combined, most households (1,446) earned only Cr$500 to Cr$999 a month, while 1,293 took home between Cr$1,000 and Cr$1,499 cruzeiros.[31]

Table 6.9
Occupations in Jacarézinho in 1948

Occupations	N	%
Operative	1,903	55.1
Domestic service	318	9.2
Commerce	447	12.9
Bricklayer	302	8.7
Laundress	144	4.1
Custodian	207	5.9
Construction	132	3.8
Total	3,543	100.0

Total rounded off to 100.0%

Source: "Existem no Rio de Janeiro 119 favelas," *O Globo*, May 21, 1948.

In the 1950s import substitution industrialization attracted medium and small Brazilian firms to the neighborhood, as well as larger establishments backed by foreign capital. The district of Méier in Zona Norte, of which Jacarézinho formed a substantial part, boasted the second largest number of industrial firms in Rio de Janeiro. This guaranteed that while other favelas rose and fell with the fortunes of the construction business or tourism, Jacarézinho would continue to grow. The 1960 census confirmed Jacarézinho's unique status among the favelas of Rio de Janeiro: 56 percent of the population over age fifteen was economically active, and over 42 percent of them worked in industry, primarily at GE, Cisper, and other nearby factories (see Table 6.10).

Table 6.10
Economically Active Population of Jacarézinho in 1960

Population over age 15: 13,568	Economically active: 7,659
Economic sectors and condition of activity	
Agriculture, livestock and extractive activities	Economically active: 91
Industrial activities	Economically active: 3,270
Other activities	Economically active: 4,298

Source: Brasil IBGE, VII *recenseamento geral do Brasil—censo demografico de 1960*, vol. 4, *Favelas do estado da Guanabara*, 39, Table 23.

The steady income earned by workers in the surrounding factories infused Jacarézinho with a degree of business activity that was the envy of other favelas. By 1960 the favela boasted one of the largest consumer markets in Zona Norte. Most stores carried a variety of goods from furniture to tires, cigarettes, construction materials, and candy. Just about anything to be found outside the favela was brought in by local entrepreneurs and resold at higher prices. Commerce was concentrated on Rua Darcy Vargas, Praça da Concórdia, and Rua Gracinho de Sá. Specialized stores thrived near the entrance to Jacarézinho, and did considerable business with customers from the more prosperous neighborhoods nearby.

Jacarézinho overlapped two neighborhoods, Maria da Graça and Jacaré, that contained large working-class and middle-class populations who often walked to the favela to purchase food and secondhand goods. Commercial establishments located close to the entrances gained access to customers denied to the rest of the favela, but they paid a price by being more closely watched by the police. The working population of Jacarézinho had sufficient buying power to keep local entrepreneurs afloat. Bakers, butchers, barbers, and beauticians converted their small shacks into part-time shops. There was really no need for the favelados to cross the river or the train tracks if they wanted efficient service; all their needs could be attended to in their own neighborhood. Local shops generated income that stayed inside the favela and provided credit for others to go into business. This situation also created a healthy political consciousness. The poor employed the poor and sold to the poor, and there was little chance they would allow themselves to be removed from their homes and places of business.

Some idea of the lively economic activity in Jacarézinho in the 1960s can be gleaned from a report filed by a social worker who came to visit in 1965.

Commercial life in Jacarézinho is fairly intense and varied, satisfactorily serving the population. A few stores leave nothing to desire from those found in the immediate suburbs. There are warehouses, butcher shops, stationery stores, shoe stores, shops for eye glasses and photographic equipment, stores for furniture, textiles, construction materials [bricks, tiles etc.], stores that sell electro-domestic equipment [TV, hi-fi, freezers etc.] and an accounting office.[32]

Thanks in part to the growth of a native commerce and service sector, Jacarézinho was slowly acquiring a privileged sector of workers. Income differences between favelados widened in the 1960s. Figures for 1962 indicate that close to half of households earned the minimum salary of Cr$12,000 to Cr$13,999, and over one-quarter earned Cr$20,000 or more—a paltry sum by the wage standards of the rest of the city, but enough to motivate some families to build permanent homes in the favela.[33]

Some in Jacarézinho lived as princes among paupers. In February 1965, 4,630 families occupied 3,933 dwellings, but many of these structures no longer resembled the shacks of yore. The favela had left behind the age of wood for good: 2,145 houses were made of stone and cement. A majority of residences had more than five rooms, and 13 percent of the homes rose two stories. Further, 81 percent of the houses had running water, 87 percent had electricity, and 78 percent had sewage facilities. The physical improvements in the squatment lifted many families to the status of homeowners and consumers.[34]

The success of the favela attracted new migrants who had to settle for second-class status, living by the riverside and hoping to rise to better jobs and homes. The attainment of class consciousness in Jacarézinho, as in Brás de Pina and Praia do Pinto, was obstructed by geographical divisions as well as income differences. Vieira Fazenda residents had a reputation for discriminating against the other inhabitants of the settlement, based on the concentration of commercial activity around their homes. Morro Azul was the birthplace of the entire favela, and homeowners there felt a certain pride in being able to literally overlook their rich and poor neighbors downhill. The riverside was always stigmatized for its plethora of primitive shanties, which sheltered a population born mostly outside of Rio de Janeiro.

At the end of the 1960s a large part of Jacarézinho had ceased to be a favela, at least according to the city government's definition. Ownership of land was legalized for many residents, streets were paved, and an infrastructure of water, sewers and electricity reached thousands of households. Conflicts arose inside the favela, based not so much on employment as on the acquisition of consumer goods and services. The shacks of the riverside were pitted against the houses of brick, stone, and marble being built every day in the more prosperous parts of Jacarézinho as migrants and old settlers competed for space. The cramped streets and alleys also made solidarity very difficult. In 1965 several favelados told the social worker that despite having lived in Jacarézinho for more than 20 years, there were parts of the favela they had never visited, and some expressed surprise that the squatment had grown so large since they moved in. Others warned her to stay away from certain parts of the favela because "the people there are not like us; they're an inferior class of folk."[35]

The most important contradiction that undermined class consciousness in Jacarézinho is that even as the favela expanded in size, it still functioned as an economic satellite of the neighborhood factories. Jané Souto de Oliveira has perceptively written that by the 1960s, Jacarézinho resembled a company town of the nineteenth century, but without any of the benefits such a relationship might produce for the inhabitants.[36] The favela depended on the factories for employment, but the industrialists of the twentieth century, unlike those of the previous era, felt no obligation to provide food, clothing, or shelter for their employees, not even on credit. Paradoxically, as will be seen in Chapter 8, although the factories have always been political allies of the favela in opposition to removal—since they do not want to see their labor force disappear—they did nothing to help the favelados on a day-to-day basis.

For the squatters the contradictions of living in a favela located next to their job site produced a complicated set of loyalties. They felt gratitude toward the factory owners for protecting the favela from the clutches of the city and the real estate developers who coveted the lands, but they also resented the fact that the survival of Jacarézinho was in the hands of their employers; they felt a duty to the favela as one of the most developed in the city, with an infrastructure others envied, yet they quarreled among themselves on the basis of housing and income differences; they maintained an obligation to the upkeep of the family but, according to visitors like the social worker, seldom visited neighbors or extended kin.

Jacarézinho's status as a proletarian encampment saved it from extinction. The inhabitants could rightly claim to be workers first and favelados second. Their ties to industry allowed them to forge a cross-class alliance with local entrepreneurs. As far back as World War I, industrialists had come to depend on Jacarézinho for cheap labor every bit as much as favelados had come to rely on them for jobs. Time and again workers here mobilized to protect their homes and force the city to grant them political autonomy.

But what did being "proletarian" mean at the end of the 1960s? Class consciousness in this favela seems to have been dissipated by the success of the inhabitants in lifting themselves above abject poverty. In Praia do Pinto the inhabitants were too poor to protest against the political and economic order in Rio de Janeiro that consigned them to a desperate fate, whereas in Jacarézinho, favelados had too much to lose by uniting as workers. Divisions among the favelados placed severe limits on their class consciousness. Favelados in Jacarézinho fulfilled family obligations first and class obligations second. Living in a huge favela constantly undergoing expansion and renovation of infrastructure split the poor along lines of geography, income, and even type of dwelling. Instead of spearheading the drive against the military dictatorship in the 1960s the working class in Jacarézinho functioned as a microcosm of the historical debilities of the Brazilian proletariat.

CONCLUSION

Favelas were the consequence of the incomplete proletarianization of the rural population that swamped the cities of Brazil after 1930. During the next 40 years a working class composed of three distinct segments came to live in the squatter settlements of Rio de Janeiro: a proletariat formally linked to the job market by contract, with stable employment and regular wages; a subproletariat with erratic participation in the labor force and insufficient remuneration; and large numbers of unemployed young males and adult females. A typical squatter might find himself or herself in all three categories in the course of one year, so precarious were the job opportunities for favelados.

The most important development in the economic history of the favelas during this generation was the growth of the proletariat that emerged out of the subproletariat. By the end of the 1960s all three settlements surveyed in this study had a substantial number of workers with a signed labor card, engaged in semiskilled work, and secure in the same job for more than one year. Remarkable, too, was the entry of women into the labor force, though seldom on a full-time basis. The favela woman was more likely to be unemployed or to work at informal jobs and earn the minimum salary than was her mate.

The location of the squatter settlement and the economic needs of the jobs and earn the minimum salary than was her mate.

The location of the squatter settlement and the economic needs of the surrounding community seem to have largely decided the fate of each favela. Praia do Pinto offered its inhabitants little more than the chance to be maids and construction workers in Gávea, Leblon, and Ipanema. The growth of a large, steadily employed labor force that could flex its political muscles came too late to save this favela from destruction in the late 1960s. Brás de Pina residents took advantage of their proximity to Avenida Brasil to go into business for themselves and acquired sufficient economic clout to force the city to urbanize the favela. Though in many ways worse off than the inhabitants of Praia do Pinto, squatters in Brás de Pina were more closely integrated with the surrounding community and could count on them as allies. Perhaps unique among major favelas of Rio de Janeiro, Jacarézinho thrived on the industrial jobs provided by a host of factories located in the same neighborhood. Yet, ironically, the proletarianization of the labor force sapped their political will to act together as workers.

7

Consumption

After examining family organization among the urban poor and the forging of the squatter workforce, this study now turns to the material world of the favelados and their physical reproduction. This chapter documents housing, education, health conditions, consumption of goods and services, and survival strategies practiced by the inhabitants of Praia do Pinto, Brás de Pina, and Jacarézinho. Though residents of all three settlements remained trapped in poverty, marked improvements in living standards occurred during this generation. The metamorphosis of the favelas from shantytowns to urban communities was largely the work of the favelados themselves, who re-created their environment to make decent homes for future generations. When the favelados were permitted to chart their own course, they behaved like other homeowners, investing time, energy, and money in the improvement of their houses and the welfare of their families. The level of self-improvement of each favela, and the degree to which the favelados assimilated the lifestyles of other Cariocas, were decisive elements in deciding its fate.

If the city had recognized the the aspirations of the favelados for middle-class comforts, much time and turmoil would have been saved. Instead, those who ruled Rio de Janeiro persisted in perpetuating the myth of the exoticism of the squatter settlements. Two diametrically opposed forces waged war over the favelas during these thirty years. The favelados' quest for acceptance from the rest of the city, manifested in the struggle to acquire property and essential services for the shantytown, was opposed by the city's concept of the favelas as static entities that reproduced only crime, marginality, and poverty. The outcome of this battle destroyed Praia do Pinto, led to the urbanization of Brás de Pina, and turned Jacarézinho into one of the largest "cities" in Brazil.

PRAIA DO PINTO

The first section of Praia do Pinto destroyed to make way for the proletarian parks in 1942 was Largo da Memória. Even the most hardened students of the favela population were shocked by the appearance of this squatment. Maria Hortencia do Nascimento Silva wrote:

This horrible ulcer is a painful sight to behold in the midst of such a prosperous neighborhood. The first-time visitor sees in front of him a curious assemblage of sordid shanties—some glued to others, or with only narrow, tortuous alleys to connect them—constructed out of old pieces of wood, full of patches, and covered with the most diverse materials.[1]

Largo da Memória contained 450 shanties in 1942, of which 434 were residences, 3 were commercial establishments, 1 was an entertainment establishment, and 12 were of mixed usage; 309 had only one or two rooms. The average number of inhabitants per dwelling was 3.5, including 1.4 children. However, even in this rustic environment some residents aspired to better living. While 69 houses in Largo da Memória were worth no more than Cr$200, 87 had cost the occupants between Cr$401 and Cr$600; 26, from Cr$801 to Cr$1,000; and 15 were worth more than Cr$1,000. Even in its darkest hour Largo da Memória had a privileged stratum of inhabitants for whom removal to the housing projects constituted a step down the social ladder.[2]

Praia do Pinto, the largest of the subunits, contained 1,779 houses in 1942. Though the average number of persons living in each home, 2.29, was lower than in Largo da Memória and Cidade Maravilhosa, the inhabitants were much poorer. Close to 90 percent of all houses were made of dirt and wood. Further, 1,697 were classified as residences, 35 served as commercial establishments, 46 were units of mixed usage, and 1 functioned as a school.[3]

Cidade Maravilhosa, the third subunit of Praia do Pinto, had 4,737 residents and 1,344 shanties, for an 3.5 occupancy rate, including 1.4 children. It was described by Dr. Vitor Moura as "one of the largest and ugliest favelas in Rio de Janeiro." In it, 1,277 dwellings were classified as residences, 21 were commercial, 2 were for entertainment, 43 were of mixed usage, and 1 was used for prayer meetings. Sixty-five percent of the homes had one or two rooms, and 70 percent were worth more than Cr$400. Half of the shacks had dirt floors, two-thirds had zinc roofs, and only a tiny number were covered with tile or can. There were 190 families who rented their homes, paying a median rent of Cr$31 to Cr$41 a month[4] (see Table 7.1).

The entire favela of Praia do Pinto lacked piped water and a sewage system. The land smelled of mud, feces and animal remains. As a consequence, many children in the favela contracted diseases that doomed them at the start of their lives. Tuberculosis, in particular, proved a deadly killer. In the 1940s, 534 children in Praia do Pinto were tested by X-ray, and 112 were found to be radiologically abnormal, indicating the presence of TB. Among 639 adults examined, 12 had moderately advanced cases of tuberculosis and 19 had advanced cases. Most child

Table 7.1
Housing in the Three Favelas in 1942

				Largo da Memória					
No of Rooms	1	2	3	4	5	6	7	7+	Total
Number	141	168	70	42	16	7	3	3	450
Percent	31.3	37.3	15.5	9.3	3.5	1.5	0.6	0.61	100.0

Cover	Zinc	Tile	Can	Diverse	Zinc-Can	Zinc-Tile	Total
Number	321	38	14	53	8	16	450
Percent	71.3	8.4	3.1	11.7	1.7	3.5	100.0

Floor	Dirt	Wood	Cement	Drt-Wd	Drt-Cmt	Cmt-Wd	Total
Number	119	281	8	33	4	5	450
Percent	26.4	62.4	1.8	7.3	0.9	1.1	100.0

				Cidade Maravilhosa					
No of Rooms	1	2	3	4	5	6	7	7+	Total
Number	370	505	232	127	67	22	11	10	1,344
Percent	27.53	37.57	17.26	9.44	4.98	1.63	0.81	0.75	100.0

Cover	Zinc	Tile	Can	Diverse	Zinc-Can	Zinc-Tile	Total
Number	858	112	123	183	47	21	1,344
Percent	63.85	8.33	9.15	13.61	3.49	1.56	100.0

Floor	Dirt	Wood	Cement	Drt-Wd	Drt-Cmt	Cmt-Wd	Total
Number	672	556	49	49	6	12	1,344
Percent	50.00	41.36	3.64	3.64	0.44	0.88	100.0

				Praia do Pinto					
No of Rooms	1	2	3	4	5	6	7	8	Total
Number	1,111	236	198	121	64	15	18	16	1,779
Percent	62.45	13.25	11.13	6.8	3.59	0.84	1.00	0.89	100.0

Cover	Zinc	Tile	Can	Diverse	Zinc-Can	Zinc-Tile	Total
Number	1,281	185	197	79	18	19	1,779
Percent	72.00	10.39	11.07	4.44	1.01	1.06	100.0

Floor	Dirt	Wood	Cement	Drt-Wd	Drt-Cmt	Cmt-Wd	Brick	Total
Number	1,036	548	83	61	29	20	2	1,779
Percent	58.23	30.80	4.66	3.42	1.63	1.12	0.11	100.0

Totals Rounded off to 100.0%

Sources: "Apuração do censo realisado na favela de Largo da Memória;" ". . . na favela de Cidade Maravilhosa;" ". . . na favela de Praia do Pinto," Moura Family Papers.

deaths in Praia do Pinto occurred before the age of two, with tetanus the biggest killer after tuberculosis. Syphilis was another major danger to men, women, and children in the favela. A survey of the inhabitants of Largo da Memória, Praia do Pinto, and two other favelas, Capinzal Olaria, and Humaita, who had migrated to Proletarian Park No. 1 in Gávea found that among children up to the age of ten, 12 percent registered positive on Wasserman tests; for those older than ten, including adults, the figure was 23 percent. Since this was a one-time examination, the true frequency of syphilis was undoubtedly higher. The children of the squatter settlements were sacrificial lambs to diseases that were on the way to being eradicated in the rest of the city.[5]

When one recalls that Praia do Pinto was the largest and best-known favela in Rio de Janeiro at this time, the situation of the inhabitants appears even more pathetic. Many migrants had moved to Praia do Pinto to escape the exorbitant rents in the rest of Rio, and although some had lived in the favela long enough to invest in the improvement of their homes, most of the inhabitants were barely surviving. Small wonder Mayor Henrique Dodsworth and Vitor de Moura thought it was safe to transfer them to the provisional proletarian parks. Who would object to the extinction of this "ulcer" located within the confines of the "Marvelous City" of Rio de Janeiro?

Dr. Moura established five criteria for those favelados allowed to move into the parks; "Homes will be rented only to those persons who have a regular job, form part of a legally constituted family, have good social conduct and have passed a medical exam in which they have been verified as not suffering from contagious diseases, as well as having had vaccines against variola and coli-typhic diseases, with their children vaccinated against diphtheria."[6] The original plans for the parks called for a total of forty-five hundred housing units to be built, at a cost of Cr$10,000 each. The land used for construction was to be exempt from taxes for twenty years, and each house rented for Cr$100 a month.[7]

The favelados relocated to Park No. 1 were promised private housing fit for a typical Carioca worker. What they received was more akin to army barracks. A former resident has left a detailed description of the houses occupied by the first families to move in from Praia do Pinto.

The units made of wood that constituted the great majority of the habitations in (Park No. 1) were formed by groups of twin houses, built always of two rooms, with measurements that varied from 2.5m x 2.5m up to 3.5m x 3.5m. . . . The houses had access only through the front entry, had no sheathing, and rooms were separated only by walls of up to 2.5m. Houses were held together by tiny concrete pillars, sheltered by 30cm boards and covered by French tiles.[8]

Moura and his collaborators had pledged to the city to build not only decent housing for the poor but also a structured environment where the favelados could be elevated to the status of proletarians. Some steps were taken in this regard. By 1945, Proletarian Park No. 1 resembled a planned village. Inside the compound the residents had access to a milk distribution center, a day-care facility, a children's recreational area, a preschool, an adult literacy school, a medical unit, a sports club, small industries (shoemaker, stucco shop), a Boy Scout unit, a fire fighting training center, a library, a worker's club, a religious education center, and an office of the Caixa Economica Federal—the government lending agency used by the poor.[9]

The park also featured a vocational center, dubbed the "workshop school," to train favelado youth for participation in the industrial workforce. The school accepted only young males aged twelve to fourteen, and illiterates were excluded. Classes lasted forty-eight hours a week, of which 40 were devoted to training in woodshop and mechanical work and eight to theoretical instruction. Teachers were told by the planners to instill a sense of responsibility in their pupils by cultivating the habits of punctuality, discipline, obedience, neatness, cleanliness, and a spirit of camaraderie to make them worthy to join the labor force.[10] The dream seems to have come true for some of the first to attend. The matriculation form from one of the professional schools set up in the park, Escola Profissional Col. Jonas Correa, proudly displays a list of names of pupils who left the school for part-time jobs in art design.[11] A vocational school for children aged seven to twelve was also contemplated by the park authorities but never completed. The Jesuino de Albuquerque school was projected to provide 247 pupils with primary education and vocational training in woodworking, carpentry, shoe repair, painting, electricity, horticulture, and gardening.[12]

The park managers were convinced that living in a regulated environment would wean the favelados from the culture that kept them poor. Speaking to an audience at the Pontifical Catholic University of Rio de Janeiro in 1945, Dr. Moura affirmed the favela had done terrible damage to the minds of the squatters.

Habits, preferences, moral and physical health, which must always be in equilibrium, are undoubtedly linked to the house or habitation. The residence—the home—where a man spends the greater part of his life resting, eating, and enjoying the comfort of his family, exercises a decisive influence on his body and spirit. Humid and squalid slum buildings, badly constructed habitations without sufficient air and space, located alongside similar structures, cause and aggravate diseases and generate bad habits with disastrous consequences. . . . They create an environment propitious to all the ills of body and spirit, with grave consequences for the individual and the collectivity.[13]

It was evident, he told his listeners, that the cramped space of the shanty was bound to produce a disordered family life, leading to the marginalization of the favelado. Only the physical destruction of the favela could prevent future generations of squatters from being contaminated by the ills of squatter living. Moura mentioned the specific example of Praia do Pinto, and how removal to Park No. 1 had actually benefited the inhabitants.

A couple from Praia do Pinto came to reside in the Proletarian Park of Gávea. The father suffered from general paralysis. The mother was syphilitic, without, however, showing any alarming symptoms. The family had lived for a long time in a shanty of only one room, which served at the same time as living room, kitchen and bedroom. One of the daughters, age seven, was constantly irritated, suffered from nocturnal fears, antisocial attitudes, and demonstrated real hatred toward her brothers, antipathy for her father and genuine love for her mother. Examine this picture and the conclusion is obvious. The doctor [in the Proletarian Park of Gávea] obtained her confidence and consequently much information from her. The exposure to intimate family scenes, the concentration of the entire family in one room, these facts certainly increased her antipathy toward her father and jealousy of her brothers, provoking her neurosis. She required psychiatric treatment only. Now this child is in primary school, [in the park]which she attends assiduously, and has no hatred of her brothers or any other children.[14]

Moura then cited examples of "promiscuous pubescents" who were subject to seizures and nervous disorders but recuperated after moving to the park. He predicted that soon no child in Rio de Janeiro would have to undergo the travail of being raised in a favela. In fact, the opposite happened. After 1945, Praia do Pinto continued to grow in population and area, whereas the parks died a slow death due to a lack of political will on the part of national and city authorities to keep them afloat. The parks had been conceived during the presidency of Getúlio Vargas, when the predominant policy in dealing with the working class and the poor was a mixture of repression and state-sponsored paternalism. The ouster of Vargas by the army in 1945 brought a new political strategy to tame the proletariat. Under the Eurico Gaspar Dutra administration (1946–1950) the favelas became suspected breeding grounds for Communists and subversives. When the national government abandoned all pretense of helping the poor, the failure of the proletarian parks was a foregone conclusion.

At the start of the 1950s, Proletarian Park No. 1 in Gávea counted 5,262 persons housed in 961 units, for an occupancy rate of 5.4 per domicile, which meant less space for more people than in most favelas. Actually the official statistics understated the shortage of housing because it was not easy to distinguish one house in the park from another; some units with three rooms or more were classified as two separate houses. Thus, while in principle the park contained 989 units, the actual number of houses occupied was 961. The park looked like an overcrowded prison: 2,214 persons lived in two-room units, with an average of four persons per house and a maximum of fourteen, and 246 resided in one room units, with an average occupancy rate of three persons and a maximum of nine.[15] Nearly all houses in the Park (914, or 92.4 percent) were built of wood, and just 15 were of stone. Only 10 percent of the homes had running water, and ten percent of these had damaged plumbing.[16] Those unfortunate souls who had left Praia do Pinto for the park had taken a giant step backward. In return for their rent payment they enjoyed less privacy and suffered more regulation and regimentation of their lives.

The typical family in the park found it harder to make ends meet than in the favela. Close to one-third of family heads earned less than Cr$1,500 per month, and 90 percent earned less than Cr$3,000. Whereas almost all residents of the favela had owned their own shack, in the park over half the families paid between Cr$40 and Cr$450 a month for rent. Park residents also had to pay for electricity, which had been obtained illegally, but free, in Praia do Pinto.[17] In order to maintain the fiction that park residents were just like other Cariocas, they were forced to pay middle-class bills with working-class wages.

The chances of climbing out of poverty by moving to the park and taking advantage of its schooling facilities were slim. Certainly the literacy level for this generation was higher than for those who had migrated to Praia do Pinto in the 1940s. Out of 1,775 residents aged 15 and older surveyed in 1952, only 16 percent were illiterate. But the education they received was of poor quality. One-third had attended three years of primary education, another third had completed primary school, but only 12 percent had finished secondary school. The children of the park fared slightly better. Among a sample group of 367 children ages 7 to 14 surveyed in 1952, 309 were attending school and 58 were not. But these figures can be misleading. The schoolday in the Park lasted only three hours, and many children spent the remainder of the day in the street, playing, working, and occasionally begging.[18]

Was the failure of Park No. 1 an isolated case or systematic? Proletarian Park No. 3 in Leblon, which was contiguous to Praia do Pinto, offers an interesting comparison. In 1962, Park No. 3 had a total population of 2,037 housed in 412 units, for an occupancy rate of 4.9 per house. The 412 families consisted of 961 adults and 1,076 children. At first the Leblon park was so poor that residents had to trek to Park No. 1 for water. But by the early 1960s the inhabitants had pried a few of the creature comforts of home from the city authorities. Most of the houses in Park No. 3 were made of wood but featured tile roofs and cement floors. Many homes had two rooms, a kitchen, and a bath-room. Park residents had access to a public school, a school for expectant mothers, a vocational school, a chapel, a recreational club, a first aid center, and a social work office.[19] Unlike Park No. 1, the Leblon Park had its own primary school, along with an adult literacy night school. A special vocational school for girls ages eight to twelve which taught crochet and needlepoint; there was no equivalent for boys. Twenty percent of the population fifteen and older was estimated to be illiterate, 50 percent literate but without formal education, and roughly 30 percent had completed primary school. The Social Service School of the Pontífica Universidade Católica maintained an office in Park No. 3 (as well as in No. 1), and social workers from the PUC paid regular visits to the residents, advising them on education, legal rights, child care, and aid for the unemployed.[20]

Despite these advantages the lack of a proper infrastructure eventually doomed Park No. 3 as well as No. 1. The physical environment was not made safe for human occupation. Frequent floods drenched the houses and bent them out of shape. The absence of proper drainage facilities and an efficient sewage system reintroduced diseases the residents had encountered in the favelas, a problem now aggravated by overcrowding. Health care was highly deficient. Only one medical unit operated inside the gates of Park No. 3—a pediatric center for children under seven that dispensed medicines and injections. The other inhabitants had to go to the Hospital Miguel Couto in Leblon, but were admitted only in emergencies.

The true reason for the collapse of both parks was the inability of the city to provide economic security for the residents. As one social worker noted: "The residents of the Parks, already adjusted to their surroundings, cannot move out; and the high rents and lack of housing in places accessible to workers makes it necessary for the Parks Service to concede them more time of residence, since otherwise, there would arise larger maladjustments with great harm done to them and society at large, establishing a cycle of adjustment and readjustment; a total negation of the objectives of the Parks in the first place."[21] The "provisional proletarian parks" were none of these things; by the 1960s they had become prison camps for another generation of favelados.

Since the government had abandoned the favelas, particularly Praia do Pinto, the Catholic Church stepped in to fill the void. If removing the favelados from their homes only resulted in the creation of new favelas, why not bring new homes to the favelados instead? That was the thinking behind the Cruzada São Sebastião, a project sponsored Dom Helder Câmara, Bishop of Recife and auxiliary bishop of Rio de Janeiro, to build an apartment complex inside Praia do Pinto during 1956–1957. The principles of the Cruzada were summed up by Dom Helder in three words—"humanization, Christianization, urbanization"—which meant treating the favelado as a human being instead of an outcast; instilling in him Christian values, especially love of family; and integrating him with the city by giving him the rights of citizenship, including housing, health care, education for him and his children, and political participation.[22]

The Cruzada was launched on September 29, 1955 with the approval of President João Café Filho and a gift of Cr$50,000 from the federal government. Dom Helder optimistically prophesied the Cruzada would spread throughout the city, with one apartment building in each favela. Instead, only two projects became fully operational, one in Praia do Pinto and one in the favela of Radio Nacional in Parada de Lucas. The apartment buildings in Praia do Pinto were located at the end of Rua Humberto de Campos, with Leblon beach to the right, Lagoa Rodrigo de Freitas to the left, and Jardim de Alá in front. On January 4, 1957, 12 families from Praia do Pinto, which by then had an estimated population of over 7,000 persons crowded into 1,546 shacks, were chosen as a "guinea pig" population to set up house in the Cruzada.[23]

Ten buildings had been built for them, each seven stories high, containing 910 apartments. Three types of dwellings were set aside for the 900 families who were scheduled to move in by the end of 1957: small apartments, with combination living room and bedroom; medium, with living room and bedroom separate; and large, with living room and two bedrooms. All apartments had a bathroom and a kitchen. Apartments could not be subleased, and no one other than those persons listed in the lease could reside in the unit. The founding families could expect to own their apartments after 180 payments of 8 to 15 percent of the national minimum salary.[24] Transferral from Praia do Pinto to the Cruzada buildings occurred on Tuesdays, Thursdays, and Saturdays between 8 and 11 A.M. In the first weeks of January an average of 36 families arrived every week, taking up residence in 144 apartments. At the same time the demolition of shanties continued in the favela; a total of 574 were destroyed the first year.[25]

The Cruzada accepted only families who met the criteria of residence in Praia do Pinto for at least four years, financial circumstances that made it impossible to rent or own a home outside the favela, and living in a legally constituted union, "or at least encompassed by natural morality, with offspring, and without 'marginal' members."[26] Dom Helder admitted that if these regulations were truly adhered to, perhaps as many as 80 percent of the Praia do Pinto families would be disqualified; hence he and his colleagues had to overlook minor infractions of the rules. But of the total number of families installed in the Cruzada only 203 required investigation by social assistants for serious violations.[27]

The directors of the Cruzada São Sebastião, wiser from the experience of previous failed efforts to integrate the favelado with the city, recognized that the road out of the favela led through the door of employment. They consciously sought to provide the residents with income strategies and ways of increasing their value in the job market. Ninety percent of the adults who moved into the Cruzada in 1957 were illiterate or semiliterate. A literacy course was started especially for them, taught at night in building block #4. From August to December 1958 approximately sixty adults participated in the course, with an increase to five hundred students by 1965. The school also taught sewing, typing, cooking, and first aid. The Cruzada offered vocational instruction in lampmaking, wiring, shoe repair, and carpentry. Student enrollment during the first year averaged two-hundred pupils. After five years of planning and delay, the Cruzada finally acquired its own high school in 1962, the Ginasio Comercial Papa João XXIII, with an enrollment of 120 students. The Cruzada also started the Escola dos Santos Anjos, a kindergarten and primary school for the children of working mothers. Housed in building block #3, the school offered educational and vocational instruction to enable youngsters to forget the stigma of having been born in a favela. One volunteer teacher with seven to nine assistants taught the ABCs plus catechism. By 1965 the school had twelve hundred pupils, and forty-two teachers, and plans were being laid for an artisanal shop.[28]

The Cruzada could attempt to rescue the minds of the favelados, but the rest of the body posed major problems. The favela of Praia do Pinto, as previously noted, was notorious in the city for tuberculosis, cardiovascular problems, rheumatism, and syphilis. With the help of a few medical volunteers, a small hospital caring for children was started in Praia do Pinto in 1957. Medical examinations led doctors to believe that as many as 96 percent of the youngsters who came to the hospital carried one to three types of worms and parasites. But there was little the staff could do except counsel patients to seek outside help. As a general rule the Cruzada staff advised residents that the practice of good hygiene at home was the best medicine. In this regard the staffers had some success. An inspection of the buildings in 1962 revealed that 10 percent of the apartments were very dirty, 20 percent were badly preserved, and 30 percent were barely preserved. But 25 percent showed some improvements in paint jobs and bricklaying, and 15 percent showed major improvements in floor plan, lighting, and other utilities.[29]

The aim of the Cruzada in providing job training, education, and health care to the favelado and his children was moral recuperation. To that extent the authorities proclaimed victory in the early 1960s. A report submitted by one staffer to the Third Brazilian Congress of Social Work in 1965 summarized the accomplishments of eight years of the Cruzada São Sebastião:

As to the most remote goal, the integration of the residents into the neighborhood of Leblon, it can be affirmed that, however slowly, this goal is being fulfilled through the transformation we see taking place in the residents and their acceptance by the inhabitants of Leblon. This transformation of habits can be felt in all aspects of life: physical, social, moral, and religious. . . . The most extensive, that is, the one pertaining to the most persons, is the one operating in the physical aspects of the residents: health and appearance [personal hygiene, order, dress].[30]

The dream of the Cruzada managers was to gain acceptance for the favelado by changing his comportment so he would be better accepted by "normal society." Reality gave cruel lie to this illusion.

In the late 1960s the city cut off funding for the Cruzada, and instead, money intended for the apartment projects was sent directly to Praia do Pinto, which once again was one of the largest favelas in Zona Sul. But the poor continued to pour into the projects, giving rise to a criminal element that terrorized both residents and neighbors in Ipanema and Leblon. Fundamentally, the demise of the Cruzada can be traced to the selfimprovement philosophy of Dom Helder Câmara. The basic problems of the favelado—lack of stable employment, the great distance he had to travel to work, payment of rent, inadequate schooling and health care—were not alleviated by building him a nicer home.[31] Unable to secure funds from the city or private sources, the Cruzada died an ignored and unmourned death in the 1970s though the buildings still stand as a monument to the futility of partial solutions to the favela problem.

Praia do Pinto underwent a rebirth after the failure of the proletarian parks and the Cruzada São Sebastião: 3,305 families resided there in 1969, and occupancy rates ranged from one to seventeen inhabitants, with an average of four persons in each house, which meant the shanties were more overcrowded than in the 1940s. But there were noticeable differences in the architecture of the shanties compared with the previous generation, reflecting the growing income differences inside the favela: 98 percent of the shacks had wooden walls, but a majority had tile roofs, followed by those with wood and zinc. Close to half of the homes in Praia do Pinto had wooden floors, and the other half were of cement (see Table 7.2). A third of the homes had running water, three-quarters had electric lighting and a little less than half had toilets. Half of all homes contained one to five pieces of furniture, while a quarter had six to ten. A surprising one-quarter of the favelados owned a refrigerator, and an equal number had purchased a television set. Clearly some squatters had acquired the trappings of the consumer society.[32]

The last generation to live in Praia do Pinto was the best-educated in the history of the favela, but access to schooling was still restricted by gender and social class. Only half the household heads had completed primary school, and one-quarter were illiterate. Among the male population over the age of 14, 2,436, or four-fifths, were literate in 1969; of 3,560 females over 14 only 2,197, or 61 percent were literate. Half of the males had completed primary school, but only one-third of the females had done so. Over 85 percent of the 2,006 children between the ages of 7 and 12 were registered in school, but this figure was based on those listed on school matriculation forms, not on actual attendance. Adolescents aged 13 to 18 had a school registration ratio of 93.3 percent, but there is no way of knowing how many graduated.[33]

Table 7.2
Housing in Praia do Pinto in 1969

No. of Rooms	1	2	3	3+	Total
Number	935	889	589	812	3,225
Percent	29.0	27.5	18.3	25.2	100.0

Cover	Wood	Zinc	Tiles	Amianthus	Other	Total
Number	402	657	1,676	44	321	3,100
Percentage	12.9	21.2	54.1	1.5	10.3	100.0

Walls	Wood	Cement	Zinc	Other	Total
Number	3,186	37	1	1	3,225
Percent	98.8	1.1	0.0	0.0	100.0

125 Did not respond
Totals rounded off to 100.0%

Source: Governo do Estado da Guanabara, Secretaria de Serviços Sociais, "Praia do Pinto," 97–98.

After the collapse of the Cruzada São Sebastião, the city ceased to provide health care to Praia do Pinto, so the squatters had to turn to private agencies for assistance. One of the most important parties who brought aid to Praia do Pinto was the Ação Social da Paroquia de São Lucas—an outpost of the Anglican Church serving the favelas of Zona Sul. The Ação Social offered food and clothing to the poor, along with courses in sewing, typing, and religious instruction. The Ambulatório da Praia do Pinto, also started by the Anglican Church, provided prenatal care to mothers and taught arts and crafts to women of all ages. The Centro Educacional de Ação Comunitaria, associated with the Brazilian Woman's Sisterhood Order, specialized in child-care and homemaking classes for new mothers. The Conferência de Nossa Senhora da Conceição da Gávea attended principally to the inhabitants of the proletarian park of Gávea, providing food, clothing, and shelter to the destitute. The Dispensário Santa Teresinha do Menino Jesus took care of the elderly and offered day care to the children of maids from the favela. The Posto de Calmetização Nossa Senhora da Aparecida aimed at eradicating tuberculosis in Praia do Pinto, and offered treatment to women and children free of charge; an examination and preventive vaccination were required for entrance. The Obra de Assistência Social e Educacional da Praia do Pinto gave the favela a nursery, kindergarten, day school, and pediatric hospital.[34]

This plethora of organizations testifies to the notoriety Praia do Pinto had acquired over four decades of existence. While other favelas were urbanized during the 1960s, housing in Praia do Pinto remained at a very primitive level. Wood, not brick, was still the building material of most shanties. Educational opportunities were unequally distributed, and females suffered the most in this regard. The favela lacked all but rudimentary health care facilities. Is it any wonder that when eradication finally became a reality in 1969, no city official could make a successful case for allowing Praia do Pinto to remain standing?

Few in Praia do Pinto wanted to see the settlement destroyed. The residents prized their primitive housing compared with the alternatives offered by city and church. Though hardly happy with their surroundings, they felt more at ease in their native environment than in the Cruzada buildings or the proletarian parks. They appreciated the advantages of squatter living on the south side of Rio de Janeiro: "no rent to pay, work located nearby, no fear of crime, an active commercial life in Leblon, and recreation for the children." They also felt more accepted by their neighbors in the favela than in the housing projects that forced them to live alongside rich and snobbish Cariocas.[35]

Though many of the inhabitants were willing to defend Praia do Pinto, the favela was the victim of its own tortured history. Due to its precarious position in Zona Sul, it had always been chosen as the first site of a proposed solution to the favela problem. But there was one catch. The founders of the proletarian parks, Dom Helder and his helpers in the Cruzada São Sebastião, and many others wanted to do things for the favelado instead of with him. Having survived various experiments conducted upon its body by the city and the church, Praia do Pinto never shed its image as a blight on the Carioca landscape. For decades, journalists delighted in portraying it as a sewer of iniquity.[36] Hardly anyone concerned about Praia do Pinto delved beneath the surface to investigate the material conditions responsible for that image. Despite the tenacity of the residents, Praia do Pinto was sacrificed to the real estate developers in 1969. A tragedy, really, when all the residents wanted was to be left alone.

BRÁS DE PINA

As one of the few favelas of Rio de Janeiro to be completely urbanized, Brás de Pina stands out as a shining example of how squatter settlements can be integrated with the city. What is more remarkable is that the urbanization of Brás de Pina, through the construction of new housing, the building of an infrastructure, and the extension of essential urban services to the poor, was accomplished with the participation of the favelados. The story of the transformation of the favela under the auspices of the Companhia de Desenvolvimento de Comunidades (CODESCO) has been told by the urban planners themselves and does not need to be repeated here.[37] This section focuses on the formation and growth of shanties in Brás de Pina before the urbanization campaign of 1967–1975. It attempts to explain why this favela was spared while Praia do Pinto was demolished around the same time.

Though first settled in the mid-1930s, as late as the 1950s Brás de Pina had a population of little more than five hundred residents. The favela lacked a water system, sewage removal, and electricity. The entire area, which belonged to the Brazilian navy, was covered with water and hills of trash. But this was an advantage to the first settlers, who used mud for bricklaying when constructing their homes. Paper cartons obtained from nearby food markets on Avenida Brasil and other workplaces provided temporary walls and roofs. The prohibition on erecting shacks on government-owned land made it necessary to work at night, but by 1960 the squatters had built fifty permanent dwellings.

One notable pioneer in settling Brás de Pina was Jorge Dionisio Barros, the president of the resident's association today. His case was somewhat unusual, in that he purchased the land for his shack from a real estate company rather than occupy it illegally. In 1947 he applied to the city of Rio de Janeiro for the right to acquire land on which to construct a house on Rua Ourique 1126. The lot measured 24 meters in front and back, and 15 meters on both sides, with an area of 360 square meters, and faced Rua Tamoio on the right and Rua do Imperador at the front. The total sale price was Cr$7,500, with a down payment of Cr$1,600, the balance to be paid in fifty-two monthly installments of Cr$112.50, starting in December 1950. Jorge obtained the building materials he needed by making weekly trips to Praça XV, located next to the harbor of Rio de Janeiro, and picking up scraps of wood and metal. He beautified his home with items bought on credit from the Casa Nova Aurora, a furniture company.

Another common tactic in obtaining a new home was to transfer land titles from one party to another. Elpidio Roque da Silva, one of the oldest continuous residents in the favela, acquired his house this way. In 1954 he purchased a plot of land for Cr$5,000 from a private party who had held it since 1934. It measured 8.57 meters in front and 8 meters in back, 25 meters on the right, and by 28 meters on the left. On this land he built his shanty, which remained standing until the favela was urbanized in 1975. But he and Senhor Jorge were the exceptions. Most of the early squatters simply occupied the land owned by the navy and dared the city to evict them.[38]

The typical shanty in Brás de Pina before 1967 was owned by the proprietor. But "ownership" meant permanent occupation unchallenged by the city, not legal registration of property. Most residents had the means to purchase building materials but they lacked money to buy their own plot of land. Nearly every shanty was built of wood (see Table 7.3). In 1967, Brás de Pina housed 4,416 persons in 812 houses, for an average occupancy rate of 5.4. Over 90 percent of the homes housed just one family. The most common type of house (219 in total) had three rooms for five to six people. The 812 houses had 2,713 closed rooms, for an occupancy rate of 1.6, and 1,563 bedrooms, for an average 2.8 persons per bed, with only one bed in each bedroom. Three-quarters of the homeowners owned a stove, but only one-third had purchased chairs, tables, or cabinets.[39]

The level of education in Brás de Pina was quite low by Brazilian urban standards. In 1967 the population over age 15 numbered 2,487. Of these, over one-quarter (691) were illiterate, 276 were literate but without formal education, one-third (927) were literate but had not completed primary school, and 375 were literate and had a complete primary education. Two hundred and nine had received instruction beyond primary school, but the overall chances of an adult in Brás de Pina obtaining an education were slim. Among the population over age 15, only 234 (9 percent) were in school, and most of them attended classes at night; 2,253 had stopped attending school altogether. These figures are alarming, yet Brás de Pina had a higher percentage of adult students than most favelas.[40]

Table 7.3
Housing in Brás de Pina in 1967

No. of Rooms	1	2	3	4	5	6	7	8	8+	Total
Number	107	127	219	193	104	40	16	3	3	812
Percent	13.1	15.6	26.9	23.7	12.8	4.9	1.9	0.3	0.3	100.0

Housing Types	Brick	Stucco	Wood	Total
Number	30	12	770	812
Percent	3.8	1.4	94.8	100.0

Total rounded off to 100.0%

Source: Pontífica Universidade Católica, Escola de Sociologia e Política, "Tres Favelas cariocas: Mata Machado, Morro União, Brás de Pina-levantamento sócioeconômico," 52.

Sadly, the generation that inherited the favela in the 1970s was off to an even worse start. Of the 1,130 children in the favela ages six to fourteen 15 percent did not attend school. Among those nine to fourteen years old, who by law had to be in school, 7 percent were illiterate and only 4 percent had completed the primary grades. None of the 512 children aged up to three was enrolled in preschool, and of 280 children ages four and five, only 2 percent received instruction.[41] Nevertheless, Brás de Pina was fortunate in that some hope existed for a child to gain an education close to the favela. A Catholic day school, Fe' de Deus, specializing in scientific and technical training, had functioned in the neighborhood of Brás de Pina since 1945 and had thirty-two hundred students enrolled in 1967, about half of them from the favela. Two nearby public schools, São Paulo and Oliveira Vianna, founded under Vargas to serve the population of the suburbs, also welcomed students from Brás de Pina.[42]

Brás de Pina was an extremely unhealthy environment in which to raise a child. The peculiar terrain of the favela, flooded for most of the year and surrounded by garbage, forced the original inhabitants to erect their shanties on stilts. But this tactic could not prevent major illnesses from spreading. The Pedro Ernesto Clinical Hospital studied 10 percent of the households in Brás de Pina in 1967 and found that over one-quarter of them suffered from worm infection. The prevalence of this disease was linked to the lack of proper sewage facilities, which forced residents to dump garbage into ditches, and the practice of raising animals like pigs and chickens to earn extra income, which infected youngsters who played in the favela during the day. A high number of residents suffered from diarrhea, arterial hypertension, sore throats, bronchitis, ear, nose, and throat problems, skin disease, and tuberculosis. Medical service was not easily available to the residents of Brás de Pina. Only one-quarter of the survey families in 1967 said they had sought the use of a government hospital within the last twelve months, while one-third had not obtained any kind of medical treatment since moving to the favela. First-rate medical assistance was available only in Hospital Getúlio Vargas, located very far away in Penha.

The threat of illness began at home. Over one-third of the houses in Brás de Pina lacked sanitary installations. As previously noted, the average bedroom occupancy in the favela was nearly three persons per bedroom and two per bed. Children may have received priority in use of the beds, but this was a mixed blessing, since it was precisely there that they were more likely to pick up contagious diseases. Still another factor contributing to the spread of illness was the diet of the favelado, which typically consisted of milk and bread in the morning and one other meal of rice, beans, manioc, and ground corn during the day. The daily caloric intake for residents of Brás de Pina and two other favelas, Mata Machado and Parque União, was estimated at an insufficient 1,880 per capita in 1967.[43]

Two private agencies, both inspired by religious ideals, offered medicine and other types of aid to the poor in the vicinity of Brás de Pina. The Liga da Boa Vontade, founded in 1950, maintained an outpost in the neighborhood on Rua Boa Viagem. It distributed free medications, food, clothes, and school supplies, and provided medical and dental treatment. The Centro Espírita Bezerra de Menezes performed similar services but under a different philosophy. Guided by the principles of spiritualism, it sought to spread its doctrine through good works in the favelas, attending to families in São Carlos, Parada Angélica, and Penha, as well as Brás de Pina.[44]

Since assistance from the state was not forthcoming, favelados had to devise their own survival strategies to maintain their homes. Interviews conducted by one of the participants in the urbanization project of 1967-1975 cataloged the kinds of strategies used for increasing family income. The head of the house sometimes sacrificed his leisure hours to take odd jobs. One family member, usually female, could work outside the home. The family might rent part of its house to strangers. Otherwise, the family stopped saving money, and the cash they had stored away was used to buy construction materials or furniture for the home. Other strategies included switching jobs, starting vocational training, going into business, and selling land.

The other form of survival strategy involved decreasing expenses. One way was to eliminate or alter leisure activities outside the favela, such as going to soccer games. Changing the mode of transportation to work also helped cut costs. Because the favela bordered Avenida Brasil, many workers could walk or bicycle to their place of employment. Reducing domestic expenses by postponing the purchase of furniture, utensils, and appliances was also tried on occasion. These strategies seem logical enough, and could easily be applied by middle-class families, but when one considers the material conditions under which the favelados lived, "belt-tightening" had an ominous ring. What was left to tighten?[45]

Despite this grim scenario, Brás de Pina nevertheless possessed certain features that assured its survival and made urbanization a viable goal. The greater stability of family life compared with other favelas certainly must have impressed city authorities. In a place with an average occupancy rate of one nuclear household per shanty, the urbanization project could be carried out with the collaboration of the household heads, and the more traditional family structure made the enterprise more salable to the press and public of Rio de Janeiro. The Cariocas who would have to pay for urbanizing Brás de Pina might feel better about it if they thought they were rescuing working class families who prized home life. Family stability, in turn, was made possible by the favela's emergence after World War II in the new economic boom zone of Rio de Janeiro alongside Avenida Brasil. Unlike the inhabitants of Praia do Pinto, who most often worked in restaurants, construction projects, and other ephemeral employment, a high number of family heads in Brás de Pina held steady jobs in industry, the service sector, and the informal economy.

Geography was of great benefit to the squatters. The neighborhood of Brás de Pina complemented the favela by serving as a role model for the favelados to imitate. The bairro (district) Brás de Pina housed industrial workers and lower-middle-class families similar to those of the squatters, but its residents had access to water, sewers, and lighting. There was no antagonism between favela and neighborhood, as in the case of Praia do Pinto. Separated by Avenida Brasil, the two communities nevertheless shared common employers, stores, entertainment, and, perhaps most important, dreams.

Though important divisions based on geography and income differences existed inside Brás de Pina, the favelados had a common reason to protect their homes from demolition. The sturdiest and most modern houses, located near the entrance to the favela facing the neighborhood of Brás de Pina, belonged to the oldest families of the settlement—those who had the strongest will to resist eviction. But an equally important constituency for urbanization was the poorest families in the favela. Arriving in the 1960s, they were forced to live at the edge of the mud pool and had an intense desire to acquire permanent housing.

The perennial complaint made by all residents was the lack of any infrastructure in Brás de Pina, above all the absence of a drainage system, sewage disposal, electricity, and paved streets. Since their requests went unanswered, the favelados were forced to build their own rustic canals, and by the mid-1960s a primitive water network served half of the favela, though it was subject to frequent breakdown when the rains came. Most of the shanties had access to electricity even before 1967, through the illegal use of fuse boxes. A crude system of paved streets also existed in Brás de Pina, serving to link the favela to nearby job sites and schools.

The urbanization project of 1967–1975 accomplished Brás de Pina's integration with the city and the reconstruction of the favela without the forced removal of residents that occurred during the proletarian parks project in Praia do Pinto. The goal of CODESCO was to create one community in Brás de Pina, making the neighborhood and the favela indistinguishable. New streets were opened and old ones realigned to make possible the installation of water and sewage systems. Seventy percent of the favela lay in swampy terrain in 1967, but by 1975 all the houses rested on stable foundations and the mud pool in the heart of the settlement was finally paved over, saving the lives of many children. Housing was revolutionized. Whereas before 1967 fewer than ten shanties in the entire favela were constructed of material other than wood, 60 to 70 percent of the houses built after 1967 were made of cement or other durable material. CODESCO financed the construction of 690 houses to be rented or owned by the inhabitants themselves; many of them featured multiple bedrooms, a bathroom, a living room, and a paved open space around the home. The economic life of the favelados was not disrupted because all new homes were built close to the job sites of the owners.

But the dream of transforming the favela into a modern community never materialized. Brás de Pina survives to this day, home to workers who have much in common physically and socially with the families who founded the settlement. The residents carved out their own little corner of Rio de Janeiro, but they were not able to escape from the plagues of low wages, inadequate diets, poor education, rampant disease, and crime that befell their parents. Many who received homes from CODESCO have been unable to keep up their payments and face the constant threat of eviction. Class divisions have widened considerably since the 1960s, and new arrivals are still met with disdain and suspicion. CODESCO itself disappeared in the late 1970s and the city of Rio de Janeiro refused to pay for any new constructions in Brás de Pina, even though the population had nearly doubled since 1967. The residents' association has lost touch with its popular base and a deep cynicism toward politics now prevails, especially among those born in the favela. The inhabitants of this "showcase" favela are still groping for a way out to the city.[46]

JACARÉZINHO

Sometimes the enemies of the favelados tell us more about squatter life than do putative friends. Unlike Dr. Vitor Moura, Dom Helder Câmara, and others who wanted to eradicate the favelas to "rescue" the poor souls who lived there, Carlos Lacerda, contentious journalist of the 1940s and governor of Guanabara in the 1960s, never hid his opinion that the squatters of Rio de Janeiro were a public menace. His bombastic series of articles on the favelas, "Batalha do Rio de Janeiro" (The Battle of Rio de Janeiro), which ran in the *Correio da Manhã* newspaper in May 1948, called on the government to rid the city of this danger once and for all.[47] To buttress his case, Lacerda had to make personal visits to the favelas, the better to know the places he wanted destroyed. The on-site impressions recorded by the crusading journalist offer the first glimpses of life in Jacarézinho, then the largest favela in Rio de Janeiro.

After his visit on May 22, 1948, Lacerda reported in his "Tribuna da imprensa" column:

The favela is a volcano. Yesterday, up on Morro de Jacarézinho, I heard the sound of Macumba ceremonies, while people danced in the street in the mud, next to ditches carved out by the rainwater—the only kind of sewage system the favela possesses. The police prohibit the building of new shanties, but for a fee, say 500 cruzeiros, they are willing to look the other way. Nearly every service available to the Carioca can be obtained in Jacarézinho—for a price. A payoff will secure your child a "school," with a professor who works for 20 cruzeiros. Nightly entertainment can be had in a "cinema" etc.[48]

Lacerda's use of quotation marks around certain nouns revealed his unwillingness to comprehend the world of the favelado. He wanted his readers to think that everything in the favela was a mockery of its counterpart in the rest of the city. Fortunately, other parties documented the early years of Jacarézinho without the jaundiced eye of prejudice.

The founding generation got off to a bad start indeed. Authorities from the Fundação Leão XIII, the Catholic aid organization dedicated to serving the squatters of Rio de Janeiro, counted 17,979 persons living in Jacarézinho in 1948, and 3,478 shanties. (631 dwellings were used for purposes other than home residence.) Fewer than 5 percent of the shanties were made of durable material. Less than half had sanitary installations, and only twenty-three had running water. One of the sadder statistics concerned child mortality: 10,144 live children were born in Jacarézinho in 1948, and 3,213 died before their first birthday, a mortality rate of 31.67 percent—an outrageous figure even for the favelas. But there were a few hopeful signs. Salaries from factory work lifted Jacarézinho above the living standards of other squatter settlements in some important ways. Only twelve households used gas in 1948, but a good number, 1,402, had access to electricity. Just one-quarter included milk in their daily meals, but 81 percent consumed meat, 83 percent had vegetables and 70 percent ate fruits.[49]

Miserable though their lives might be compared with other Cariocas, the employment available to squatters in Jacarézinho in nearby factories poured enough money into the favela to allow many residents to purchase their own plot of land and build a home. Land deeds dating from the 1940s and 1950s record cases of those for whom this wish came true. They also reveal much about the growing class divisions inside Jacarézinho. Many favelados looked upon their homes as an investment. A typical land transfer document reads: "I received from SJS the sum of Cr$19,000 from the sale of a house, with improvements, on Rua Gloria, in Jacarézinho. A house with 4 rooms and covered with French tiles. Dated: Rio de Janeiro, 3 of April 1956." Another noticeable difference was that poorer dwellings were termed "shacks," while those priced above Cr$10,000 were designated as "houses." By the late 1950s Jacarézinho was no longer just a collection of shanties on Morro Azul but a full-blown settlement the city recognized by validating land titles in a place with no legal existence.[50]

The proletarians of this favela were determined to attain the living standards of workers in the rest of the city. The population in 1960 came to 22,646, living in 4,620 permanent private residences, for an occupation rate of 4.9, and below the average for Praia do Pinto and Brás de Pina at that time. The houses contained a total of 16,440 rooms, the typical unit featured three and one half rooms for five people and a bed for three persons. Further, 2,211 homes had running water and 132 tapped into wells. A high number of homes (3,982) utilized electricity and 3,445 had sanitary installations on the premises. Over 4,000 used gas or other fuel. Only 322 had a refrigerator, but most had a radio and 45 were pioneer purchasers of television sets.[51]

Surprised by the stupendous growth of Jacarézinho in the 1950s and early 1960s, city housing authorities drew up plans for the full urbanization of the favela. Unfortunately, these designs never left the drawing board, but the survey conducted in Jacarézinho in 1965 by the state housing agency (COHAB) did contain important findings on the ongoing transformation of the favela: 4,630 families lived in Jacarézinho in 1965, housed in 3,933 dwellings, 2,145 of the houses were made of stone and cement, 417 of wood, and 1,371 of other material (see Table 7.4). As space in the favela ran out due to the constant arrival of new migrants, houses got bigger and structures were built further up. The most common type of residence in 1965 had more than five rooms, and 13 percent of all houses had two stories.

Table 7.4
Housing in Jacarézinho in 1965

No. of Rooms	1	2	3	4	5	5+	Undetermined	Total
Number	170	180	360	1,031	934	1,254	4	3,933
Percent	4.3	4.5	9.1	26.2	23.7	31.8	0.1	100.0

Housing Type	Stone/Cement	Wood	Stucco/Brick/Concrete	Total
Number	2,145	417	1,371	3,933
Percent	54.5	10.6	34.8	100.0

Total Rounded off to 100.0%

Source: Pereira, "O serviço social e a urbanização da favela de Jacarézinho," 12.

The favela gradually acquired a privileged group of residents as income differences between favelados widened in the late 1960s. One member of this lucky group was João Gomes Filho, a long-time resident and prominent community leader still living in the favela today. Listed in Table 7.5 are his expenses for the month of May 1969. Senhor Gomes has always been an active participant in local politics and the labor movement, so some of his outlays are not typical of other favelados. But the list is useful in indicating the high priority favela families gave to the care of their children and household maintenance. Also impressive is the variety of consumer items—including a television set, refrigerator, and pressure cooker—within the purchasing range of a favelado by the end of the 1960s.

Education in Jacarézinho also showed some improvement during the decade. Roughly two-thirds of the population was literate, but few attended school on a regular basis. In 1960 the total population over five years of age came to 19,035, of whom 11,929 were literate but only 3,617 appeared on school registries. Among those used 7 to 14 (4,096), the mandatory school age range in Brazil, 2,541 could read and write and 2,810 were registered as students. Children still had to go outside the favela for instruction, since it was not until 1985 that Jacarézinho had its own primary school, Alberto Montegro de Carvalho, operated by the Catholic Church.[52]

Jacarézinho still lacked proper medical facilities in the late 1960s. The closest medical centers were Hospital Getúlio Vargas, located in Penha (which also served patients from Brás de Pina), Hospital Carlos Chagas in Vila Proletária Marechal Hermes, which specialized in pediatrics; and Ambulatório Méier, built in the 1930s to serve the poor in Zona Norte. Diarrhea, worm and parasite infections, bronchitis, and hepatitis were still common diseases among children, according to city officials.[53]

Table 7.5
Sample Budget for a Resident of Jacarézinho in May 1969

Expenses		Curzeiros
Domestic expenses		270.00
(Illegible)		10.00
(Illegible)		5.00
Refrigerator/TV		35.00
Pressure cooker		25.00
Children's shoes		96.00
Children's clothes		30.00
Notebook		3.00
Entertainment		10.00
Magzs./newspapers		4.50
Haircut		1.50
Shave		1.00
Soap		.90
I.N.P.S.*		24.00
Labor union		1.20
Residents association		5.20
Bridge (contribution)		3.00
Lottery		2.00
Lunches		22.00
Travel		23.00
Subtotal	572.30	
Medicine		85.90
Income	658.50	
Expenses	658.20	

*Instituto Nacional de Previdencia Social.

Source: João Gomes Filho Papers, Jacarézinho.

The Catholic Church maintained two agencies in Jacarézinho to make up for the lack of government concern with health care and adult education. Obras Profissionais e Sociais de Santa Rita de Cássia, located at Rua Darcy Vargas no. 12, was started in 1959 under the auspices of the parish church of Jacarézinho, Nossa Senhora Auxiliadora. Founded by Padre Nelson Carlos del Monaco, it offered catechism, primary school for children and literacy classes for adults, as well as courses in sewing, flower arrangement, and music. It also distributed food, medicine, and clothing to the destitute. Closely involved in the political life of the favela, Obras has always been in the forefront of the fight for urbanization, especially the installation of electricity and water. Equally important in the social and political life of the favela was the local outpost of the Fundação Leão XIII, the Centro Social Carmela Dutra. Started in 1948 during the "Batalha do Rio de Janeiro" newspaper campaign of journalist Carlos Lacerda, it served multiple functions. Clients had a variety of services to choose from, including courses in domestic work, sewing, embroidery, mechanics, and sports. Expectant mothers received prenatal care and attended child-rearing classes. The Centro also ran clubs for men, women, and children to promote social life in Jacarézinho.[54]

One notable survival strategy practiced in Jacarézinho, also sponsored by the Catholic Church, was the *mutirão*, or mutual aid effort. In rural Brazil the mutirão usually involved farmers helping one another gather the harvest or families getting together to erect a home for a new neighbor, but in the favela it more often was collective work to improve the infrastructure and collective services. One such project, carried out in September 1967, is detailed in the minutes of meetings of the Centro Social Carmela Dutra:

We received a solicitation from some homeowners on Rua Getúlio Vargas to begin work on improvements on said street [for sewage removal and pavement]. They themselves called a meeting to discuss the issue. At this meeting a commission to oversee the work was elected and a decision made to visit the rest of the inhabitants of the street to make clear to them the necessity of such a project. A sum of two new cruzeiros was requested from each homeowner to purchase the material to be utilized.[55]

Episodes like these, repeated many times a year throughout the favela, showed the squatter his neighbors could serve as an army of labor under the direction of church or government agencies. Mutual aid groups also provided political protection to the favelado, because they belied the myth that squatters were helpless creatures who had to be taught by outsiders how to improve their lives. The founders of Jacarézinho could be proud that despite their puny resources, they handed over the favela in better shape to a new generation in the 1970s. By the start of the 1970s, three-quarters of their homes were made of durable material, four-fifths were linked to the water system, over nine-tenths had sanitary facilities on the premises and almost 100 percent had access to electricity.[56]

CONCLUSION

Poverty is not a static condition but a dynamic process. Differences in living conditions among the poor are often as wide as those that separate them from the rich. Praia do Pinto, Brás de Pina, and Jacarézinho experienced three different fates in the course of one generation. The hardest blow struck Praia do Pinto. This favela died many times only to be reborn, each time poorer than before. Once the most populous squatter settlements in Rio de Janeiro, large segments of Praia do Pinto were razed in 1942 to make way for the proletarian parks. Over time the parks themselves became new favelas. The Cruzada São Sebastião of the 1950s, which wanted to bring the city to the favelado, instead proved the futility of trying to reform the favela piecemeal. In the 1960s Praia do Pinto became a superfavela, featuring the original decrepit shanties, the Cruzada São Sebastião buildings, and the satellite settlements of Proletarian Parks No. 1 and No. 3. The history of Praia do Pinto is an example of refavelization: the partial destruction and subsequent regeneration of the favela, due to the failure of city authorities to address the problems that had caused migrants to move to the squatter settlements in the first place.

Brás de Pina is an example of the successful urbanization of the favela. Although it originally contained a tiny population, this did not prevent Brás de Pina from reproducing some of the worst ills of favela life: unemployment and underemployment, miserly remuneration for the labor force, houses made from primitive materials, education limited to a relative handful of residents, and inadequate medical facilities. But Brás de Pina functioned effectively as a community even before the urbanization project began in 1967. Unlike Praia do Pinto, which grew to monstrous size to serve the labor needs of the middle class of Leblon, this favela was the poor adjunct of a working-class neighborhood. The favelados here could make a compelling case that the city owed them the chance to rise to the status of their counterparts in the surrounding community.

Jacarézinho stood somewhere between these two extremes. It grew so large in the 1950s that no one dared seriously tackle the prospect of building new homes and bringing city services to the favela, so the favelados did the job themselves. By the 1960s Jacarézinho boasted thousands of homes made of cement and brick, many having plumbing, electricity and even television sets. The whole process may be dubbed defavelization—the improvement of the favela carried on by the residents themselves which proved an important factor in motivating the resistance of the squatters against city authorities bent on the favela's destruction. The growth of Jacarézinho foreshadowed the development of other large favelas in Rio de Janeiro like Rocinha and the gradual transformation of dozens of shantytowns into urban communities.

8

Representation

The favelados are in many ways the perfect foil for those who blame poverty on the poor. Like Voltaire's God, if they did not exist, they would have to be invented. The idea that the masses of the poor are responsible for the nation's backwardness is a perennial theme in Brazilian political discourse. Particularly in Rio de Janeiro, government authorities composed a catalog of how and why the city was cursed with the "problem" of the favelas. Acting on these premises, politicians, clergymen, urban planners, and journalists painted a grim portrait of the squatters and their milieu. But the favelados refused to act out their assigned role; taking matters into their own hands, they battled tenaciously against official stereotypes and for the right to run their own lives. This chapter focuses on public policy toward the favelas and political activity by the Favelados from the early 1940s to the late 1960s in Praia do Pinto, Brás de Pina, and Jacarézinho. The history of three squatments during one generation shows the evolution of government policy from favoring eradication of the favelas to the granting of partial autonomy to some settlements. These years also saw a progression from the favelado being seen as a plaything to be reshaped in his attitudes toward family life, work, and politics, to the conquest by the squatter of the right to represent his own interests.

The three settlements under scrutiny fought for thirty years to stay alive. Praia do Pinto residents relied on the Mayor's Office and the Catholic Church to protect them from rich neighbors in Leblon and Gávea who coveted their land. However, city officials and Catholic aid agencies saw Praia do Pinto as the logical testing ground for experiments in doing away with the shantytowns. When these failed, the favela was sacrificed to the real estate interests of Zona Sul and demolished. The squatters of Brás de Pina formed an alliance with politicians, urban planners, and members of the clergy to rescue their settlement from destruction, and then persuaded the city to build them new homes. The working class of Jacarézinho united with local businessmen and politicians hungry for votes to legalize their settlement and obtain a limited degree of freedom from government intervention. A review of the history of the three favelas forces a reassessment of the notion that squatters were politically dormant until recent times. The political options exercised by the favelados during these three decades ranged from clientelism to independent mobilization. Their efforts to preserve their homes formed the historical backdrop to the growth of neighborhood organizations and religious-based communities that surged in the shantytowns of Rio de Janeiro in the 1970s and 1980s.[1]

PRAIA DO PINTO

Praia do Pinto possessed three qualities that earned it local notoriety and provided the justification for government authorities in Rio de Janeiro who wished to eradicate the favelas. The land occupied by the favela on the edge of Lagoa Rodrigo de Freitas was coveted by local industry, and blocked the expansion of the residential area of Leblon. Second, the population included many recent migrants unable to find decent jobs in Rio de Janeiro. Lacking resources, they had been forced to construct their shanties on the worst side of the favela, directly facing the lagoon; many of them would jump at the chance of removal to better dwellings. Third, the settlement was grossly overcrowded. At the start of 1942, an estimated four thousand people were packed into two square blocks of shacks, compared with two hundred per two square blocks in the apartment area next to the squatment. Overcrowding produced the usual diseases associated with urban poverty: 10 percent of the population was said to be stricken with tuberculosis. Fear of the spread of the dread disease into Leblon, Gávea, Copacabana, and Ipanema led residents of these neighborhoods to call on Mayor Henrique Dodsworth to eradicate Praia do Pinto, Cidade Maravilhosa, and Largo da Memória.[2]

Mayor Dodsworth's close friend, Dr. Vitor Tavares de Moura, a physician who had treated many favelados since his arrival in the city from the Northeast in the 1920s, was made overseer of the destruction of Praia do Pinto in 1942. Because his opinions on the squatter settlements coincided neatly with those of the mayor, who in turn worked closely with president Vargas on this question, his pronouncements offer the best insight into public policy toward the favelas during the Vargas years. The Moura Commission was determined not to repeat the mistakes of past administrators who had failed to give the favelados incentives to leave the shantytown for good. If the city was to be rid of the favelas once and for all, the squatter had to be retrained to become a useful member of society. The good doctor claimed he had a clear idea of why the city had not been able to eliminate this scourge before:

In sum, what we have in the favelas is a high number of illiterate youth, of low health standards, without the documents required by our military and labor laws, who moved to Rio de Janeiro to find work. Those who build the shanties do so by necessity or from lack of education, but all contribute to perpetuate the social ill of living in the favela. And so this vice continues to besmirch the city, simply because the land for building the shanty is so easy to acquire and because our sentimentality prevents us from prohibiting such a state of affairs, and so everything remains as before.[3]

Moura saw the population of the favelas as deadweight around the neck of the city; for the sake of the metropolis, not the favelados, the squatter settlements should be eliminated.

This was the guiding principle of the provisional proletarian parks— "temporary housing project for the residents of Largo da Memória, for an estimated 700 families who would be removed from their shacks into spanking-new barracks buildings," according to Moura. The aim of the project was to "put the favelados in houses made of wood, above damp ground, with sanitary toilets, showers, tubs, running water, clinics, a kindergarten, night classes, a postal service, restaurant and dairy service; all under police control." The construction of two thousand parks was contemplated by the commission, but Moura felt the city might need forty thousand in total to abolish the favelas forever.[4]

Moura proposed that the first step towards demolishing the favelas should be the compilation of a detailed census to find out who lived there and under what conditions.

Among the measures I would recommend to solve the problems of the favela is a study of the shanty dweller as to his nationality, age, color, sex, profession, instruction, auxiliary aptitudes, married life, religion, school attendance, employment, income, types of salary, method of remuneration (in kind, contract, or day laborer); does he own the shanty, how much did it cost him, does he pay taxes, does he pay rent and how much. In short, everything there is to know in order to evaluate the favelado, his family, his shanty, his land, etc.[5]

The doctor was not sanguine as to what such a survey might reveal. A visit to Morro da Favela, the first squatter settlement founded in Rio de Janeiro, had convinced him that "everything evil and pernicious exists up there: gambling reigns day and night, and samba and other forms of diversion are irrigated with alcohol."[6]

Moura's impressions of Praia do Pinto during his visits in 1942, particularly regarding family life, have been cited in previous chapters. But one item that merits special attention is his outlook on the future of the favela as foretold in the lives of its children. He believed the primary reason to go ahead with the demolition of the settlement was to give these youngsters a second chance in life. He described the young people he came across in Praia do Pinto in gloomy terms:

How many times during our visits to Praia do Pinto did we not find a gang of youth huddled around a shack playing games for money and force them to disperse by our presence. In a quick survey we made of minors ages 10 to 15, when asked what they wanted to be in life, around 25 percent responded that they wanted to be outlaws, because a scar on the cheek, a sign of courage, was a pretty sight. One such case was Robalo, an outlaw already at age 28, but kind to us. He became so docile that shortly before his death, a consequence perhaps of many bodily fights, he sent us a message of his last wish. He wanted to die in one of the houses in Proletarian Park No. 1, scene of his former escapades. A few hours after we moved him, he died, comforted by young outlaws like himself, who, with a train of 56 automobiles, escorted his body to the cemetery.[7]

Moura was sure that the key to preventing a repetition of such tragedies was to refashion the favelado by moving him into a radically different environment. "Our interest is not in building homes, it is in building people," he approvingly quoted a fellow commissioner.[8]

Since the squatter was his own worst enemy, Moura proposed to mold a new kind of person through the correction of bad habits, legalization of marriages, proper documentation for employment, and systematic medical examinations. For the favelado to be born again under the aegis of the proletarian parks, his environment had to be cleansed of the bad influences that had corrupted him. Moura instructed the managers of the parks: "Exclude, and give the most appropriate treatment to: (a) the ill; (b) exploiters, criminals, and certain types of marginals (loan sharks, outlaws etc.); (c) those who have failed to adapt to the ways of the city, or can be convinced to return to their native states; (d) those with high income."[9]

Squatters who met these qualifications and settled in the Parks signed a contract once they moved into their homes.

Those who occupy house number _____ of group _____ in this park promise to:
1. Pay rent on time, on or before the fifth of each month, plus light and radio bills.
2. Authorize, if necessary, that rent be deducted from the salary earned.
3. Keep the house in perfect condition . . . , washing the floor at least once a week.
4. Report immediately any faulty boards, faucets, or other defects, and help to do repairs.
5. Collect garbage and dispose of it in the dumps at specified hours.
6. Not to stick paper, photographs, posters, decorations, etc. on walls.
7. Not to use an electric iron or any light that is not electric, and to cook only with coal.
8. Not to spit on the floor or walls.
9. Keep the ground around the house well paved, and not allow the accumulation of garbage underneath.
10. Maintain cordial relations with family and neighbors, avoiding grounds for arguments and fights.
11. Make sure that children attend school, workshops, and physical education courses offered by the park.
12. Legalize one's conjugal life, before the state and one's religion, as well as obey military and labor laws.
13. Make sure the family observes patriotic and religious holidays.
14. Submit to all health regulations.
15. Not allow illegal substances into the park or get drunk.
16. Find a job that will provide for the decent subsistence of one's family.
17. Not permit outside persons or nonregistered family members to reside in the home.
18. Belong to the consumer's cooperative planned for the park.

I understand that violation of any of these obligations constitutes just cause for my immediate expulsion from the park.[10]

Unabashedly, the park planners hoped to churn out a new kind of favelado, a content worker who got married, raised children, kept a steady job, and paid his bills on time. Behavior modification would be the the key to ensuring his survival in a new setting. But to demand prerequisites for quitting the favela and staying in the proletarian parks was putting the cart before the horse. Migrants had moved to Praia do Pinto because they could not find decent jobs, secure housing, or maintain a family anywhere else.

Moura and the other commissioners grasped part of this truth by writing off large segments of the adult population of Praia do Pinto as beyond salvation. They thought they might have better luck with the children and adolescents, who constituted nearly half of the population of the parks: "The child of school age [residing in the parks] was born in the favela, where the law of the jungle dominates. The reeducation of the adult happens only under exceptional circumstances—therefore it is with the minor that we must work, seriously and intensely, finding ways to occupy all his free time with continuous and efficient action." A child in the Proletarian Park No. 1 in Gávea had his whole day programmed for him. Classes ran from 7 to 9 for the morning group and 4 to 6 for the afternoon students. Gym class followed school, then a shower and snack. Leisure hours were occupied by attendance at a combination play park and workshop, featuring carpentry and electrical repair for boys and sewing for girls. Moura stressed the sense of responsibility and discipline the child would learn:

1. The child will spend his free time off the streets, and outside the shanty, where he is often exposed to antihygienic conditions and the antieducational attitude of his parents.
2. His duties will instill in the child a sense of self-worth, and help to overcome his feeling of social and often racial inferiority.[11]

If the park administrators thought they could do away with the favelas by remolding the younger generation before it was corrupted by the environment, they were destined to be disappointed. All three parks died a slow death from neglect by the city even while more poor people poured in from other parts of Rio, lured by the prospect of obtaining state-sponsored housing. By 1952, park No. 1, the showpiece of the project, had a population of 5,262, considerably beyond original estimates for maximum capacity. It soon collapsed into a new favela overlapping its "mother" settlement of Praia do Pinto.

While the park administrators dreamed that their experiment would lead to the extinction of the favelas, Praia do Pinto languished. A new wave of evictions occurred in the summer of 1948, but this time the purpose was to "save" them from the menace of Communist subversion. The overthrow of Vargas in 1945 had been accompanied by a radicalization of Brazilian politics. The Communist party, enjoying new freedom and popularity due to its participation in the war effort, mobilized the poor and homeless in Rio de Janeiro and São Paulo in the fight for decent housing.[12] The city government and the press reacted with panic. During July 1948 the former Communist, and now crusading journalist, Carlos Lacerda, in his newspaper column "Tribuna da imprensa," called on the city fathers to remove the favelados from their homes "before the Communists get to them."[13] Invoking his recent series of newspaper articles Lacerda dubbed the campaign "A Batalha do Rio de Janeiro," and called for expelling the Communists from the favelas, the destruction of those squatments known to the police as breeding grounds for subversive agitation, and the incorporation of the squatters into the city under the watchful eye of the Fundação Leão XIII of the Catholic Church.

Once again Praia do Pinto was picked as the showcase of the city's favela policy. Mayor Angelo Mendes de Moraes ordered the destruction of what remained of the settlement and the expansion of the proletarian parks to house the refugees. But the squatters were no longer so submissive as when they had moved in. Residents met the threat of eviction with defiance, as on reporter found out:

In Praia do Pinto the atmosphere is one of alarm. Almost all the inhabitants are upset. They are ready to quit the favela, provided they are guaranteed some other living arrangements. "Otherwise," one female resident told me, "we will not leave. They would have to step over our dead bodies. I have four sons. The oldest is three. They can not stay outdoors. A man can withstand everything, but women and children can't cope. This won't do. We live in misery and promiscuity. This place is not ours. We are ready to leave the favela, but we want a place to live." [14]

The city saw the threat of upheaval on the horizon. On July 20, 1948, a week after "D-Day" of the battle, the mayor promised to build up to five hundred homes for the favelados in Proletarian Park No. 1. One city engineer made them sound positively charming: "There will be three types of homes, depending on the number of family members: one, two, or three bedroom units with living room and kitchen. The disposition of the bathrooms is still to be decided by the Department of Social Assistance." Needless to say, these dream cottages were never built, but just to make sure "subversive elements" did not warn the favelados they were being deceived, the police rounded up "Reds and agitators" known to be active in neighborhood committees in Zona Sul.[15]

Praia do Pinto was not destroyed. The other side of the equation to eliminate Communist influence among the favelados involved the Catholic Church. Vargas's successor, Eurico Gaspar Dutra, had signed legislation on January 22, 1947, calling for the creation of the Fundação Leão XIII, a Catholic aid agency operating under the sponsorship of the city of Rio de Janeiro to bring urban services to the favelados while ensuring their political loyalty to the regime. But to do this, the church had to listen to the favelados and work alongside them. The Fundação created neighborhood block organizations, called "social action centers," inside the favelas to pressure the city to provide health, education, and social facilities to squatters. The favelas thereby became the bailiwick of the Catholic Church, and thus gained a small degree of political influence with city hall. The social action center in Praia do Pinto, perhaps the largest in the city, acted as the rallying point of opposition to removal.[16] The growing discredit of the Dutra administration, caused by the massive postwar inflation and corruption scandals, made the favelas of Rio de Janeiro, and particularly Praia do Pinto, a battleground for votes in the presidential election of

1950. No local politician could afford to alienate both the Catholic Church and the growing ranks of the urban poor. The "Battle of Rio de Janeiro" was called off, and Praia do Pinto breathed a collective sigh of relief.

Thanks in part to the "Batalha," Praia do Pinto regained national attention in the 1950s, after having been almost forgotten following the failure of the proletarian parks. Presidential candidate Brigadier Eduardo Gomes visited the favela on June 28, 1950, and offered to donate funds totaling 3,785 cruzeiros from his party—the União Nacional Democratica—directly to the residents. Gomes stopped at several shanties in Praia do Pinto, the social action center, and Proletarian Park No. 1 in search of votes.[17] Despite all the publicity the visit engendered, the city broke its promise to build new homes for the favelados, and instead threatened the entire settlement once more with eradication. A city ordinance forbade residents to build new shanties, and government officials made regular rounds of the favela to warn inhabitants that their days as squatters were numbered.[18]

Undaunted, the favelados clung to their homes, taking their case against eviction straight to city hall. The new mayor of Rio de Janeiro, João Vital, a political ally of President Vargas, paid a visit to Praia do Pinto in May 1951. Newspapers quoted him as saying that he could not imagine how such a "monstrosity" could exist in the middle of civilization. Like his predecessors, the mayor promised a greater commitment to "proletarian" housing—expansion of the parks. Typically, editorialists of the leading Rio dailies used the visit to decry the misery and malnutrition found in the favela. They also criticized the inhabitants for their lack of hygiene. Nevertheless, Praia do Pinto was spared on orders of Mayor Vital, and the enemies of the favela had to devise new methods to bring about its demise.[19]

Since the city had failed to eradicate Praia do Pinto, and the inhabitants had won a small measure of political power in their contest with city officials, demolition of the settlement was no longer a feasible option by the mid-1950s. Residents were so resentful of government authorities that the city willingly turned Praia do Pinto over to the Catholic Church. In 1956 Dom Helder Câmara, bishop of Recife, launched the Cruzada São Sebastião, a campaign to build an apartment complex inside the favela with the help of the city and federal governments. The Crusade was inspired in equal measure by anticommunism, paternalism, and an underlying assumption that the favelado was like any other Carioca, but had been corrupted by evil influences. One participant elaborated on the attitude of the Cruzada towards the squatters:

The people who live in the favela, the majority, wish to better themselves socially and live honestly. If they live in the favela, it is because they cannot pay . . . to acquire their own houses. If many do not lead honest and decent lives, it is because they let themselves be led astray by bad examples, and suffer the influence of the sub-human environment of the favela that leads them to depreciate themselves. Not having received any formal education or moral formation, they have no weapons to defend themselves against such influences.[20]

Quite a contrast to the attitude prevalent in the days of the proletarian parks, when the favelado had been seen as a wastrel. Yet much more explicitly than the proletarian park managers, the planners of the Cruzada São Sebastião set out to invent a new kind of favela family.

The triad of goals set by the Cruzada was "to urbanize, humanize and Christianize" the inhabitants of Praia do Pinto. Overall the Cruzada aimed at integration of the squatter with the city; not by taking him out of the favela as in the Proletarian Parks experiment, but by bringing the city to the favelado. Starting in 1956, a year before the inauguration of the first building of the Cruzada in Praia do Pinto, men and women religious along with lay assistants began paying calls on the favelados, much in the manner of missionaries. Outdoor Mass was held every Sunday, and Dom Helder himself frequently visited Praia do Pinto to prepare the inhabitants for "a new home and a new way of life."[21]

The reproduction of "truly Christian families" was a major concern of the Cruzada staff. Special care was taken to ensure that all residents living together legalize and sanctify their unions. Two associations were formed specifically to monitor the moral of life of the favelados, the Cavaleiros de São Sebastião for men and Legionarias de São Jorge for women. Their members had to swear to abide by a family code of honor. For women this entailed the following:

1. Maintain a clean, tidy house.
2. Don't argue. Remember, it takes two to fight.
3. Be an angel of peace, not a demon of intrigue.
4. Do not turn away just because your husband is wrong.
5. If the husband is missing, be both mother and father.
6. Educate by truth, without swear words or hitting.
7. Be a link between your child and his teachers.
8. Do not be a negative person, be agreeable. With the right attitude you can go as high as the moon.
9. There is nothing sadder than a degenerate woman.
10. A woman without religion is worse than a man who is an atheist.

Men swore to a slightly different set of obligations. The statutes for them, unlike those for women, emphasized public as well as private obligations.

1. Be a man of your word.
2. Help your neighbor.
3. Beating a woman is an act of cowardice.
4. Educate by example.
5. A real man does not drink to excess.
6. When it comes to games, stick to soccer.
7. It is more difficult to command yourself than others.
8. Communism is not the answer.
9. I want my rights, and fulfill my obligations.
10. Without God we are nothing.[22]

The Cruzada broke new ground by giving the favelados a degree of political autonomy. In January 1957 the residents agreed to form a common fund, the Caixa de Fundo Comunal, to finance repairs on the buildings. Each apartment dweller was expected to donate a part of his or her monthly salary to the fund, as a sort of tax. Two years later, in September 1959, the Caixa officially became the *Associação Civil dos Moradores do Bairro São Sebastião* (Residents' Association of the Neighborhood of São Sebastião). Each block of buildings had its own Association, and after 1960 the Council of Presidents of all the buildings met every two weeks to settle communal disputes. Though members of the Residents' Association fought among themselves many times, mostly over misuse of the common fund, they learned a valuable lesson in local democracy, that other favelados would learn in the 1960s.

A record of the minutes of a meeting of the provisional Residents' Association, held on July 23, 1957, has survived. The items for discussion that day were "(a) closing down the fourth floor of Bloco No. 1; (b) the Caixa de Fundos; (c) Faucets; (d) the light at the front entrance [of the Bairro São Sebastião]; (e) the cinema." From 1957 to 1965 the Residents' Association tackled collective problems of the bairro, including repair of stairs, cleaning water deposits, clearing sewage pipes, repaveing of unstable ground, and promoting the Cruzada high school.[23]

Political life in the Bairro São Sebastião was not limited to the Residents' Association. Occasionally the household heads were called together to deal with problems like garbage removal. The female residents sometimes met to discuss such concerns as child safety, the quality of the kindergarten, and the duties of a spouse. In one instance, the men gathered to contemplate "maintenance of the family" and the dangers of egotism in a communal environment. Reports from Cruzada staffers give the impression that these assemblies were a combination of owners' meeting, pep rally, and religious revival.[24]

The Cruzada sought to convince the favelado that if he behaved properly, he would be accepted as an equal by his neighbors in Leblon. This never happened. In the mid-1960s, while Dom Helder held out the promise of gradual integration of the bairro into the surrounding community, the favela of Praia do Pinto continued to grow, sending its excess population to the Bairro São Sebastião. The great impediment to the success of the bairro was that it was still too close to Praia do Pinto, so that the two populations could never be fully separated, and too dependent on Leblon and Gávea, where its men and women held tenuous jobs and were looked down on by their rich white employers. Moved by complaints from neighborhood residents, in the 1970s the police and press in Rio de Janeiro accused the bairro of breeding crime and delinquency, the same charge that had always been made against the favela of Praia do Pinto.[25] By not treating the root cause of the favelas, an economic regime designed to exclude the majority, the Cruzada merely gave favelados a brief chance to run their own slum.

The poor who stayed behind in Praia do Pinto and the proletarian parks fared little better in the fight for recognition of their rights. Government and church agencies operating in the favela and the parks in the 1950s and 1960s pursued a contradictory set of aims by promising to incorporate the favelado into the life of the city without educating him about the conditions that had made him a squatter. The political experience of residents of Proletarian Park No. 3, located next to Praia do Pinto in Leblon, is instructive. The Catholic Church had been active in the park since the 1940s through the Social Service Institute of the *Pontífica Universidade Católica do Rio de Janeiro* (Pontifical Catholic University). The work of the Social Service Institute was guided by the principle that the favelado should be "educated and readjusted to the social milieu to which he will one day belong." In the judgment of the managers of Park No. 3, the poor had to be motivated to improve their own lives and gain a sense of participation in community life. "It is important that the residents feel that they are responsible for the reforms or modifications introduced [in the park]; that these not be brought in from the outside, but arise out of their own investigations. Reforms must be strengthened by their sweat and made concrete through a desired ideal and the global development of the community," wrote one volunteer.[26] But the social workers had no intention of expanding the political vision of the residents beyond their immediate surroundings. The favelado was expected to accept the socioeconomic system of Brazil and learn how best to live within it.

Proletarian Park No. 3 seemed an ideal place to experiment once again with the favelados of Praia do Pinto. The inhabitants were described by social workers as exhibiting "good conduct and a relative spirit of solidarity, which assures a well-disciplined environment, rarely troubled by fights, drunkenness, or other disorderly conduct."[27] Social workers promoted the creation of a *Comissão de Moradores* (Residents' Commission) to improve the spirit of individual initiative and collective responsibility by allowing the residents to help run the Park. They felt it was important that the idea for the commission seem to come from the residents themselves, and at a meeting held on October 23, 1961, debated the best way to have the favelados "suggest" such a proposal to the park authorities.

Elections for the commission were held in the week of November 5–12, 1961. The ideal candidate for commissioner had to demonstrate outstanding qualities of citizenship, "promote group cooperation, show good personal conduct in his family life, work, and community service, respect and esteem the other residents, interest himself in the problems of the Park, show a spirit of initiative, be of calm temperament, maintain a clean, orderly house, and have an organized private life—responsible to his family and conscious of his duties as husband and father." A commissioner was expected to motivate residents to participate in collective work, report to the Serviço Social those residents who did not show initiative, contact homeowners who had made unauthorized modification to their homes and note complaints of inefficient gas, light, and water service.[28]

The park managers may have fooled themselves into thinking that at last democracy had been brought to Park No. 3, but many residents expressed grave misgivings about the Comissão de Moradores and its alleged powers. On the eve of the election, one longtime occupant offered a prophetic critique of the notion that political participation would revive the favelados' shattered spirits: "All this [about elections] is very pretty, and yes, we know that unity is strength, but we have already lost hope of anyone listening to our ideas concerning the problems that afflict us."[29] He was right, because the major ills that plagued the park, such as the lack of a sewage system and garbage removal, were not subject to local solution but depended on the dedication of city authorities, who by the 1960s had given up on the proletarian Parks and other showplace experiments designed to solve the favela problem.

After the failure of the Cruzada São Sebastião and the proletarian parks, the fate of Praia do Pinto was sealed. The military coup of 1964 strengthened the hand of politicians and urban planners who wanted to destroy the favela altogether. The land for Proletarian Parks 1 and 3 had been purchased by the Federal District from the Instituto Nacional de Previdencia Social (INPS) in the 1940s, but the sale had never been finalized. No one cared about or remembered this loophole until 1968, when real estate developers in Leblon decided to purchase the land. The area of Praia do Pinto, though it contained some of the most insanitary land in the entire city, represented prime property for real estate agencies that were running out of space to put up new apartments for the wealthy in Leblon.[30] Previously the susceptibility of civilian regimes to public opinion in Rio de Janeiro had staid the real estate interests, but the coup of 1964 gave the latter what they wanted—a city administration afraid to defy the national government. In 1968 the state of Guanabara purchased from the INPS the property originally allocated for the proletarian parks, and all the terrain estimated by city planners—approximately 96,000 square meters—to encompass the favelas of Ilha das Dragas and Praia do Pinto, for the sum of NCr $150 million. The money from the sale was supposed to be used to eradicate other favelas and to build seven thousand units of public housing for the former residents.[31]

The government of Guanabara issued an official white paper to explain the case for removal. After paying tribute to Praia do Pinto, "a foundation of the vivacious and spirited Carioca folklore," city planners made their views plain: the favela was "a criminal haven and a threat to public health; an assemblage of distortions provoked by social marginality, promiscuity, and disease. Urbanization is not an option in this case, due to the swampy terrain."[32]

Plans for eradication were drawn up on March 4, 1969, but encountered unexpected resistance from the favelados. Residents of Praia do Pinto were not happy after visiting the apartment buildings in Cordovil and Cidade de Deus in Zona Norte, built for them by the city housing agency, which turned out to be dozens of miles from their jobs. Resentment against removal hardened, and a carnivalesque tune soon was heard around Praia do Pinto: "Daqui não saio/ daqui ninguém me tira" (I'm not leaving here/No one is throwing me out). City authorities blamed this passive resistance on "demagogic exploiters of poverty and persons with evil intentions," but in fact opposition to eviction became more widespread as the favelados learned more about the fate intended for them.[33]

On hearing that eradication was imminent, several residents of Praia do Pinto paid a call on Guanabara Governor Francisco Negrão de Lima, hoping that he would intervene on their behalf, as he had done on past occasions when other favelas were threatened, notably Brás de Pina in 1967. In the summer of 1969 a delegation from the Federação das Associações de Favelas do Estado da Guanabara (FAFEG), the federation of favela residents' organizations formed in 1963, visited the governor to make one last plea on behalf of Praia do Pinto.

Journalist Guida Nunes describes the scene:

Negrão de Lima swore that their new homes would not be too far from their workplaces. At this moment he was interrupted by an aide who reminded him that he was not in a position to promise anything. The governor stopped talking, and the favelados left with the impression that the power to decide [the fate of Praia do Pinto] was no longer in his hands.[34]

Why didn't Negrão de Lima step in to save this favela, as he had for Brás de Pina? The strong lobby of real estate developers was certainly one obstacle to rescuing Praia do Pinto, but there were several other difficulties. The favelados' request that their homes be spared could not have come at a more inconvenient time for a governor elected on an antimilitary platform in 1965. The crisis over Praia do Pinto came during the "hard-line" period of military rule in Brazil, when the armed forces were bent on destroying all forms of popular organization. The mayor no doubt felt he had to sacrifice some favelas in other to protect others. But the location and history of Praia do Pinto also conspired against its survival. The men, women, and children who lived there depended almost entirely on the service sector of Leblon and Copacabana for employment. They were a disposable element of the economy that most employers in Zona Sul were not sad to lose. The middleclass men and women who gave jobs to the favelados probably knew little about them except their first names. The rich inhabitants of Leblon and Gávea stared across Lagoa Rodrigo de Freitas at Praia do Pinto and saw an ugly outpost of barbarism amid civilization. Residents of the luxurious apartment buildings and the favela shopped, ate, and drank in completely different establishments, so that Praia do Pinto lacked the kind of organic ties with the surrounding neighborhood found in Brás de Pina and Jacarézinho.

The residents of Praia do Pinto wielded little political clout. Lacking stable jobs and consumer power in the neighborhood, they had usually looked to outsiders to guarantee their safety. Every time the settlement had been threatened with demolition, they had run to the Mayor's Office or plead with the church to help them keep their shanties. But Henrique Dodsworth, Dr. Vitor Moura, and Dom Helder Câmara had all proved to be fair weather friends. No responsible authority spoke out now that the favela faced extinction. The pleas of the delegation that went to see Negrão de Lima did them no good. At the cost of their homes, the favelados had learned too late the limits of relying on paternalistic protectors to save them.

Praia do Pinto did not die a natural death. At the midpoint of removal during March 1969, when seven thousand out of the total seventeen thousand favelados had been transferred to the housing project of Cordovil, a mysterious fire broke out that destroyed all the remaining shanties, leaving ten thousand people without shelter, water, or food. Even today day former residents swear the fire was started on the orders of Sandra Cavalcanti, an aide to former governor Carlos Lacerda, who had been plotting the destruction of the favela since 1961.[35] Whether true or not, such a claim exposes the deep loathing favelados had toward those politicians who wrecked the homes they had built in the course of thirty years.

Officially, of course, "Operation Praia do Pinto," as the removal project was dubbed by the city, was proclaimed a great success. "Today the favelado moves out of his home with satisfaction," claimed a government panegyrist. "A community of 17,000 persons made a climb toward more decent standards of life. With the money earned from the sale of their lands, the government will carry out similar operations, turning shanties into homes and marginalized Brazilians into citizens perfectly integrated into the collectivity."[36] A multilingual book published by the city stated that "Criminals once found hiding places among the dwellers of the Praia do Pinto slum, who lived in promiscuous misery, but now one of the most beautiful residential districts in Rio's southern zone will rise on the land."[37] Perhaps the author of this report was cynical enough to believe such mendacity, but any squatter, young or old, could have guessed that prospects for a better life outside the favela were bleak.

Although the favelados had a written promise from the city that "they would be removed to localities as close as possible to their current job market," the distant housing projects selected for them in Cordovil and Cidade de Deus in Zona Norte forced residents to catch buses that ran at four and five in the morning to commute to their old jobs in Leblon and Copacabana.[38] Cordovil, the larger of the two projects, is still grossly overcrowded and crimeridden, according to some inhabitants. To those who rescued them from the favela, many former residents of Praia do Pinto say "Thanks, but no thanks."

BRÁS DE PINA

Mass political mobilization was the key to protecting the favelas from demolition, as the residents of Praia do Pinto learned too late. Rio de Janeiro had a proven example of the efficacy of this type of action. The fight against eviction in Brás de Pina from 1964 to 1967, and gaining the right to integration with the rest of the city, demonstrated the power of the favelados to intervene in local, state, and national politics. It can even be said that the upheaval in this tiny community helped derail the presidential ambitions of one of Brazil's most prominent politicians.

Guanabara Governor Carlos Lacerda had never forsaken his dream of doing away with the favelas of Rio de Janeiro. The desire had festered inside him for more than two decades, ever since his days as a contentious journalist in the 1940s. Brás de Pina, which in 1964 counted less than one thousand families, seemed an ideal location to renew his efforts. Lacerda's administration built three housing projects on the outskirts of Rio during 1961–1963 with money provided by the Alliance for Progress—Vilas Aliança, Kennedy, and Esperança. Early in 1964, Lacerda ordered the Secretaria de Serviços Sociais, which handled favela affairs, to begin removing families from Brás de Pina to the projects.

Lacerda claimed he had the backing of many squatters in Brás de Pina. According to a report filed with the city by the state housing agency, Companhia de Habitação Popular da Guanabara (COHAB), "Among the 323 families who reside in shanties declared uninhabitable by the Secretaria de Serviços Sociais, 219 spoke of their desire to move to any project built by COHAB."[39]

Some in the favela truly welcomed Lacerda's decision. At the end of November

1964, 100 residents, representing the first 280 families scheduled to be relocated to the housing projects, visited the Governor's Palace and were received by Lacerda's chief of staff, Marcio Garcia, who promised them that transfer to Vila Aliança would begin before Christmas. The 323 "uninhabitable" shanties were to be destroyed during the first phase of the operation, with the rest to follow in 1965.[40] But despite this show of support for Lacerda, trouble was already brewing for the government.

One notable feature of Brás de Pina that distinguished it from Praia do Pinto and many other favelas was its close connection to the Catholic Church, dating back to the 1950s when it was chosen by the clerical hierarchy as a test area for charity work on behalf of the favelados. This relationship paid off when clergymen rallied to the defense of Brás de Pina in 1964. On November 24 of that year, twenty-five priests engaged in favela work and and fifty-five clerics from all over Rio de Janeiro presented a petition at the office of Governor Lacerda, calling for an end to the threat of eviction, branding such action "inhuman and anti-Christian." The manifesto began by declaring that the favelas were a product of the rural exodus in Brazil, and the natural solution to the problems of high rent, inflation, and low salaries that burdened the migrant once he arrived in the city. Removal of the favelado from his habitat amounted to segregation. A better solution was urbanization of the favelas. In the case of Brás de Pina, instead of relying on the word of a minority of families who wanted transfer to the Vila, it would be better to cooperate with those who remained behind to try to solve the pressing problems of the community, such as flooding. But Lacerda, his mind already made up, did not accept the petition and the priests were told to go home.[41]

Also scheduled to visit the governor that day was a more radical cleric who actually lived in Brás de Pina, Padre José Artola, an outspoken leader in the fight against eradication. Aware that it was too late to stop Lacerda from carrying out his threat, Padre Artola took the case of Brás de Pina one step higher and organized a march on the former Presidential Palace of Laranjeiras, hoping to catch President Humberto Castelo Branco, who was passing through Rio de Janeiro. On December 3, 1964, he and other priests led 654 Brás de Pina residents, including 306 family heads, to see the chief executive. After a candlelight procession outside the Church of Glória, the crowd, carrying signs and bearing the national flag, marched on the Palace of Laranjeiras, but instead of being received by the president, they were confronted by his personal bodyguards—the Polícia do Exército—armed with machine guns.[42]

Unable to meet with Castelo Branco, the favelados instead had an audience with his chief of staff, Luis Viana Filho, who accepted the protest letter they had written with the help of Padre Artola. "We do not know how to properly express ourselves," it began, "because we are illiterate, but Your Excellency, who has studied and lived much, and still has the good health to study further, understands the aspirations and rights of the people."[43] Padre Artola reminded Viana Filho that "The voice of the people is the voice of God," and told him that the favelados' demands were simple: "They want the Ministry of the Navy [which owned most of the land where Brás de Pina had been erected] to turn over the land to them, which they intend to urbanize, so they will not be obligated to move to Vila Aliança and Vila Kennedy, as Governor Carlos Lacerda wants."[44]

For his trouble Padre Artola spent several hours in jail and earned the condemnation of the church hierarchy. Speaking on behalf of Cardinal Jaime Câmara, who had established the Fundação Leão XIII in 1948, Friar Cassiano Vilrosa told the press, "We priests must mainly side with those [inhabitants of the city] who are actually employed because if, on the contrary, we endorsed unpopular causes, we would lose the support of public opinion. If there are, in Guanabara, ten priests spending most of their time working in the favelas, that is enough."[45] But many clergymen who had contact with the favelas felt otherwise. Fifty of them signed a manifesto in support of Padre Artola.

The visit to the Presidential Palace revealed the growing political power of Brás de Pina residents. In addition to the church, another important source of support was from FAFEG. At a meeting held on November 27, 1964 in the favela of Esqueleto, which also was threatened with eradication by Lacerda, the president of FAFEG, Justino de Oliveira, promised the residents of both settlements that he would mobilize his members on their behalf. "The fight for a just way of life is a natural right of free men—the favelados of Brás de Pina do not accept removal to Vila Aliança," he told the crowd that night.[46]

The alliance of parish priests, FAFEG, and the squatters was put to the test as evictions began during the last two weeks of 1964. When forty trucks sent by the Secretaria de Serviços Sociais and the Fundação Leão XIII arrived in Brás de Pina on Christmas Eve to begin demolition of the settlement they were met by fifty priests, dressed in cassocks, forming a human shield around the shanties. Behind them stood the members of over eight hundred families who were resisting eviction. The presence of fifty policemen equipped with machine guns did not deter the crowd from shouting its opposition to eradication and their repudiation of Lacerda.[47]

Hearing of the disturbance at Brás de Pina, the governor decided to pay a visit to the place he had earlier dismissed as a "mud hole." Lacerda brought with him Cardinal Câmara, a close political ally whose role in creating the Fundação Leão XIII might help persuade the residents that the governor's intentions were all for the best. He was soon disappointed. After engaging in a shouting match with several of the priests, Lacerda found the inhabitants, especially the elderly ones, no more receptive to his plans than before. Losing his temper, the governor shouted to his assistants, "If they want to live like pigs, let them!" and withdrew for a two-week vacation. Meanwhile, he planned the extinction of Favela de Esquéleto in Maracanã. But news of the incident in Brás de Pina was flashed around Brazil by the press, and when Lacerda returned to Guanabara, he spent some anguished moments before the state assembly, explaining his actions.[48]

Quietly, the Catholic Church and the state government had agreed that only those families who truly wished to leave Brás de Pina would do so. But while the threat of eviction had ended at least temporarily, the favela was still vulnerable to destruction because the squatters, except a lucky few, did not own the land under their shanties. Residents pinned their hopes of protecting their homes on Negrão de Lima, running as an opposition candidate in the gubernatorial elections of 1965, the first test of popularity for the military regime installed the year before. Negrão de Lima needed an issue to use against the Lacerda administration, and the resistance of Brás de Pina to eradication had received national publicity, even though the dictatorship had begun to muzzle the press. Both Negrão de Lima and Amaral Neto, another candidate in the race, visited Brás de Pina during the electoral campaign, but the former scored points with the residents when he promised to urbanize the favela. Elected by a fairly sizable majority in a protest vote against the military, Negrão de Lima kept his word and ordered the land of Brás de Pina transferred to the jurisdiction of the State Housing Authority, the Companhia de Progresso do Estado da Guanabara, which was empowered to create an agency called Companhia de Desenvolvimento das Comunidades (CODESCO) to begin urbanization.[49]

The families of Brás de Pina built a powerful political alliance to save their homes. Catholic priests from within the favela and without, politicians hungry for votes, and young architects and engineers promoting urbanization of the favelas joined forces with the community to stand up to Lacerda and pressure the city government to legalize and improve their community. Propaganda was a powerful tool at their disposal, and the favelados took advantage of the political conjuncture. Lacerda did not dare risk a scandal that might cost him the presidency, and the military dictatorship could not tarnish its image by suppressing a revolt involving hundreds of poor men, women, and children. The survival of Brás de Pina proved to all squatters in Rio de Janeiro that successful resistance to authority—those who claimed to know what was best for the favelados—was possible. Their reward was not only the urbanization of their homes but also the example they set for others to emulate.

Urbanization grants the favelado his greatest wish, a home to call his own. The experience of helping to turn Brás de Pina from a favela into a community strengthened group solidarity. Interviewers for CODESCO noted the frequent references to "we the people" and "us folks" in the residents' talk. But favelados still felt inferior to the other inhabitants of the city. The stigma of living in a squatter settlement was drilled into the heads of the poor in Rio de Janeiro, and those in Brás de Pina were not immune. This contradiction was evident in such statements as "Maybe we are favelados, but we're also people you can count on any hour of the day" and "For favelados, we at least show a little dignity."[50]

Several household heads who had lived in the Vilas and had chosen to return to Brás de Pina mentioned the maintenance of group solidarity as an important reason for staying in the favela. Relocation to a housing project, two family heads told the CODESCO interviewers, would be all right "if they had one building for inhabitants from each favela," but living with strangers "on the other side of the wall" was not their idea of a happy home life.[51]

The changes in social and political relations that resulted from urbanization were impressive. In some ways the community was brought closer together. The three residents' associations fused in the 1970s and today operate under one command, working closely with the powerful alliance of favela organizations, the *Federação de Associações de Favelas do Rio de Janeiro,* to which all politicians must pay heed. The Fundação Leão XIII has expanded its activities in Brás de Pina to provide assistance to the founders of the favela—it runs a free milk program for the elderly—and to the new generation of toddlers. The favela has been sealed off by a brick wall that keeps out both the police and troublemakers. Residents express confidence that they will hand over the community in better shape to their children, and many have turned down offers to purchase lots elsewhere.

But the urbanization project also accentuated contradictions inside the favela. Many families could not continue making rent payments to the city housing agency after 1975 and were forced to leave Brás de Pina for good. Other families paid their rent on time but never earned enough money to purchase the land from the city, though they had been given twenty years to pay back their construction loans. Sparkling new homes now coexist with premises collapsing for lack of repairs, inflaming jealousy among neighbors. The Residents' Association fell victim to its own success. The sway it held over members depended on close collaboration with city authorities. But CODESCO was dissolved in the 1970s due to internal bickering, and the new Guanabara housing authority, the Companhia Estadual do Estado da Guanabara, withdrew its representative in Brás de Pina once urbanization was complete. The community is deeply divided by the legacy of urbanization. A bitter rivalry pits those who worked with CODESCO, including the current leadership of the Residents' Association, against Padre Artola and his supporters, who feel the favela lost its independence by accepting government tutelage. Political fights go on all the time between these two factions on the question of whether to occupy more land to make way for new settlers, or to shut off further migration with the help of the police. Brás de Pina no longer looks like a favela, but it shares many of the same problems of other poor communities. The generation now coming of age will have to decide whether these problems can be resolved through collaboration with other favelados or by striking out on their own.

What made this favela privileged is that it contained a combative population that struggled for twenty-five years to protect and improve their homes while subsisting on starvation salaries. Perhaps it is appropriate to close this section by recounting the experiences of an anonymous resident interviewed by CODESCO in 1967. Born in Minas Gerais, he migrated to the favela in 1943. At first he rented his shanty, but was forced to move out when he could not make payment. Determined to stay put, he erected a shack of his own but was told to take it down by city authorities, who warned him that squatting was illegal. He persisted in defending his home but eventually lost it to floods. In 1947 he built another, laying the foundation himself. Once his house was secure from the waters, he proceeded to construct new walls and a roof made from stones. When the threat of eviction arose in 1964, he was prepared to fight for his home once again. The urbanization project had his full cooperation. "It was worth the sacrifice," he told CODESCO. Brás de Pina was built and saved by thousands like him.[52]

JACARÉZINHO

The history of Jacarézinho, the largest squatter settlement in Rio de Janeiro from the 1950s until the late 1960s, demonstrates the possibilities and limits of the political strength of the favelados. Several unique qualities of this favela have contributed to its survival. Geography served the interests of the inhabitants by joining their fortunes to the more prosperous surrounding communities. Bordered by the Linha Auxiliar of the Central do Brasil railroad and the Jacaré river, Jacarézinho spilled over into the neighborhoods of Maria da Graça and Jacaré, both of which contained large working-class and middle-class populations who often walked to the favela to purchase food and second hand goods. The residents of Jacarézinho operated one of the most important consumer markets in the district of Méier, and won the respect of fellow Cariocas through their hard work. The eradication of the favela would therefore have dealt a hard blow to many of the neighboring communities.

The large industrial labor force living inside Jacarézinho and the mutually beneficial relationship between the favelados and the industries of Méier also helps to explain the longevity of the favela. The large number of industrial jobs held by residents of Jacarézinho was noted by census takers, who counted close to two thousand factory workers living there in 1948. Industrial activity could also be found within the favela, from shoe repair shops to slaughterhouses. While cooperatives were the most common form of industry, some workshops employed wage laborers, so the favela could be said to contain home-based capitalists and proletarians.

Jacarézinho also possessed a petty bourgeoisie. Many residents owned small commercial establishments. Nearly every shanty located near the entrances to the favela threw its doors open during the day to customers wanting food, drink, cigarettes, haircuts, and just about anything else. Some businesses generated enough income to lend money to their customers, allowing debtors to pay off loans either in cash or in labor service. Eventually the success of these establishments turned the nearby favelas, such as Manguinhos, into economic satellites of Jacarézinho. Poorer favelados trekked to Jacarézinho in search of work, loans, and cheap goods. This network of service sector, credit establishments, cooperatives, and industries forged unity across class lines and developed ties between the favela and the neighborhood of Jacaré that proved crucial in preserving the settlement.

The first serious attempt to destroy Jacarézinho came in the early 1940s, initiated by one of the original owners of the land, a Portuguese named Mario de Almeida. This episode combined tragedy with farce. Beginning in 1942, Almeida used his considerable political clout to order evictions. A genuine battle ensued in Jacarézinho for the next three years, with the police using horses and vans to demolish shanties. The favelados erected primitive barricades to protect their homes. New shacks went up as fast as the police could destroy them, and neither side could prevail.

Almeida had not counted on the political savvy of the favelados. One of the few privileges that squatters shared with more affluent residents of Rio de Janeiro was direct access to government agencies and politicians. As seen in Brás de Pina, squatters did not shrink from the authority of even the president of Brazil, but thought of him and other government officials as potential allies in the fight against eradication. On somewhat dubious grounds, the political leaders of Jacarézinho told the press and the Mayor's Office that the first lady of Brazil, Darcy Vargas, had promised them ownership of the land. To make this unfounded claim come true, some two hundred residents organized a march on the Presidential Palace in Catête in 1945, to speak with Getúlio Vargas. They were received by the chief executive, who agreed to live up to his wife's "promise." Shortly thereafter, Vargas gave orders that the inhabitants of Jacarézinho occupied the land by "consent" of the city, and that further settlements must be legalized by the Liga Brasileira de Assistência, a government aid agency for the poor run by Dona Darcy. The favelados were so grateful that they renamed one of the principal streets in Jacarézinho "Rua Darcy."

The overthrow of Vargas in 1945 created an unusual scenario in the favelas, Jacarézinho in particular. As the Estado Novo collapsed, so did the paternalistic policies of the government of Rio de Janeiro toward the squatter settlements. Whereas in the early part of the decade favelados were deemed worthy of being saved through experiments like the proletarian parks, now the political mood was one of overt hostility toward the poor and working-class followers of Vargas. Demagogues such as Carlos Lacerda called for the physical destruction of the favelas, which he despised as bailiwicks for both Vargas and the powerful Brazilian Communist party.

History was not on the side of Lacerda. The eradication of the favelas was no longer feasible because they had grown too large to demolish. Further complicating matters for the government, the squatter settlements of Rio de Janeiro now contained large numbers of voters who had to be courted by politicians aspiring to local and national office. During the presidential campaign of 1946, Eurico Dutra, Vargas's stand-in, promised community leaders in Jacarézinho that their homes would be secure if he won the election, and the squatment voted for him overwhelmingly. But, once elected, he endorsed the call to eliminate the favelas as seedbeds of radicalism.

At first Dutra and the appointed mayor of Rio de Janeiro, Angelo Mendes de Moraes, seemed to encourage urbanization as the answer to the favela problem. The president attended the inauguration of the Fundação Leão XIII post in Jacarézinho, the Centro Social Carmela Dutra, and promised residents he would build a water network for them. But when the Companhia Concórdia Imobiliaria, a real estate firm that owned much property in and around Jacarézinho, filed a claim with the city in 1949 to recover land lost to squatters, the president and Mayor Mendes equivocated in their response.

Companhia Concórdia was well known to the thirty thousand residents of Jacarézinho; in fact, one of the busiest byways of the favela still bears its name. But in 1949 it proved a deadly enemy. In the winter of that year the company, in conjunction with two local factory firms, Unidas de Tecidos and Bordados S.A., filed a petition before Federal Judge Augosto de Moura to expropriate the land of Jacarézinho, claiming it had originally been intended as the site for factory workers' housing and was now illegally occupied by squatters.[53]

The mayor countered with his own petition, calling on the judge to reject Concórdia's request, asserting that the city had first claim on the property. But the mayor was not about to concede the right of residents of Jacarézinho to defend their homes. Even as he argued their case before the courts, more police were stationed inside the favela to prevent the building of new shanties, and Mendes de Moraes publicly endorsed a federal government report that called for the expulsion of all the squatters in Rio de Janeiro to their home states. He also suggested to the City Council that it consider the forced removal of favela families whose household income exceeded the minimum wage.[54]

Judge Moura ruled in favor of Concórdia, arguing that the city had failed to register its domain over Jacarézinho in proper fashion by not submitting an evaluation of the current worth of the property. He also acceded to the company's demand for two hundred policemen to be dispatched to Jacarézinho to begin evictions.[55] But the judge was no political naif. Realizing the danger posed to the favelados should his ruling be taken as precedent, Moura stressed in his decision the need to avoid "demagogic outbursts" over the favelas, insisting that the social question involved, the future of squatter settlements in Rio de Janeiro, was not within the competency of the judiciary.[56]

Knowing just how crucial the vote in Jacarézinho was to politicians, the favelados contacted members of the City Council and asked them to speak out in their defense. On June 27 the council passed a resolution that a telegram be sent to the mayor directing him to turn "his attention to the unexpected assault" facing Jacarézinho.[57] A month later Councilman Luiz Paes Leme spoke of the "women who had stopped crying and children who had gone back to playing [in Jacarézinho], in the naive belief that their homes were safe after the government's promise of protection," only to be confronted once again with the specter of eviction.[58]

Editorials for and against the rescue of Jacarézinho appeared in the press. Most emphasized the possible harm to the city, and not the squatters, if the settlement were to be swept away. The popular daily newspaper *A Manhã* warned:

Eviction would leave thousands of people without a roof, creating a serious social problem to be conveniently exploited by extremist, demagogic elements. . . . A sword of Damocles hangs over ten thousand people [sic] and there are only two possible ways to save them: either the city comes up with the money to purchase the land or it finds a way to house the mass of favelados after eviction. The first solution seems more viable. No matter how much the land costs, the price is not as high as the onerous consequences of eviction."[59]

Those who clamored for the destruction of the favelas naturally used the uproar over Jacarézinho to blame the city authorities for having allowed squatter settlements to spread in the first place. The editors of *O Jornal* took an "I told you so" line: "This case should be a warning to the people [in the favelas] and the authorities. To the latter, for not having prevented the illegal occupation of land belonging to a third party, and to the former, for their naïveté in building shanties on property that did not belong to them and trusting the government to act like their 'good daddy.'"[60] Some in the press championed the cause of government intervention in the squatter settlements as a way of redeeming the favelados from their own vices. One editorial in the *Jornal do Brasil* pontificated: "The favela of

Jacarézinho, where thousands of men, women, and children live in condemnable promiscuity, is in desperate need of intervention by the city authorities." Much of the public in Rio de Janeiro, according to the editors, concurred with their assessment that favelados should be treated as wards of the state.[61]

A few dissenting voices questioned the notion of the favela as a den of iniquity. The explosive growth of Jacarézinho in the late 1940s forced outside observers to paint a more complex picture. In 1950 *O Jornal*, which the previous year had condemned the city government for allowing favelas to spread, was sufficiently impressed with the campaign to save Jacarézinho to reconsider its verdict. The editors now tried to impress readers with the accomplishment of the squatters.

The favela houses 35,000 people in 7,000 shanties. It is larger than 83% of existing Brazilian cities, and only 21 cities, including sixteen state capitals, have a larger population. To be sure there are pockets of outlaws and evil-doers, but most favelados are hard workers. Jacarézinho has 600 commercial establishments, including jewelry stores, but only three schools, and two of these are for samba music.[62]

Still, the paper could not refrain from calling the residents "a marginal population, waiting for incorporation into the city."[63]

The dispute over the future of Jacarézinho was still a combustible topic in local and national politics when Getúlio Vargas returned to the presidency in 1951. At the start of the 1950s the fight centered on electricity. Mario de Almeida had forsaken his claim to the land of Jacarézinho in 1945, but not to several electrical outlets he claimed to have installed. In 1950 he took his case to court and threatened to cut off light to the favela unless his lands were restored. Shanty dwellers were shocked, but their response was not long in coming. Seven associations of residents, calling themselves Light and Energy Companies, with up to four hundred members each, sprang up in Jacarézinho almost overnight to deal directly with the city electrical company and bypass Almeida. They remained in operation until the late 1960s when Rio de Janeiro officially extended electrical service to Jacarézinho.[64]

The favela confronted myriad other problems as the decade progressed. In 1951 the estimated population stood at forty-five thousand to fifty thousand persons. The inhabitants had to share six water spigots. Only seven National Guardsmen watched over the settlement. Electricity reached only a relatively few families at a cost of 300 cruzeiros for installation and 11 cruzeiros per month. Jacarézinho lacked any sort of sewage disposal, and one medical post, run out of the Fundação Leão XIII, served the entire population.[65] Community leaders decided it was time once again to go to the top of the city bureaucracy and seek official backing for urbanization, playing the votes of Jacarézinho as a trump card.

In response to the squatters' efforts during the second Vargas administration (1951–1954) many local and national politicians canvassed Jacarézinho. Early in 1951 Vice President João Café Filho climbed the Morro Azul and inspected the shanties. The pro-government press of Rio de Janeiro used the occasion to present the vice president as a "messenger of peace and joy" to a depressed area and to blast the previous city administration of "the demagogue" Mendes de Moraes for having neglected the favelas. Getulista newspapers told the favelados to put their trust in the new mayor, João Vital, who had the ear of Vargas.[66]

Café Filho told those he met in Jacarézinho that if they wanted to receive services from the city, they had to begin improving the favela themselves. This meant first of all expelling local entrepeneurs—"sharks"—who illegally dispensed goods and services to the residents while cheating the government of revenue. The newspaper *A Notícia* cited one such type:

The fat man Joaquim Modena is the owner of a fairly sizable warehouse, with monthly income of 30,000 cruzeiros. He pays no taxes, but promises to do so in the future. His goods are not inspected for hygiene, nor are his prices regulated by the government. Modena is no fool, and does pretty much as the other 200 owners of commercial establishments in Jacarézinho do: he charges what he can get away with.[67]

Such reportage reinforced the popular stereotype of the favelado as a lamb easily fleeced by con artists. Jacarézinho was described by much of the press in the 1950s as a "stagnant environment" where thousands of souls were condemned forever.[68] A typical newspaper account of the times read: "There are shanties in Jacarézinho of only one room used to house eight to ten people. The promiscuity is astounding. Residents have no sanitary installations and throw garbage in a common ditch. No ambulance serves the favela, and the sick often die for lack of attention."[69] This stereotype of the favelado as a helpless victim who needed assistance from guardian angels of the government expressed the political philosophy of Vargas to grant services to the poor in return for their loyalty.

The dangers of relying on government saviors to come to the aid of the favela was made clear when Jacarézinho was once again confronted with demolition. In July 1951, just after Café Filho's visit, the Companhia Administradora de São Paulo, owner of much of the land in Jacarézinho in the vicinity of Rua Viuva Claudio, filed suit in municipal court to evict the squatters living there within ten days. The area in question housed 30,000 persons in 452,000 square meters.[70]

The residents targeted for removal told the press they would leave "in pine boxes" rather than give up their homes, and scheduled a meeting with President Vargas. Though the chief executive was indisposed, his spokesman promised the delegation who came to the Palacio do Catête that the president would appoint a commission to address their demands and would send Mayor Vital to the favela to rally the favelados against eviction. In the meantime, to forestall immediate action by the Companhia de São Paulo, a City Council member, Edgar de Carvalho, introduced a bill to offer the company other land owned by the Federal District in exchange for its property in Jacarézinho.[71]

Back in the favela, community leaders were busy organizing the public to turn out for the mayor's visit. Upon his arrival he promised an end to the threat of eviction, and the fulfillment of every other desire of the favelados: transportation to the rest of city, widening of public streets, a primary school, and legalizing commercial activity inside the favela.[72] The newspaper *Diario trabalhista*, organ of the Partido Trabalhista Brasileiro (PTB) of President Vargas, declared that the president and João Vital would succeed where previous politicians had failed. "Perhaps with Mr. João Vital the problems of the hillside populations will be concretely resolved, putting an end to the quixotic and melancholic 'Battle of Rio de Janeiro' [campaign of Carlos Lacerda]."[73]

The favelados were more politically sophisticated than Vargas assumed. Community leaders wondered how they could preserve the favela for future generations. Many outside parties besides the Companhia de São Paulo had a claim on some segment of the favela. The only way to stop the cycle of threats of eradication was to fully urbanize the settlement. Spokesmen for the favela made their concerns known to the press, and their campaign elicited favorable if not always accurate coverage. In July 1951 the influential newspaper *Gazeta de noticias* ran an editorial titled "A Medical Post for Jacarézinho!" claiming "that of all their problems the favelados of Jacarézinho consider the lack of a medical post the most crucial. The creation of such a structure, in our view, would prevent a repetition of the tragedy that occurred a few days ago—when [the old woman] Arquiminia Vitoria died for lack of immediate assistance."[74] A few days later the favelados extracted from President Vargas a promise to build a thousand new houses for them in the vicinity of the favela should they be expelled from their shanties.[75] As in the case of the "proletarian homes" in Praia do Pinto that were never built, the pro-government press excelled in describing imaginary domiciles: "One thousand prefabricated houses will be built close to Jacarézinho, with two to three rooms, bath, and kitchen. Construction should take up to four to six months, including water installation. Favelados living here will pay a small monthly fee for each house."[76]

As eviction day drew closer, enemies of the favela grew bolder. At the start of August 1951, the police, apparently acting without authorization of the mayor, temporarily closed down all commerce in the favelas. This struck a hard blow at Jacarézinho in particular, which housed eight hundred commercial stores. A courageous federal deputy, Breno de Silveira, protested directly to the Mayor's Office, and the order was revoked.[77]

This temporary victory could not dissipate the dark cloud that hung over the favela. Stopping the evictions permanently demanded bold and massive popular repudiation of the Companhia de São Paulo's scheme to grab a piece of Jacarézinho. In the middle of August, the *Centro de Melhoramentos de Jacarézinho* (Jacarézinho Improvement Center), the union of residents' associations, staged a self-proclaimed "monster rally" in the soccer field on Rua Viuva Claudio to demand the expropriation of the favela by the city. The residents called up their electoral debts accumulated over the years and brought out every public figure who owed Jacarézinho a vote: Deputy Breno da Silveira, City Council members Cotrim Netto, Venerando da Graça, Edgar de Carvalho, and Council President João Machado. Speaking for the favelados were Francisco Santos of the Improvement Center, Zulmira Rocha on behalf of women, and Antonio Simões for the children of Jacarézinho. President Vargas was not present at the rally, but all the speeches were directed at him; as one old lady reminded a reporter: "Young man, tell Dr. Getúlio we all voted for him."[78]

The "Father of the Poor" did not disappoint his children. City authorities arrived at a solution to the crisis inspired in part by a petition filed in 1948 by two lawyers, Viana and Benicio Fontenele, to "authorize the mayor to expropriate the land situated on Rua Viuva Claudio #362, or part of the same, where the conglomeration known as 'Favela de Jacarézinho' is installed. Once expropriated, the land should be turned over to the Fundação da Casa Popular, and sold to the current occupants at cost, to be paid off in twenty years. The Fundação will help each occupant finance the construction of a new home, up to the cost of 30,000 cruzeiros."[79] Using this proposal, Mayor João Vital, acting under instructions from Vargas, had the Federal District assume ownership of Jacarézinho, but forbade the construction of any new shanties.

What had the favelados really gained? In an editorial published in the newspaper *O Radical* in 1952, Venerando da Graça, one of the featured speakers at the previous year's rally, described what he saw the morning after the demonstration in Jacarézinho: "The mayor had left. Spigots functioned here and there inside and outside the favela, but water was not generally available. Sewage disposal never materialized. Public lighting was limited to sprucing up the lamp posts. Meanwhile, thousands of children continue to live as beggars, left to their own fate, playing with the future of Brazil."[80] For the sake of the children, the favelados had to take a more agressive political stance.

Organized political activity still flourished in Jacarézinho at the start of the 1960s, but to a large degree surreptitiously. The Partido Trabalhista (Labor Party), formed by Vargas to facilitate his return to power in 1950, remained active in the favela, as shown by the many references to Jacarézinho found in the pages of the party press, *A voz trabalhista* and *Diario trabalhista*. The propaganda work of the party in Jacarézinho indicates that the president kept a watchful eye on the favela, but there is no record of overt recruitment to the party. Instead, the Getulistas sought to infiltrate their cadres into the favela to serve as ward bosses for Vargas. Although the Labor party lost most of its membership after Getúlio's death in 1954, it continued to play a part in Jacarézinho politics for the next ten years.

The Brazilian Communists appear to have been busy in Jacarézinho, if the hysterical accounts published by Carlos Lacerda and other anticommunists are to be believed, but there is no firsthand record of any significant recruitment among the favelados. At this time the Communist party was still pushing for a united front with Vargas and his followers, and the housing question was not a top priority on the its agenda. Still, the Communist party, like the Labor party, provided valuable political training for the community leaders of Jacarézinho in organizing meetings and utilizing propaganda.

The larger established political parties also turned their eyes to Jacarézinho. The fight to save the favela had demonstrated the growing political clout of what was now the largest squatter camp in the city. A startling sign of new times was the visit of Carlos Lacerda, *bête noire* of the squatters, to Jacarézinho during his gubernatorial campaign in 1960. Lacerda's mouthpiece, the newspaper *Tribuna da imprensa*, recorded the moment for posterity: "Entering Jacarézinho by way of

Avenida dos Demócraticos, Lacerda delivered his first speech of the day standing on top of a chair. He began by speaking only to a few, but little by little people began to crowd around him. When he finished, he was surrounded by a small multitude, applauded and hugged. As he strode forward, everyone followed."[81] If one believed the press, Lacerda had undergone something akin to a religious conversion in his feelings toward the favela, but in fact the one-time general of the "Batalha do Rio de Janeiro" shrewdly calculated that he had more to gain politically by posing as a friend of the poor. Soon after his election as governor of Guanabara, Lacerda had his staff devise a plan to urbanize Jacarézinho. Eradication, he assured skeptical squatters, had been a folly of his youth.

Lacerda's plans for the complete urbanization of Jacarézinho never materialized, because the election of 1965 swept him and his allies from the gubernatorial palace. His successor, Francisco Negrão de Lima, was not willing to finance such an ambitious project. It was one thing to order the upgrading of Brás de Pina, which Negrão could use as a sign of the break from the policies of his predecessor, and quite another matter to bring city services to Jacarézinho under the watchful eyes of the military dictatorship. The election of Negrão de Lima as governor of Guanabara in 1965, with the support of the favelados, had convinced the military that the return to civilian rule in Brazil should be postponed and all popular opposition, actual or potential, must be crushed. Future elections were canceled, the press was muzzled, and military police began to patrol the favelas.

The imposition of dictatorial rule under Humberto Castelo Branco and his successors cowed many politicians into not speaking out on behalf of the favelas during the 1960s, but it did not dampen the political spirit of Jacarézinho. By 1965 the favela had already been substantially urbanized by the residents, so the dictatorship did not dare attempt to demolish it, as it did Praia do Pinto. More important, Jacarézinho possessed a higher degree of political cohesion than almost any other favela in the city. In 1966 a single political organization representing the entire population was formed—*the Associação Pro-Melhoramento do Jacarézinho* (Association for the Improvement of Jacarézinho). The association's charter pledged leaders to "solicit, among other things, the legalization of the favela of Jacarézinho, so that all 150,000 of its inhabitants can be the legal owners of their homes, and to make an appeal that there be only one Association in the favela."[82] Once it received the approval of the city government and the Fundação Leão XIII, the Associação Pro-Melhoramento transformed itself into the Provisional Commission of the Residents' Association of Jacarézinho on November 2, 1966, and set direct popular elections for this body for the end of 1967.[83]

The Residents' Association was the most important political and social group working inside the favela. Ostensibly, it was to act as the voice of the squatters before the state of Guanabara. The statutes of the association declared five goals:

I. To fight alongside competent state or federal authorities for assistance pertinent to the improvement of public services in the interests of our members. II. Grant members all assistance within our reach. III. Promote social activities such as recreation and sports. IV. Act as a link between legally constituted authorities and the local population, helping the former in the resolution of all problems pertinent to the community. V. Watch over and legally act for the maintenance of order, security, and tranquillity of families in the favela.[84]

In practice, the association became the city council of Jacarézinho. Residents of the favela petitioned the association on a host of grievances and requests. A typical letter read:

Rio de Janeiro 20 of April 1967. To the Residents' Association of Jacarézinho: I solicit permission to build a new roof for my shanty, already constructed, measuring 2 meters up front and more or less 4 in the back; total area 16 square meters, for said shanty is in an irregular state, situated on Rua Amaro Rangel No. 4. Awaiting your approval, and thankful for the attention you have granted me.[85]

The Residents' Association was not the only political agency at work in Jacarézinho. Other institutions with overt or covert political agendas were active in the late 1960s and three merit special attention. The importance of electricity to commercial establishments in Jacarézinho was alluded to earlier. Some businessmen had formed their own "light commissions" back in 1950 to attach the favela to the city electrical supply. In the 1960s these groups merged to form the "Light Commission of Jacarézinho" and signed a contract with the Rio de Janeiro Light Company to bring electricity directly to all parts of the favela. As an elected body, the Light Commission gained enormous authority, since it acted as a combination chamber of commerce and political lobby. The commission occasionally sent out "information bulletins" to its patrons that read very much like politicians' handbills. One read: "The Commission has illuminated all the streets of Jacarézinho, bringing tranquillity to residents and merchants. Let's demonstrate to city authorities that commerce in Jacarézinho is united behind progress and the welfare of this populous neighborhood."[86]

Religious organizations came to play an even larger role in Jacarézinho as the decade came to an end. The hold of the Catholic Church over the favela was challenged by Protestant evangelicals eager to win converts. In principle none of these groups was explicitly political. Clergymen from the Assembly of God, Baptist, Methodist, and other churches proclaimed that their ends were solely spiritual, and that they placed themselves squarely on the side of law and order. The Association of Evangelical Leaders of Jacarézinho announced to the city that its aims were "to congregate believers for the achievement of giant meetings of a purely Evangelical sense, and to cooperate with constituted authorities for the moral, social, and spiritual welfare of the community." Though the sects claimed they had no political mission in Jacarézinho, as their membership grew larger, no candidate for office in the Residents' Association could afford to ignore them.[87]

However disparate their membership and aims, all these institutions opened up space for political dialogue and protected the rights of citizenship of the favelados. Jacarézinho was better prepared politically to enter the *linha dura* (hard-line) period of military rule in Brazil after 1968, when the mere mention of the problem of the favelas was banned from the media. The urbanization of the favela at the hands of its inhabitants had created a fortress too difficult to destroy. For the city to do away with shanties built on stilts, as in Praia do Pinto, was one thing, but to destroy dwellings that in many respects now resembled middle-class homes proved politically impossible. Even more critical to the survival of Jacarézinho was the symbiotic relationship that developed between organizations inside the favela and different constituencies with the same end: the preservation of the homeland. The Light Commission lobbied the city on behalf of businessmen. Protestant sects, which claimed to be apolitical, challenged the authority of the Catholic Church and its paternalistic practices. The Residents' Association performed acts that by law belonged to the state, such as authorizing land deeds. The seeds for the social movements that would sweep the favelas in the 1970s had been sown.[88]

CONCLUSION

During the Estado Novo of Getúlio Vargas, government policy called for destruction of the favelas and the remolding of the moral character of the favelado. The proletarian parks project of the 1940s, which sought to abolish Praia do Pinto, was the first attempt to implement this philosophy. When it became evident that the favelas could not be eliminated by altering the comportment of their occupants, a new view of the favelado emerged that depicted him as the victim of forces beyond his control. The Cruzada São Sebastião of the 1950s was launched on the premise that the squatter lacked certain qualities that prevented his integration with the city. Social clubs, vocational schools, and the Residents' Association supervised by the Cruzada staff were created to fill in the missing pieces in his life. What they could not give him was what every other citizen of Rio de Janeiro expected—a secure job at adequate wages.

During the 1960s, when the favela population of Rio de Janeiro tripled, squatters took up the fight to preserve and renovate their homes. Resistance to removal transformed their image before the world. No longer could their passivity be taken for granted. As a result, the favelados started to be treated by many journalists, intellectuals, and politicians as decent citizens, with the same rights and prerogatives as other Cariocas. The urbanization of Brás de Pina, begun in 1967, was conducted by architects, engineers, and urban planners who shared a vision of the favela as a microcosm of the problems that plagued nearly all Brazilian cities. The completion of the project in 1975 represented the triumph of voluntary integration as the solution to the squatter problem. At the same time, Jacarézinho residents convinced the city their interests could best be served if they were left alone to upgrade the favela.

Political consciousness in each favela derived largely from local factors. The inhabitants of Praia do Pinto were perennially manipulated by both Church and state. Their weakness in the face of authority stemmed from Praia do Pinto's vulnerable position as an old and huge favela located in plush Zona Sul, where most jobs available fell into the category of domestic services. Without job security, inhabitants could not mount a defense of their homes, and the favela vanished in 1969, though not without outcry.

Brás de Pina contained one-quarter the population of Praia do Pinto in the 1960s, but the favela was closely connected to the surrounding neighborhood, where squatters worked, shopped, and made friends. Taking advantage of governor Carlos Lacerda's vulnerability on the charge of being callous toward the poor, they forged a strong alliance with churchmen, politicians, and the press to defy Lacerda and pressure the city to give them decent homes.

Jacarézinho had an industrial working class living within its borders. That class flexed its political muscles when the favela was threatened with extinction in the 1940s and 1950s. Residents rushed to the defense of their homes when faced with eviction, but later they did something even more remarkable by building a minicity, complete with local government, urban services, and even lobbying groups. Jacarézinho embodies the political union of worker and favelado, who often are in fact the same person.

Conclusion

Persona means "mask" in Latin, and over the years mystery fiction writers have had fun with stories in which characters blend with the masks they are assigned to wear, so that face and disguise become indistinguishable. Something similar has happened to the favelado over the past fifty years. The masks Brazilian society has placed on him have clung to his person, and only with the utmost difficulty has he been able to strip them away. What a variety of costumes the squatter has worn! Outlaw, sociopath, home wrecker, leech, bum, scavenger, and other labels of abuse were regularly assigned to him by the public. Intellectuals, churchmen and churchwomen, social workers, and politicians came up with the less offensive but equally misleading notion that the favelado was a victim of personal circumstances who should be allowed in decent society only when he had reformed himself.

Misperceptions about the favela remain prevalent to this day. Economist Martin Katzman has written: "Crowded jerrybuilt dwellings are the most permanent and photogenic characteristics of poverty. Slums generally horrify the middle class, both those who sympathize with the poor and those who fear the poor. Because of its visibility, poor housing has tended to define urban problems and policies throughout the world." Most observers, including urban experts, see only the surface of the favela, and assume that the demolition of squatter settlements is the first decisive step toward the eradication of urban poverty. Nothing could be more misleading. First, the housing "problem" is not a problem at all, but the solution the ruling strata of Brazil have found to the influx of migrants from the countryside. Second, for favelados themselves the problem is not lack of housing but the absence of steady jobs at decent wages. Taking the squatter out of his habitat fails to resolve the complex of high rents, unstable employment, low salaries, poor medical facilities, and inadequate education that made him turn to self-built housing in the first place.

There was nothing strange or inexplicable about the growth of shantytowns in Rio de Janeiro. Favelas represent the nightmare side of Brazilian economic growth in the twentieth century. They arose not out of the failure of modernization but out of its completion. In order to compete economically with the developed nations, the elites of Rio de Janeiro restructured the Carioca landscape by casting hundreds of thousands of men, women, and children into the hills, beaches, lakes, swamps, and back lots of the city.

Another reason why many observers failed to grasp the truth about squatter life is that they were looking at the wrong subject. Focusing on the lone individual makes the favela seem anarchic. It was the obsession with the idiosyncratic "type" of favelado that gave birth to the myth of marginality. The household is the proper unit for examining the shantytown. When family structure, economic activity, living standards, and political participation are subject to analysis at the household level, the favela emerges as a functioning community.

Favela residence *ipso facto* did not prescribe a peculiar kind of family life. All sorts of living arrangements could be found in the squatter settlement, depending on the economic circumstances of the parties involved. Analysis suggests that individuals trapped in poverty maintain the family values of the world around them, but also construct uncommon means to relate to one another, and that such unions may be as stable as those of the more privileged classes.

Patterns of family formation in the three favelas of this study did not differ greatly from the rest of Rio de Janeiro. The favela household was subject to the same process of nuclearization as those of the working and middle classes. The extended family was unusual in the squatter camps, and typically limited to one elderly relative living in the same shanty. Households headed by a male and usually counting three to five members were the most common. The average size of the household shrank as squatters became part of the urban labor force, and favelados tended to have fewer children the longer they lived in the city. Marriage between favelados was far more widespread than generally supposed, and few adults in the favela remained unattached for very long. Consensual unions, seen by outsiders to be a sign of social disorganization, served an economic purpose. For women, such unions represented a chance to gain a breadwinner for the home, while men felt they offered a more flexible family structure. Female-headed households were exceptional during this generation, and flourished only where women could attain a minimum level of financial independence.

The location, economic activity, and degree of poverty in each favela to a large part determined household composition. In Praia do Pinto, the most wretched of the three settlements, 40 percent of household heads remained unmarried and one-quarter were living in consensual unions in 1969. The service economy of Zona Sul offered more job opportunities for women, and females headed one-third of the households when the favela was demolished that year. Brás de Pina, comfortably situated on Avenida Brasil, was populated almost entirely by nuclear households similar in size and composition to those of the surrounding neighborhood. Nearly all households were headed by males married to their partners, and virtually every woman was attached to a male. The proletarian squatment of Jacarézinho, despite its huge size, housed as large a percentage of married persons as Brás de Pina. Consensual unions were rare, and few female-headed households existed in this working-class favela.

While most favelados were joined in families, the household did not serve as an important unit of production in the favela. The surge of squatter settlements in Rio de Janeiro after 1940 was the result of the elimination of traditional methods of agriculture in Brazil during the 1930s, which sent a human throng of rural laborers into the metropolises. But these migrants could not form the basis of a proletariat because industrialization in the Federal District created only a small industrial labor market. Many migrants to Rio de Janeiro and other cities came to sell their labor power but found no one who wanted to purchase it. Favelados constituted a subproletariat, that portion of the rural population that had lost access to the means of production but had not attained stable employment in the cities. Praia do Pinto provided the clearest example of this phenomenon. Prosperous Zona Sul provided only temporary employment to men in construction, bartending, and cooking, while their mates took jobs as maids in the middle-class apartments of Ipanema, Leblon, and Copacabana.

The informal labor sector employed relatively few favelados on a full-time basis. Gainful employment in the biscate depended on the geographical location of the favela, the purchasing power of customers in the neighborhood, and the acquiescence of the city. Praia do Pinto was unfortunate in that its neighbors were too wealthy to demand goods from the informal sector, and the city was hostile to the survival of the favela. Squatters in Jacarézinho made their money largely from wage labor in industry. Only Brás de Pina contained a significant segment of male street vendors who sold their goods alongside Avenida Brasil, while women engaged in home production—cooking, sewing, craft work—to supplement the family income. But the availability of the biscate had harmful consequences for the favela. Income from informal labor in Brás de Pina produced deep class divisions and a petit bourgeois political consciousness that blocked unity with other favelados after the favela was urbanized.

The favelado workforce did not remain static but, ironically, became more proletarian as the city economy deindustrialized. At the end of the 1960s the squatments housed large numbers of workers formally linked to the job market by contracts and wages. One of the paradoxes of urbanization in Rio de Janeiro is that high rents in the core of the city center forced both the rich and the poor to seek cheaper land on the outskirts. The factory and the favela were not rivals but siblings. Where one went, the other followed. Industrialists came to appreciate the advantage of having a large source of inexpensive labor located next to their establishments, and factory owners and favelados formed an unstable but mutually beneficial political union to defend the shanties from destruction. Though both Praia do Pinto and Brás de Pina contained a significant share of full-time wage laborers by the end of the 1960s, Jacarézinho was the model for the proletarianization of the favelados. Ever since the 1930s, industrial workers constituted the majority of the economically active population of Jacarézinho, employed mainly in the factories located on the borders of the favela. The two communities, employers and employees, developed a close relationship that allowed them to thrive.

The favelados could boast, to paraphrase what Augustus Caesar said about Rome, that they had started with habitations made out of cardboard and left them brick. In the 1940s many squatters lived like foragers, utilizing whatever material was discarded by their neighbors to erect shanties, and their homes had not much more security than those of a forest creature. But it was all they had. The favelados invested in the future and made a commitment to improve the lives of their children. By the end of the 1960s even the poorest favelas, such as Praia do Pinto, featured houses made from tile and marble, while Brás de Pina and Jacarézinho boasted homes with radios, television sets, and other middle-class comforts. The climb from subproletarian to proletarian and even bourgeois accommodations was also a political investment that made it harder for the city to demolish the favelas.

Favelados were experienced political players who understood the nuances of local and national politics. Praia do Pinto proved incapable of saving itself, but Brás de Pina and Jacarézinho residents joined with members of the clergy and politicians sympathetic to their cause to fight off eviction. But squatters made no long-term political commitments. Quick to spot an enemy (Carlos Lacerda, Sandra Cavalcanti) and thank a friend (Getúlio Vargas, Francisco Negrão de Lima) with their votes, the favelados had little patience with refined political ideology. The president of the Residents' Association who collaborated with the Communists one day would sit down with the mayor in city hall the next morning if it would benefit his favela.[2]

Squatters possessed a sharp political eye, but their horizon was limited to their immediate surroundings. Contrary to the assertions of many on the left, the urban poor in Brazil at the end of this generation were not potential recruits for a new Fidel Castro. The political life of Praia do Pinto, Brás de Pina, and Jacarézinho did not evince radicalism. When a political figure arose inside the favela who questioned the socioeconomic origins of poverty, such as Padre José Artola in Brás de Pina, he was condemned by his superiors and ignored by the bulk of the population. Indirectly, though, the favelados did represent a challenge to the existing order. The residents' associations formed in the 1950s and 1960s resisted the military dictatorship installed in 1964 and paved the way for the social movements of the 1970s.

The experience of one generation of favelados in Rio de Janeiro from the 1940s to the 1960s documents the process of the production and reproduction of the poor in an underdeveloped society. The favela household was beset by disease, illiteracy, and crime, and some in positions of power questioned the very existence of the family unit among the urban poor. The favela workforce was untrained, poorly paid, and often unemployed and underemployed. The shantytown lacked adequate water and sewage facilities, schools, hospitals, and even legal recognition. The favelados constantly faced threats of eviction, endured repression at the hands of the police and army, and withstood mistreatment by both enemies and do-gooders.

But the process of reproduction bred resistance. Favela men and women found mates for long-term relationships to protect themselves against the ravages of poverty. The squatter was willing to do whatever job the city handed him or her, from digging ditches to washing dishes. Brás de Pina and Jacarézinho, along with many other favelas, were transformed from squalid shantytowns to modern communities. Every politician of importance in the city, from Communist to fascist, was forced to come to the favelas and earn the vote of the most humble citizens of the Cidade Maravilhosa. The political and economic regime of Rio de Janeiro persists in reproducing the favela, but the relationship of forces between city and squatter is more favorable to the favelado today. For this the current residents of the squatments must thank the men, women, and children of the boom generation of the 1940s.

The favela has been transformed, but it will not vanish in the foreseeable future. Abolition of the squatter settlements is a chimera unless substantial changes are made in Brazilian society. The signs are not hopeful. According to a report by the Instituto Brasileiro de Geografia e Estatística published in 1990, thirty-one million children in Brazil live in poverty, seventeen million live in misery, and eight million are abandoned on the streets. Seven million young people between ages ten and seventeen are economically active, and of these 58 percent earn less than 25 dollars a month. Twelve percent of those who work are responsible for 30 percent or more of their family's income, and only 33 percent are covered by a legal labor contract.[3] These youngsters will be the inheritors of the favela in the twenty-first century. The shantytown will survive until the Old Testament prophecy of Isaiah comes true:

There shall be no more thence an infant that lives but a few days nor an old man that hath not filled out his days. They shall not build and another inhabit. They shall not plant and another eat. They shall not labor in vain, nor bring forth trouble, and it shall come to pass that before they call, I shall answer. While they are speaking, I will hear. (Isaiah, 65:22-24)

This is the lesson the inhabitants of Praia do Pinto, Brás de Pina, and Jacarézinho teach us.

Notes

ABBREVIATIONS

EL Papers	Elizabeth Leeds, Cambridge, Massachusetts
GB Papers	Gilda Blank Papers, Rio de Janeiro
OB Papers	Olga Bronstein Papers, Rio de Janerio
CCD	Centro Carmela Dutra, Jacarézinho, Rio de Janeiro
MF Papers	Moura Family Papers, Rio de Janeiro
PN Papers	Padre Nelson Papers, Jacarézinho, Rio de Janeiro
JAR Papers	José Artur Rios Papers, Rio de Janeiro

INTRODUCTION

1. Pastore et al., *Mudança social e pobreza*, ix.

2. See Medina, *Família e mudança*, for a critical bibliography.

3. See Ianni, *Industrialização e desenvolvimento no Brasil*; López, *Sociedade industrial no Brasil*.

4. See Lefevbre, *The Survival of Capitalism;* Bourdieu and Passernon, *Reproduction in Education, Society, and Culture*; Dickinson and Russel, eds., *Family, Economy,and the State*.

5. Karl Marx, *Capital*, Vol. 1, 723.

6. See Folbre, "Exploitation Comes Home."

7. "Crece población de favelas de Rio de Janeiro," *Diario las Américas* (Miami), May 22, 1994.

8. Perlman, *The Myth of Marginality*.

9. For the theory of marginality see Lewis, *The Children of Sanchez;* and *La Vida*; Kowarick, *Capitalismo e marginalidade na América Latina*; Germani, *Política y sociedad en la época de las masas*.

10. For the methodological problems involved in classifying the urban poor in Latin America, see Musgrove and Ferber, " Identifying the Urban Poor," 25-53.

11. Kriegel, "Generational Difference."
12. Ravelo, "Blessed are the (Un)meek for they Shall Inherit the Earth."

CHAPTER 1: THE FAMILY

1. Cancian, Goodman, and Smith, "Capitalism, Industrialization and Kinship in Latin America," 323.
2. Meillassoux, *Maidens, Meal, and Money*, xiii.
3. Engels, *Origins of the Family*. For an opposing view see Mount, *The Subversive Family*.
4. See Prado, "Conceito de família e domicilio," 7–8.
5. Schmink, "Household Economic Strategies," 88.
6. Jelin, "Formas de organização." See also Portes, "Latin American Class Structures."
7. Schmink, "Women and Urban Development in Brazil," 143–44.
8. Arguello, "Estratégias de supervivência," 192.
9. Fausto Neto, *Família operária*, 143.
10. Kuznets, "Economic Growth," 1 ff.
11. Macedo, *A reprodução da desigualdade*, 144.
12. Rainho, *Os peões do ABC*, 18.
13. Firestone, *The Dialectic of Sex*, ch. 4.
14. Stone, "The Rise of the Nuclear Family in Early Modern England."
15. Blachman, "Selective Omission," 251.
16. Vianna, *Instituições políticas brasileiras*, vol. 1, 237–74.
17. Azevedo, "Family, Marriage and Divorce in Brazil"; Willems, "The Structure of the Brazilian Family."
18. Freyre, *Casa grande e senzala*, 22, 64–66.
19. For a critique of Freyre, see Mendes de Almeida, ed., *Pensando a família no Brasil*.
20. Schwartz, *Sugar Plantations*, 303–8, 313–17, 379–412.
21. Prado Junior, *The Colonial Heritage of Brazil*, 328–33, 409–10.
22. Kuznesof, *Household Economy*, 54–71.
23. Russell–Wood, *The Black Man*, 172–97.
24. Ramos, "Single and Married Women," 263–65.
25. See Conrad, *Children of God's Fire*, 178–80.
26. See Freyre, *Sobrados e mucambos*.
27. Stolcke, "A família não é sagrada."
28. See Fernandes, *The Negro in Brazilian Society*.
29. Andrews, *Blacks and Whites in São Paulo*, 76–77.
30. Bibliographical references for a study of the family and underdevelopment in twentieth century Brazil are scarce. Two excellent sources, both difficult to obtain, are Alcantara, "Estudos e pesquisas sobre família no Brasil"; and Medina, "Família e desenvolvimento."
31. Rosen and Berlinck, "Modernization and Family Structure."
32. See Iutaka and Bock, "Urbanização e família extensa."
33. López, *Desenvolvimento e mudança*, vol. 1, esp. 127–40; Medina, "Família e desenvolvimento."
34. Nogueira, "A organização da família."
35. Shirley, *The End of a Tradition*, 38–40, 142–46.
36. Correa, "Repensando a família patriarcal brasileira," 34.

37. Laslett, *Household and Family*; Zaretsky, *Capitalism, the Family and Personal Life*; Anderson, *Family Structure in Nineteenth Century Lancashire*; Goode, *World Revolution and Family Patterns*.

38. Macedo, *A reprodução*, 145.

CHAPTER 2: THE CITY

1. See Baran, "The Political Economy of Growth"; Kuznets, "Underdeveloped Countries"; Bendix, "What is Modernization?"; Lacoste, *Geografia do subdesenvolvimento*; Löwy, *The Politics of Combined and Uneven Development*; Gershenkron, "Economic Backwardness"; Sahlins and Service, *Evolution and Culture*.

2. Industrialization in the Third World is covered in Evans, *Dependent Development*; Amin, *Unequal Development*; Sutcliffe, "Imperialism and Industrialization"; Gunder Franke, "The Development of Underdevelopment"; Kowarick and Campanaro, "São Paulo"; Cardoso and Falleto, *Dependency and Development*.

3. See Pereira, *Desenvolvimento e crise*; Brum, *O desenvolvimento brasileiro*; Fishlow, "Origins and Consequences of Import Substitution"; Oliveira and Sá, Jr., *Questionando a economia brasileira*; Francisco de Oliveira, *A economia da dependência*; Versiani and Mendonça, *Formação económica*.

4. Arque, "O Rio de Janeiro."

5. Bernardes, "Importância da posição."

6. Estado da Guanabara, *Rio de Janeiro em seus quatrocentos anos*, 75ff; Maria Beatriz Silva, *Cultura e sociedade*, 41–48.

7. See Stein, *Vassouras, passim*.

8. Renault, *Rio de Janeiro*, 18–56; and *O dia–a–dia no Rio de Janeiro*, 83ff.

9. Topik, *Political Economy of the Brazilian State*, 131; Hahner, *Poverty and Politics*, 200.

10. Geiger, *Evolução*, 15.

11. See Dean, *Industrialization of São Paulo*.

12. Coniff, *Urban Politics in Brazil*, 94.

13. Lobo, *História do Rio de Janeiro*, 2: 858.

14. Ibid., 859.

15. Sylvio Abreu, *O Distrito Federal*, 154.

16. Cunha, *O novo Rio de Janeiro*, 36.

17. Geiger, *Evolução* , 156.

18. Brasil, Conselho Nacional de Geografia, *Área central*, 93–96.

19. Rocha, "Indústrias."

20. Mauricio Abreu, *Evolução urbana* , 115.

21. Cunha, *O novo Rio de Janeiro*, 35.

22. Lobo, *História do Rio de Janeiro*, 2: 863–64.

23. Azevedo, "O comércio carioca," 130–31.

24. Geiger, *Evolução da rede*, 160–61.

25. Cunha, *O novo Rio de Janeiro*, 38.

26. Azevedo, "O comércio carioca," 128.

27. Pedroso and Porto, *Rio de Janeiro*, 39–40, 44. See also Camargo, *O êxodo rural*, 85–86.

28. This survey of the workforce in Rio de Janeiro from 1940 to 1960 is based on Costa, *População economicamente ativa*, esp. 26, 29, 32–35, 37, 39, 41, 47, 48, 56.

29. See Oliveira, "A economia brasileira"; Santos, *A pobreza urbana*, 50–51; Nun,

"Superpoblación"; the reply to Nun by Cardoso, "Comentários sobre os conceitos da superpopulação"; Kowarick, *Capitalismo e marginalidade*, 147–74.
30. Lobo, *História do Rio de Janeiro*, 2: 871; Romero, *O salário mínimo*, 59–60.
31. Saboia, *Salário mínimo*, 44.
32. Oliveira and Sá Jr., *Questionando a economia brasileira* , 41.
33. Castro, *O problema da alimentação*, 216–217
34. Mortara, *Tábuas brasileiras*, 64–73.
35. Smith, *Brazil: People and Institutions*, 199.
36. Schurz, *Brazil: The Infinite Country*, 230.
37. Abreu, *Evolução urbana*, 124. For census purposes the city of Rio de Janeiro was demarcated this way in 1960: nucleus: Centro + Área Periférica, Central [The neighborhoods of Gamboa and Rio Comprido] + São Cristovão, Santa Teresa, Zona Sul, Zona Norte; immediate periphery: Zona Suburbana, Ilhas and Jacarépagua, Niterói. Intermediate periphery: Zona Suburbana II, Zona Rural, Duque de Caxias, Nilópolis, Nova Iguaçu, São João de Meriti, São Gonçalo.
38. Brasil, *Estudo sobre a alfabetização*, 147–49.
39. Brasil, *Sinopse regional do ensino*, 101, Table 1.

CHAPTER 3: THE SHANTY

1. Cortes, *Favelas* , 5.
2. Abrams, *Squatter Settlements*, 1–3.
3. Rios, "As favelas"; Bonilla, "Rio's Favelas."
4. Fundação Leão XIII, *Favelas: Um compromisso*.
5. Leeds and Leeds, *A sociologia do Brasil urbano;* Mangin, "Latin American Squatter Settlements"; Parisse, "Las favelas"; "Favelas do Rio de Janeiro"; "Favelas de l'agglomeration de Rio de Janeiro."
6. Perlman, *Myth of Marginality*. Perlman's book is usually assumed to be the first revisionist study of the favela, but in fact it was neither the first nor the most original. See Barcellos, *As favelas;* Casaco, "The Social Functions of the Slum"; Leeds, "The Significant Variables"; Leeds and Leeds, "Brazil and the Myth of Urban Rurality "; Medina, "A favela como estrutura atomística"; Salman, "Housing Alternatives for the Carioca Poor"; Silberstein, "Favela Living".
7. IBGE, *VII recenseamento geral do Brasil*, v.
8. Needell, "Making the Carioca *Belle Epoque* Concrete."
9. Guimarães, "As favelas do Distrito Federal," 250.
10. Estado da Guanabara, *Rio de Janeiro em seus quatrocentos anos*, 145.
11. Lobo et al., *Questão habitacional, passim*; Hahner, *Poverty and Politics*, 166–68.
12. Goulart, *Favelas do Distrito Federal* , 21–22.
13. Henrique Dodsworth, "As favelas," Moura Family Papers. Mimeo. (Rio de Janeiro), October 17, 1945.
14. Brasil, Comissão Nacional de Bem–Estar Social, *Favelas e habitação popular*, Tables 3, 4; Robert, "As favelas do Rio de Janeiro."
15. See Centro de Coordenação Industrial para o Plano Habitacional, "A interpenetração das áreas faveladas e áreas industriais."
16. Distrito Federal, Prefeitura, *Censo das favelas*, 14, 15.
17. Ibid.,7.
18. *Censo demográfico de 1o–VII–1950*, "População presente, segundo o sexo, por favelas," in Goulart, *Favelas*, 72.

19. Guanabara, Comissão Executiva para o Desenvolvimento Urbano, *Guanabara*, 136–41

20. Bezerra, *Alagados, mocambos e mocambeiros*; Estado de Minas Gerais, Secretaria do Trabalho e Cultura Popular, *Levantamento da população favelada de Belo Horizonte;* Sachs, "Croissance urbaine et favelisation des metropoles."

21. Cox, *Os párias*, 47–48.

22. Portugal, "Favelas: Problema administrativo."

23. Distrito Federal, Prefeitura, *Censo das favelas*, 9.

24. IBGE, *VII recenseamento geral do Brasil*, 40, Table 24.

25. Distrito Federal, Prefeitura, *Censo das favelas*, 27, Table 6; *Censo de 1o-VII-1950*, in Goulart, *Favelas*, 59, Table III; IBGE *VII recenseamento geral do Brasil*, 3, Table 2.

26. Distrito Federal, Prefeitura, *Censo das favelas*, 17; *Censo de 1o–VII–1950*, in Goulart, *Favelas*, 60, Table IV.

27. Siqueira, "O centro Nossa Senhora das Graças," 39.

28. Pinto, *O negro no Rio de Janeiro*, 130–33.

29. Lopes, "Duas favelas."

30. Louzeiro, *Assim marcha a família*, 11.

31. IBGE, *VII recenseamento geral do Brasil*, 9, Table 9.

32. Consorte, "A criança favelada."

33. See Medina and Valladares, *Favela e religião*.

34. Bombart, "Les Cultes protestants dans une favela."

35. Instituto de Pesquisas e Estudos de Mercado, *A vida mental dos favelados*, 15–19.

36. Coniff, *Urban Politics*, ch.7; See also Medina, *A favela e o demagôgo*.

37. IBGE, *VII recenseamento geral do Brasil*, 83, Table 1.

38. Ibid., 84, Table 2.

39. União Pro–Melhoramentos dos Moradores da Rocinha, *Varal de lembranças*, 98.

40. Estado da Guanabara, *O problema sanitário das favelas*, 5.

41. de Jesús, *Child of the Dark*.

42. Machado, "O significado do botequim."

CHAPTER 4: ONE GENERATION

1. Schlesinger, *Cycles of American History*, 29–31.

2. Parisse, "Favelas de l' agglomeration de Rio de Janeiro," 108, 125; "Favela oficial é ruim como a original," *Jornal do Brasil*, May 19, 1968; "Favelados deixam felizes a Praia do Pinto que ajudaram construir," *Jornal do Brasil*, July 23, 1968. I shall use "Praia do Pinto" when speaking of all three units, and "the subunit of Praia do Pinto" to refer to the settlement known by that name in the 1940s and 1950s.

3. "Favelas," *Correio da manhã*, July, [n.d]. 1965; Maria Hortencia Silva, *Impressões de uma assistante*, 19–22.

4. Kliman, "Acabar com as favelas"; Violich, *Cities of Latin America*, 76–77; Vitor Tavares de Moura, untitled note, 1945, MF.

5. "Cordovil recebe as primeiras familias da Praia do Pinto," *Jornal do Brasil*, March 28, 1969; "Praia do Pinto acaba e deixa Ipanema que ajudou construir," *Jornal do Brasil*, May 11, 1969.

6. "Urbanization" in this context means raising a shantytown to the status of an urban community by building an infrastructure and giving the residents access to city services. For the urbanization of Brás de Pina, see Carlos Santos, *Tres movimentos sociais urbanos no Rio de Janeiro*, 55–57; on CODESCO see Leeds, "Political Considerations and Social Effects";

"Um plano de habitação popular—julho 1970," OB.

7. Governo do Estado do Rio de Janeiro, *Relatorio de atividades do projeto de eco–desenvolvimento*, 2.10–2.17.

8. Sociedade de Análises Gráficas e Mecanográficas Aplicadas aos Complexos Sociais, "Aspectos humanos da favela Carioca," parte geral, 17.

9. Pereira, "O serviço social e a urbanização da favela de Jacarézinho," 7–8.

CHAPTER 5: ORGANIZATION

1. Centro de Planejamento Social, Pontífica Universidade Católica, "Família e menor internado no estado da Guanabara." Cited in Corwin, "Afro-Brazilians: Myths and Realities," 411.

2. One exception is Souto de Oliveira, "A reposição do suor."

3. Maria Hortencia Silva, *Impressões de uma assistente* , 43–44, 50–56.

4. Moura, "Favelas do Distrito Federal"; Cidade Maravilhosa': Onde a vida tem duas faces," *Revista do globo* (November 1944).

5. Adelaide Silva, "Estudo sobre um inquerito social realizado no Parque Proletário Provisório No. 1," 6, 3, 34.

6. Ibid., 9ff., 30.

7. Bogado, "Parque Proletário Provisório No. 1," 24.

8. Ibid., 15–17.

9. Ibid., 17–19.

10. Silva, "Estudo," 49–54.

11. Comissão Executiva de Projetos Específicos, "Dados estatísticos referentes à favela Praia do Pinto."

12. Secretaria de Serviços Sociais, Governo do Estado da Guanabara, "Praia do Pinto," 86, 88–90.

13. Ibid., 79, 82.

14. Interview, Brás de Pina, March 26, 1990.

15. *Censo de 1o–VII–1950*, in Goulart, *Favelas do Distrito Federal*, 72; IBGE, *VII recenseamento geral do Brasil*, 34.

16. Carlos Santos, "Tres movimentos sociais," 34

17. Pontífica Universidade Católica, "Tres favelas cariocas," 47–48.

18. Ibid., 132–33.

19. Carlos Santos, "Some Considerations," 32.

20. "Existem no Rio de Janeiro 119 favelas," *O Globo*, May 21, 1948.

21. Fundação Leão XII, *Morros e favelas*, 14.

22. *Censo de 1o–VII–1950*, in Goulart, *Favelas do Distrito Federal*, 72.

23. IBGE, *recenseamento geral do Brasil*, 78.

24. "Jacarézinho—Quarterly Report," EL.

25. Centro Médico Sanitário da XII R.A. Meiér, "Fichas de cadastro domiciliar," EL.

26. "Ante–projeto de urbanização da favela do Jacarézinho: Memória descritiva,1962," EL.

27. Sociedade de Análises Gráficas e Mecánogáficas Aplicadas aos Complexos Sociais, "Aspectos humanos da favela Carioca," parte geral, 17.

28. Ibid., 10.

29. Pearse, "Integração social das famílias," 249. See also Pearse, "Notas sobre a organização social."

30. "Radiografia da Favela," *Síntese social*, (Jan.–Mar. 1964): 66.

31. Perlman, *The Myth of Marginality*, 146.
32. Estado de Minas Gerais, Secretaria do Trabalho e Cultura Popular, *Levantamento da população favelada de Belo Horizonte*, 16–17.
33. Bezerra, *Alagados, mocambos e mocambeiros*, 83.
34. Safa, *The Urban Poor in Puerto Rico*, 36–41.
35. Safa, "The New Women Workers."
36. Lomnitz, *Networks and Marginality*, ch. 5
37. Lloyd, *Slums of Hope?*, 131.
38. Roberts, *Organizing Strangers*, 114ff.

CHAPTER 6: PRODUCTION

1. Moura, "Reunião de 8 de janeiro, 1957, Rotary Club, Rio de Janeiro," MF.
2. Moura, "Apuração do censo realisado na favela Largo da Memória," MF.
3. Maria Hortencia Silva, *Impressões de uma assistente*, 29.
4. Ibid., 28.
5. Moura, "Para o Senhor Secretário Geral," MF.
6. Moura, "Apuração do censo realisado na favela Praia do Pinto," MF.
7. Moura, "Apuração do censo realisado na favela Cidade Maravilhosa," MF.
8. Moura, "Apuração do censo realisado na favela Largo da Memória," MF.
9. *Observador economico e financeiro*, "O censo retrata as favelas," (1951): 73–74.
10. Adelaide Silva, "Estudo sobre um inquerito social," 26.
11. Bogado, "Parque Proletário Provisório No. 1," 26.
12. "Favelas da Lagoa são as piores que temos," *Correio da Manhã*, May 21, 1964.
13. Secretaria de Serviços Sociais, Governo do Estado da Guanabara, "Praia do Pinto," 34–35, 38–40.
14. Ibid., 63–64, 71.
15. Ibid., 118–121.
16. Ibid., 73.
17. "Ilusões se perdem nas favelas de muitos planos sem aplicação," *Correio da Manhã*, March 17, 1967.
18. Interview, Brás de Pina, March 26 and April 25, 1990.
19. Interview, Brás de Pina, April 25, 1990.
20. Companhia de Habitação Popular do Estado da Guanabara, "A COHAB através de números e imagens."
21. "Brás de Pina—Dados da pesquisa feita em 1967," GB.
22. Carlos Santos, "Some Considerations," 32.
23. Pontífica Universidade Católica, "Tres favelas cariocas," 129.
24. Blank, "Experiencia de urbanização," 148–49.
25. Pontifica Universidade Católica, "Tres favelas cariocas," 138.
26. Ibid., 69.
27. Carlos Santos, "Some Considerations," 31.
28. "Avaliação do plano da urbanização de Brás de Pina," OB.
29. Souto de Oliveira, "Favelas do Rio de Janeiro," 151–52.
30. "Existem 119 favelas no Rio de Janeiro," *O Globo*, May 21, 1948.
31. Fundação Leão XIII, *Morros e favelas*, 15.
32. Pereira, "O serviço social e a urbanização da favela de Jacarézinho," 18.
33. José Artur Rios, "Coordenação dos serviços sociais, projeto de financiamento do programa de recuperação de favelas e habitações anti-higiênicas, 1961." Table III.

34. Pereira, "O serviço social," 12–13.

35. Ibid., 17

36. Souto de Oliveira, "Favelas do Rio de Janeiro," 154–55.

CHAPTER 7: CONSUMPTION

1. Maria Hortencia Silva, *Impressões de uma assistente*, 19.

2. Moura, "Apuração do censo realisado na favela Largo da Memória," MF.

3. Moura, "Apuração do censo realisado na favela Praia do Pinto," MF.

4. Moura, "Apuração do censo realisado na favela Cidade Maravilhosa," MF.

5. Nascimento and Alvim, "Luta contra tuberculose na favela," See also "Transformadas as favelas nos maiores e mais perigosos focos de tuberculose," *O Globo*, May 22, 1948; Moura, "Palestra–Universidade Católica," MF.

6. Moura, untitled note, 1945, MF.

7. Moura, "Demonstrativo," MF.

8. Ney Oliveira, "Parque Proletário da Gávea," 60.

9. Moura, "Parques Proletários," MF.

10. Moura, "Plano para a organização de uma escola–oficina," MF.

11. Moura, "Escola Profisional Col. Jonas Correa," MF.

12. Moura, "Esboço de organização de uma escola de trabalho para menores," MF.

13. Moura, "Palestra–Universidade Católica," MF.

14. Ibid.

15. Adelaide Silva, "Estudo sobre um inquerito social," 9–12.

16. Ibid., 18–19.

17. Ibid.

18. Bogado, "Parque Proletário Provisório No. 1," 25a.

19. Pacheco, "Uma experiência de desenvolvimento e organização," 23.

20. Ibid., 32.

21. Dr. Eitel de Oliveira Luma, quoted in Pacheco, "Uma experiência de desenvolvimento e organização," 5.

22. "Não seriamos cristãos se desprezassemos as favelas do D. Federal," *O Globo*, July 9, 1957. "Uma cruzada e um paladino," *Visão* , December 21, 1957.

23. Coutinho, *Um ensaio de aplicação*, 23.

24. Congresso Brasileiro de Serviço Social, 3, "Cruzada São Sebastião," 2.

25. Coutinho, *Um ensaio de aplicação*, 33.

26. Guarnieri, "Uma experiência de promoção social," 2–4.

27. "Uma cruzada e um paladino," *Visão*, December 21, 1957, 21.

28. Congresso Brasileiro de Serviço Social, 3, "Cruzada São Sebastião," 6–9.

29. Guarnieri, "Uma experiência de promoção social," 52–54.

30. Congresso Brasileiro de Serviço Social, 3, "Cruzada São Sebastião," 13–14.

31. See the editorial "O que se tem feito pelo favelado?" *O Metropolitano*, January 25, 1959.

32. Secretaria de Serviços Sociais, Governo do Estado da Guanabara, "Praia do Pinto," 92, 94–104.

33. Ibid., 37, 116, 112–15.

34. Ação Comunitaria do Brasil, "Guanabara—Catálogo de obras."

35. Interview with former residents of Praia do Pinto at Cordovil, May 17, 1990.

36. See "Dois reporteres voltam da selva de Copacabana," *Ultima Hora*, March 24, 1961.

37. See Blank, "Brás de Pina.

38. Interview , Brás de Pina, March 26, 1990.

39. Gilda Blank, "Brás de Pina: Dados da pesquisa de 1967," GB.

40. Ibid.

41. Ibid.

42. Henrique Cruz, *Os suburbios cariocas,* 20–21.

43. "Levantamento médico-sanitário do Hospital de Clínicas Pedro Ernesto da FEM/UEG—favelas Mata Machado, [Morro] União e Brás de Pina," OB.

44. Ação Comunitaria do Brasil, "Guanabara,—Catálogo de obras."

45. Blank, "Experiência em urbanização de favela carioca—Brás de Pina," 160–65.

46. "Projeto Brás de Pina, nove anos depois," *Jornal do Brasil,* May 27, 1977.

47. Carlos Lacerda, "Batalha do Rio de Janeiro—crônicas," *Correio da Manhã,* 19–30 May 19–20, 1948.

48. Carlos Lacerda, "Jacarézinho," *Correio da Manhã,* May 23, 1948.

49. Fundação Leão XIII, *Morros e favelas,* 14–15.

50. Sample of land transfers in Jacarézinho 1945–64:

A. "Received from Sra. S. the quantity of Cr$2,150.00 from my sale of a shack situated on Rua Claudia, no. 362–back. Sold for the price of Cr$2,500, with Cr$350 to be paid within two months."
Rio de Janeiro
October 4, 1945

B. "Declaration. I, DAS, resident of the Morro do Jacarézinho, declare that I sold to JIS a shack for the value of Cr$8,800."
Rio de Janeiro
May 28, 1946

C. "I declare that I sold, in the Morro do Jacarézinho, on the Travessa Sra. do Bom Fim, a house with improvements, to JFC, for the price of Cr$850."
Rio de Janeiro
(Illegible) 1952

D. "I received from JCC the sum of Cr$10,000 for a house with four rooms and a veranda, from my own property, which I sold to him on the Morro de Jacarézinho."
Rio de Janeiro
February 7, 1954

E. "I received from SJS the sum of Cr$19,000 from the sale of a house, with improvements, on Rua Gloria, in Jacarézinho. A house with 4 rooms and covered with French tiles."
Rio de Janeiro
April 3, 1956

F. "I received from D. RV a shack, situated in Morro de Jacarézinho on Rua Gloria, for the sum of Cr$11,000."
Rio de Janeiro
July 7, 1956

G. "I declare that the shack on Travessa Esperança no. 8, house 8, owned by AH and NAR, is transferred for the sum of Cr$10,000 to SMP and Dona MBP."
Federal District
February 8, 1957

H. "I received from MB the sum of Cr$70,000 corresponding to the sale of a house on Rua Esperança in Jacarézinho, state of Guanabara. This sale is without coercion and free of all onus, signed by me, stamped and witnessed."

Guanabara
December 30, 1960.

I. "I declare that I received from SFS the sum of Cr$70,000 for the sale of a house on Rua Beco da Glória, in Jacarézinho, with five rooms and covered by French tiles, with access to the backyard."

Guanabara
September 30, 1961

J. "I declare that I sold a house to JGS, situated on Rua João Pinto no. 4, for the value of Cr$700,000; this house is on the first floor."

Rio de Janeiro
January 21, 1964

Source: Archive of the Associação de Moradores-Jacarézinho, Rio de Janeiro.

51. Brasil, IBGE, *VII Recenseamento Geral do Brasil—censo demográfico de 1960,* 89, Table 5.

52. Ibid., 56, Table 25.

53. Cruz, *Os suburbios cariocas,* 19–23.

54. Padre Nelson Carlos del Monaco, "Obras profissionais e sociais Sta. Rita Cássia," PN.

55. The *mutirão* proceeded as follows:

July 11–14, 1967

"We went from house to house, explaining the motive behind our visit, and asked for their contribution of NCr$2 to purchase material. Thirty–five residents signed the list to provide aid. We also explained to them the necessity of the family heads being present at a subsequent meeting to put together a labor detail."

July 15, 1967

"The number of residents present at the meeting fell below our expectations, which will set back our work. There was much discussion and many suggestions from those present. The sum of money collected up to this moment is NCr$35. The treasurer noted that many residents felt it was enough to contribute money [and saw no need to donate their time]."

July 17, 1967

"The foreman hired by the Fundação Leão XIII addressed the meeting, and explained that the project would require thirty-five pipes, one [cubic] meter of stone no. 2, one [cubic] meter of clean sand, fifteen hundred massive bricks, two [cubic] meters of very black dirt, ten iron bars (3/16), ten bags of cement."

July 18–26, 1967

"We sent the foreman to investigate the costs of the material for the project, and learned that the money collected would suffice to purchase only half the necessary items, corresponding to fifty meters of the street. We decided, therefore, that it would be more convenient to begin work on that part of the street most in need of repair, just those fifty meters; therefore we reduced our supply request by half.

"Note: The material has already been purchased and is stored in the residence of a homeowner living on that part of the street."

August 13, 1967

"Work began as scheduled, and the pipes were transported from Largo do Cruzeiro to Rua Getúlio Vargas. We brought the truck, and four men to help us in the transportation, as well as some residents from Rua Vargas. The work got started by opening up the old pipes (one meter in depth) at the beginning of the street for inspection. We cleaned the pipes and an old sewage disposal unit, removed the debris from within, and installed a new cover.

"To our delight, ten more residents came by and worked with great spirit, oriented by our foreman, who . . . demonstrated perfect adaptation to them and showed a specific understanding of his function."

August 20, 1967

"The work has proceeded in a harmonious climate between the residents, not withstanding their reduced number."

September 10, 1967

"Seven more pipes were installed today."

September 17, 1967

"Five more pipes were installed today." *Source:* CCD

56. For an update on the urbanization of Jacarézinho since the 1960s see Governo do Estado, Rio do de Janeiro, *Relatório de atividades do projeto de ecodesenvolvimento.*

CHAPTER 8: REPRESENTATION

1. The best review of federal and city government policy toward the favelas after 1930 is in Valla, *Educação e favela.* Gay, *Popular Organization and Democracy in Rio de Janeiro,* is typical of those who believe that favelado protest movements and political mobilization began in the 1970s.

2. Violich, *Cities of Latin America,* 76–77.

3. Moura, "Esboço de um plano para o estudo e solução do problema das favelas," Rio de Janeiro, Novembro 1940, MF.

4. Violich, *Cities of Latin America,* 148–49. See also Kliman, "'Acabar com as favelas.'"

5. Moura, "Esboço," MF.

6. Ibid.

7. Moura, "Palestra–Universidade Católica," MF.

8. Ibid.

9. Moura, "Parques proletários," MF.

10. Moura, "Secretaria Geral de Saúde e Assistencia–Serviço Social, Parque Proletário Provisório No. 1," MF.

11. Moura, "Plano para a reintegração social do menor nos parques proletários," MF.

12. See Bonduki, "The Housing Crisis in the Postwar Years."

13. Valla, *Educação e favela,* 43.

14. "Reunidas as varias comissões para começar a execução do programa," *Correio da manhã ,* July 13, 1948.

15. "Construção de 500 casas para os favelados," *Correio da Manhã,* July 20, 1948.

16. Fundação Leão XIII, *Morros e favelas,* 21.

17. "Na favela do Pinto o Brigadeiro Eduardo Gomes," *Diario de notícias,* June 28, 1950.

18. "É proibido consertar barracos nas favelas," *Diário carioca,* July 2, 1950.

19. "Esteve na Praia do Pinto o prefeito João Vital," *Diário da noite,* July 17, 1951; "Casas para os favelados de Praia do Pinto," *Diário de notícias,* May 18, 1951; "Casas proletárias para os favelados," *A Manhã,* May 18, 1951; "Casas populares para substituir a favela de Praia do Pinto," *Diário do povo,* May 19, 1951; "Habitações para Praia do Pinto," *Diário popular,* May 18, 1951; "O prefeito inspeciona," *O Globo,* May 19, 1951.

20. Congresso Brasileiro de Serviço Social, 3, "Cruzada São Sebastião," 16.

21. Guarnieri, "Uma experiência de promoção social," 55–56.

22. Coutinho, *Um ensaio de aplicação,* 48–49.

23. Ibid., 40–41; Guarnieri, "Uma experiência," 12.

24. Coutinho, *Um ensaio de aplicação*, 46–47.

25. "Cruzada São Sebastião responsavél por 70 por cento dos crimes na Zona Sul," *Jornal do Brasil*, December 16, 1973.

26. Pacheco, "Uma experiência de desenvolvimento e organização," 42.

27. Ibid.

28. Ibid., 61–62.

29. Ibid., 64.

30. Governo do Estado da Guanabara, Instituto de Engenheria Sanitária, *Levantamento sanitario da Lagoa Rodrigo de Freitas*, 8–9.

31. "Nova mentalidade presta mais serviços sociais," *Correio da Manhã*, January 9, 1968; Estado da Guanabara, "Alguns problemas sociais da Guanabara."

32. Governo do Estado da Guanabara, *Rio: Operação favela*, 63, 67.

33. Ibid., 69.

34. Nunes, *Favela: Resistência*, 88.

35. Interview, Cordovil, Rio de Janeiro, 17 May 1990.

36. Estado da Guanabara, *Rio: Operação favela*, 71–74.

37. CHISAM, *Metas alcançadas*, 42.

38. CHISAM, *origens, objetivos, programas, metas*, 28.

39. "Governo reexamina remoção das favelas," *Jornal do Brasil*, November 25, 1964.

40. "Favelados querem ir para Vila," *Correio da Manhã*, November 24, 1964.

41. "Brás de Pina," *Última hora*, November 24, 1964.

42. "Castelo atarefado mandou Luis Viana ouvir Voz de Deus," *Diario Carioca*, December 4, 1964; "Favelado vé armas em vez de Castelo," *Correio da manhã*, December 4, 1964.

43. "Frei Cassiano faz crítica ao manifesto dos padres contra derrubada de favela," *Jornal do Brasil*, December 4, 1964.

44. Padre Artola, interview, Brás de Pina, March 26, 1990; "Metralhadoras calam a voz de Deus," *Ultima hora*, December 4, 1964.

45. "Frei Cassiano," *Jornal do Brasil*, 4 December 1964.

46. "Povo de Esquéleto não quer a mudança," *Correio da manhã*, November 28, 1964.

47. Interview, Brás de Pina, May 8, 1990.

48. Nunes, *Favela: resistência*, 71.

49. See Companhia de Progresso do Estado da Guanabara, *COPEG: Primeira década*, 85–87; *Boletim de informações*, 5, 73–74.

50. "Avaliação do plano de urbanização de Brás de Pina," OB.

51. Ibid.

52. Ibid.

53. "Nova ameaça sobre Jacarézinho," *O Mundo*, June 27, 1949.

54. Souto de Oliveira, "Favelas do Rio de Janeiro," 161.

55. "Ainda não foi suspenso o despejo da favela de Jacarézinho," *Diário da noite*, June 24, 1949; "Serão demolidos os barracos de Jacarézinho," *Diario carioca*, June 25, 1949; "Novamente ameaçados de despejo os moradores de Jacarézinho," *Diretrizes*, June 24, 1949; "Novo pedido de força para o despejo de Jacarézinho," *O Jornal*, 21 July 1949; "Na pasta da secretaria a solução do drama do Morro de Jacarézinho," *Vanguarda*, July 21, 1949; "60 milhões para depropiar o Morro do Jacarézinho," *Correio da noite*, July 23, 1949.

56. "O prefeito, o juiz e o Morro de Jacarézinho," *Diario da Noite*, July 21,1949.

57. "C. legislativa," *Jornal do Brasil*, June 28, 1949.

58. "Jacarézinho," *Diário carioca*, July 22, 1949.

59. "Outra vez em foco o despejo de Jacarézinho," *A Manhã*, July 23, 1949.
60. "A prefeitura toma as últimas providências para a transação," *O Jornal*, July 27, 1949.
61. "Os martírios da população de Vieira Fazenda," *Jornal do Brasil*, October 5, 1949.
62. "Mais populosa que 1,200 cidades do pais a favela do Jacarézinho," *O Jornal*, May 20, 1950.
63. Ibid.
64. "Vai ser cortada a luz no Morro de Jacarézinho," *Tribuna da Imprensa*, May 30, 1950.
65. "Café Filho sobe o Morro de Jacarézinho," *A Notícia*, May 4, 1951.
66. "O vice-presidente no Morro de Jacarézinho," *O Jornal*, May 4, 1951; "O vice-presidente da república visitou ontem o Morro de Jacarézinho," *O Radical*, May 5, 1951.
67. "Café Filho," *A Noticia*, May 4, 1951.
68. See, for example, "O vice-presidente da república visitou ontem o Morro de Jacarézinho," *Diário da noite*, May 4, 1951.
69. "Fome, doença e cadeia," *Diário de notícias*, July 6, 1951.
70. "Os moradores de Jacarézinho fizeram um pacto para defender com a própria vida a soleira de seus barracos," *Diário da noite*, July 6, 1951.
71. "Remédio para o drama de Jacarézinho," *Vanguarda*, July 6, 1951; "Solução para o despejo de Jacarézinho," *Diario da Noite*, July 7, 1951; "Morro do Jacarézinho," *Gazeta de Notícias*, July 5, 1951.
72. "Melhoramento em Jacarézinho," *O Jornal*, July 14, 1951; "Visita do Prefeito à favela de Jacarézinho," *Correio da manhã*, July 14, 1951; " O prefeito visitou a Fundação Leão XIII," *A Voz trabalhista*, July 14, 1951.
73. "Um pouco de conforto aos favelados," *Diário trabalhista*, May 31, 1951.
74. "Posto médico para Jacarézinho," *Gazeta de notícias*, July 16, 1951.
75. "Mil casas para os moradores de Jacarézinho," *O Globo*, July 18, 1951; "Serão construidas no Jacarézinho as casas populares," *Tribuna da imprensa*, July 18, 1951.
76. "Mil casas para os moradores de Jacarézinho," *Diario do povo*, July 19, 1951.
77. "Fechado o comercio das favelas," *O Dia*, August 2, 1951.
78. "Defende–se o Morro de Jacarézinho," *O Globo*, August 13, 1951; "Aclamado pelo povo o governador da cidade," *Diário do povo*, August 15, 1951.
79. For the text of the proposal see "Jacarézinho," *A Manhã*, September 22, 1948.
80. "Da licença para um aparte?" *O Radical*, January 5, 1952.
81. "Jacarézinho e Bangu aplaudiram Carlos Lacerda," *Tribuna da imprensa*, August 8, 1960.
82. "Copia autentica do livro número um de um ata na fundação da Associação Pro–Melhoramento de Jacarézinho," CCD.
83. Associação de Moradores de Jacarézinho, "Diário de atas de reuniões da Comissão Provisória, reunião de Dezembro 9, 1967," CCD.
84. "Estatutos da Associação dos Moradores de Jacarézinho," CCD.
85. Letter dated April 20, 1967, CCD.
86. Comissão de Luz, "Boletim Informativo," CCD.
87. "Regimento interno da Associacão dos Líderes Evangélicos de Jacarézinho," CCD.
88. The best theoretical discussion is Assies, "Urban Social Movements." A comparative overview of social movements can be found in Escobar and Alvarez, *The Making of Social Movements*.

CONCLUSION

1. Katzman, "Urbanization since 1945," 130.

2. See Boschi and Goldschmidt, "Populações faveladas do estado da Guanabara" for the political views and activities of favelados in the 1960s.

3. "48 millones de jóvenes brasileños en la miseria," *Diario las Américas,* (Miami), December 21, 1990.

Bibliography

Abrams, Charles. *Squatter Settlements: The Problem and the Opportunity*. Washington, D.C.: Division of International Affairs, Washington, D.C.: Department of Housing and Urban Development,1966.

Abreu, Mauricio de. *Evolução urbana do Rio de Janeiro* (The urban evolution of Rio de Janeiro). Rio de Janeiro: Zahar, 1987.

Abreu, Sylvio Frões. *O Distrito Federal e seus recursos naturais* (The Federal District and its natural resources). Rio de Janeiro: IBGE, 1957.

Ação Comunitaria do Brasil. "Guanabara—Catálogo de obras e recursos assistênciais do estado da Guanabara" (Guanabara—A catalog of aid work and resources of the state of Guanabara). Rio de Janeiro: Ação Comunitaria 1968. (Mimeo.)

Alcantara, Aspasia Brasileiro. "Estudos e pesquisas sobre a família no Brasil" (Studies and investigations on the family in Brazil). *Dados* 2 (Summer-Fall 1966): 176-179.

Amin, Samir. *Unequal Development*. New York: Monthly Review Press,1976.

Anderson, Michael. *Family Structure in Nineteenth Century Lancashire*. Cambridge: Cambridge University Press, 1971.

Andrews, George Reid. *Blacks and Whites in São Paulo, Brazil, 1888–1988*. Madison: University of Wisconsin Press, 1991.

Arguello, Omar. "Estratégias de supervivência: Un concepto en busca de su contenido" (Survival strategies: A concept in search of its content). *Demografia y economia* (Mexico City) 15, no. 2 (1981): 190–203.

Arque, Paul. "O Rio de Janeiro e seus suburbios" (Rio de Janeiro and its suburbs). *Boletim geográfico* (Rio de Janeiro) 14, no. 184 (Jan.–Feb. 1965): 3–6.

Assies, Willem. "Urban social movements in Brazil: A debate and its dynamics." *Latin American Perspectives* Issue 81 (Spring 1984) volume 21, no. 2: 81–105.

Azevedo, Oswald Benjamín. "O comércio carioca: Sua função regional e sua posição no âmbito nacional—a rede bancária" (Carioca commerce: Its regional function and its position in the national sphere of action—the banking network). In Associação dos Geógrafos Brasileiros (Secção Regional do Rio de Janeiro) Conselho Nacional de Geografia, *Aspectos da geografia carioca*. (Aspects of Carioca geography). Rio de

Janeiro: IBGE, 1962.

Azevedo, Thales de. "Family, Marriage and Divorce in Brazil." In *Contemporary Cultures and Societies in Latin America*, edited by Dwight B. Heath and Richard Adams. New York: Random House, 1963.

Baran, Paul. "The Political Economy of Growth." In *Two Worlds of Change*, Ed. Otto Feinstein. New York: Anchor Books, 1964: 328–47.

Barcellos, Fernanda Augusta Viera Ferreira. *As favelas: Estudo sociólogico* (The favelas: A sociological study). Niterói: Livraria Universitaria,1951.

Bendix, Richard. "What Is Modernization?" In *Developing Nations: Quest for a Model.* Edited by Willard Belling and George Totten. New York: Van Nostrand Reinhold, 1970.

Bernardes, Lisa Maria Cavalcanti. "Importância da posição como fator no desenvolvimento do Rio de Janeiro" (The importance of location as a factor in the development of Rio de Janeiro). In Associação dos Geógrafos Brasileiros. (Secção Regional do Rio de Janeiro), Conselho Nacional de Geografia, *Aspectos da geografia carioca* (Aspects of Carioca geography). Rio de Janeiro: IBGE, 1962.

Bezerra, Daniel Cavalcanti. *Alagados, mocambos e mocambeiros* (Shantytowns, shantytown dwellers and the destitute). Recife: Imprensa Universitaria, 1965.

Blachman, Morris. "Selective Omission and Theoretical Distortion in Studying the Political Activity of Women in Brazil." In *Sex and Class in Latin America*. Edited by June Nash and Helen Safa. New York: Praeger, 1976.

Blank, Gilda. "Brás de Pina: Experiência de urbanização de favela" (Brás de Pina: Experience in the urbanization of a favela). In *Habitação em questão* (Housing in question). Edited by Licia do Prado Valladares. Rio de Janeiro: Zahar, 1980.

———— "Experiência em urbanização de favela carioca — Brás de Pina" (Experience in the urbanization of a Carioca favela—Brás de Pina). Master's thesis, Universidade Federal do Rio de Janeiro, 1977.

Bogado, Laura Torres. "Parque Proletário Provisório No. 1: Planejamento de um serviço social" (Provisional Proletarian Park No. 1: A plan for social service). Rio de Janeiro: Pontífica Universidade Católica, Escola de Serviço Social, 1953 (Mimeo).

Bombart, Jean Pierre. "Les Cultes protestantes dans une favela de Rio de Janeiro" (Protestant cults in a favela of Rio de Janeiro). *América Latina*. (Rio de Janeiro) 12, no. 3 (July–Sept. 1969): 137–59.

Bonilla, Frank. *Rio's Favelas: The Rural Slum Within the City.* East Coast South America Series 3, no. 3 (Brazil) New York: American University Field Staff, Reports Service, 1961.

Bonduki, Nabil G. "The housing crisis in the postwar years." In *Social Struggles and the City: The Case of São Paulo.* Edited by Lucio Kowarick. New York: Monthly Review Press, 1994.

Boschi, Renato and Rose Goldschmidt. "Populações faveladas do Estado da Guanabara" (Favela populations of the state of Guanabara). Rio de Janeiro: Instituto Universitario de Pesquisas e Estudos do Rio de Janeiro, 1970. (Mimeo).

Bourdieu, Pierre, and Jean-Claude Passernon. *Reproduction in Education, Society, and Culture.* London: Sage, 1977.

Brasil, *Estudos sobre a alfabetização da população do Brasil* (Studies on the literacy of the population of Brazil). Rio de Janeiro: IBGE, 1955.

Brasil, *Sinopse regional do ensino primário fundamental comum: Dados retrospectivos, 1940–1957* (Regional synopsis of primary fundamental common education: Retrospective data, 1940–1957). Rio de Janeiro: Ministerio de Educação e Cultura, 1959.

Brasil, Comissão Nacional de Bem-Estar Social. *Favelas e habitação popular: Uma nova política para enfrentar o problema da habitação popular* (Favelas and public housing: A new policy to confront the problem of public housing). Rio de Janeiro: Comissão Nacional de Bem-Estar Social,1954.

Brasil, Conselho Nacional da Geografia, Divisão de Geografia. *Área central da cidade do Rio de Janeiro* (Central area of the city of Rio de Janeiro). Rio de Janeiro: IBGE, 1967.

Brasil, Instituto Brasileiro de Geográfia e Estatística, Serviço Nacional de Recenseamento. *VII recenseamento geral do Brasil—censo demografico de 1960. Vol. 4, Favelas do estado da Guanabara* (Seventh general census of Brasil—demographic census of 1960. Favelas of the state of Guanabara). Rio de Janeiro: IBGE, 1968.

Bresser Pereira, Luiz. *Desenvolvimento e crise no Brasil* (Development and crisis in Brazil). São Paulo: Brasiliense, 1970.

Brum, Argeiro. *O desenvolvimento brasileiro* (Brazilian development). Petropolis: Vozes, 1982.

Camargo, José Francisco de. *O êxodo rural no Brasil* (The rural exodus in Brazil). Rio de Janeiro: Conquista, 1960.

Cancian, Francisca M., and Louis Wolf Goodman and Peter H. Smith. "Capitalism, industrialization and kinship in Latin America." *Journal of Family History* 3, no. 4 (Winter 1978): 319–36.

Cardoso, Fernando Henrique. "Comentários sobre os conceitos da superpopulação relativa e a marginalidade" (Commentaries on the concepts of relative overpopulation and marginality). *Cebrap* (São Paulo) 1 (1971): 99–130.

Cardoso, Fernando Henrique, and Enzo Falleto. *Dependency and Development in Latin America*. Berkeley: University of California Press, 1979.

Casaco, Juan. "The Social Functions of the Slum."*America Latina* (Rio de Janeiro) 12, no.3 (July–Sept. 1969): 87–109.

Castro, Josué de. *O problema da alimentação no Brasil* (The problem of nutrition in Brazil). 3rd ed. São Paulo: Companhia Editora Nacional, 1939.

Cavalcanti, Sandra. *Rio: Viver ou morrer.* (Rio: To live or to die). Rio de Janeiro: Expressão e Cultura, 1978.

Centro de Coordenação Industrial para o Plano Habitacional. "A interpenetração das áreas faveladas e áreas industriais no estado da Guanabara" (The interpenetration of favela areas and industrial areas in the state of Guanabara). Rio de Janeiro: IDEG, 1968. (Mimeo).

Comissão Executiva de Projetos Específicos, Serviço de Estatística. "Dados estatísticos referentes à favela Praia do Pinto, Ilha das Dragas, CHS-1, CHS-3" (Statistical data referring to the favelas of Praia do Pinto, Ilha das Dragas, CHS-1, CHS-3). Rio de Janeiro: CEPE, 1967. (Mimeo).

Comitê Brasileiro da Conferência Internacional de Serviço Social. "Levantamento bibliográfico—favela" (Bibliographical survey—favela). Rio de Janeiro: CBCISS, 1979. (Mimeo).

Companhia de Habitação Popular do Estado da Guanabara. "A COHAB através de números e imagens" (COHAB through numbers and figures). Rio de Janeiro: COHAB, 1965. (Mimeo).

Companhia de Progresso do Estado da Guanabara. *COPEG: Primeira década* (COPEG: First decade). Rio de Janeiro: COPEG, 1967.

Congresso Brasileiro de Serviço Social, 3. "Cruzada São Sebastião: Duas experiências de promoção humana, bairro São Sebastião e favela de Radio Nacional." (Cruzada São Sebastião: Two experiences of human promotion, the São Sebastiã neighborhood and the favela Radio Nacional). Rio de Janeiro, Congresso Brasileiro de Serviço Social, 1965. (Mimeo).

Coniff, Michael. *Urban Politics in Brazil: The Rise of Populism in Rio de Janerio, 1925-45.* Pittsburgh: University of Pittsburgh Press, 1981.

Conrad, Robert Edgar. *Children of God's Fire. A Documentary History of Black Slavery in Brazil.* Princeton: Princeton University Press, 1983.

Consorte, Josidelth Gomes. "A criança favelada e a escola pública " (The favela child and the public school). *Educação e ciencias sociais* (Rio de Janeiro) 6, no.11 (Aug. 1959): 45–59.

Coordenação de Habitação de Interesse Social da Área Metropolitana do Grande Rio de Janeiro. (CHISAM). *Metas alcançadas e novos objetivos do programa.* (Goals reached and new objectives of the program). Rio de Janeiro: Banco Nacional de Habitação, 1969.

———. *Origens, objetivos, programas, metas.* (Origins, objectives, programs, goals). Rio de Janeiro: Banco Nacional de Habitação,1969.

Correa, Mariza. "Repensando a família patriarcal brasileira " (Rethinking the patriarchal family in Brazil). In *Colcha de retalhos: Estudos sobre a família no Brasil* (Quilt of shreds: Studies on the family in Brazil). Edited by Maria Suely Kofes et al. São Paulo: Brasiliense, 1982.

Cortes, Geraldo de Menezes. *Favelas.* Rio de Janeiro: Ministerio da Educação e Cultura, Serviço de Documentação, 1959.

Corwin, Arthur F. "Afro—Brazilians: Myths and Realities," in *Slavery and Race Relations in Latin America.* Edited by Robert Brent Toplin. Westport, Conn.: Greenwood Press, 1974.

Costa, Manoel. *População economicamente ativa da Guanabara* (The economically active population of Guanabara). Rio de Janeiro: INPES, 1971.

Coutinho, Nadyr. *Um ensaio de aplicação das técnicas de organização social de comunidade de um projeto piloto de conjunto residencial para ex-favelados* (An attempt to apply techniques of community social organization for a pilot project of a residential building for ex-favelados). Rio de Janeiro: Serviço Social de Comercio, 1959.

Cox, Dilermando Duarte. *Os párias da cidade maravilhosa* (The pariahs of the marvelous city). Rio de Janeiro: José Olympio, 1950.

Cruz, Henrique Dias da. *Os suburbios cariocas no regime do estado novo* (Carioca suburbs in the regime of the Estado Novo). Rio de Janeiro: D.I.P., 1942.

Cunha, Murillo Alves da. *O novo Rio de Janeiro: geografia e realidade sócio-económica* (The new Rio de Janeiro: Geography and socioeconomic reality). Rio de Janeiro: Francisco Alves, 1975.

Dean, Warren. *The Industrialization of São Paulo, 1880–1945.* Austin: University of Texas Press, 1969.

Dickinson, James, and Bob Russel, eds. *Family, Economy, and the State: The Social Reproduction Process Under Capitalism.* New York: St. Martin's Press, 1986.

Distrito Federal, Prefeitura. *Censo das favelas: aspectos gerais* (Census of the favelas: General aspects). Rio de Janeiro: Departamento de Geografia e Estatística, 1949.

Engels, Frederick. *Origins of the Family, Private Property and the State.* New York: New World, 1972.

Escobar, Arturo and Sonia E. Alvarez, eds. *The Making of Social Movements in Latin America: Identity, Strategy, and Democracy.* Boulder: Westview Press, 1992.

Evans, Peter. *Dependent Development.* Princeton: University of Princeton Press, 1979.

Fausto Neto, Ana Maria Q. *Família operária e reprodução da força de trabalho* (The working family and the reproduction of the labor force). Petropolis: Vozes, 1982.

Fernandes, Florestan. *The Negro in Brazilian Society.* Translated by Jacqueline D. Skiles, A. Bruel, and Arthur Rothwell. New York: Columbia University Press, 1969.

Firestone, Shulamith. *The Dialectic of Sex: The Case for Feminist Revolution.* New York: Morrow, 1970.

Fishlow, Albert. "Origins and Consequences of Import Substitution Industrialization." In *International Economics and Development: Essays in Honor of Raul Prebisch.* Edited by Luis Eugenio di Marc. New York: Academic Press, 1972.

Folbre, Nancy. "Exploitation Comes Home: A Critique of the Marxian Theory of Family Labour." *Cambridge Journal of Economics* 6 (1982): 317–329.

Freyre, Gilberto. *Casa grande e senzala: Formação da família brasileira sob o regime da economia patriarcal* (The big house and the slave quarters: Formation of the Brazilian family under the regime of the patriarchal economy). 22nd ed. Rio de Janeiro: José Olympio, 1983.

———. *Sobrados e mucambos: Decadência do patriarcado rural e desenvolvimento urbano* (Mansions and shanties: The decline of rural patriarchy and urban development) 2 vols. 5th ed. Rio de Janeiro: José Olympio, 1977.

Fundação Estadual de Engenheria do Meio Ambiente. *A favela e o meio ambiente da comunidade* (The favela and the environment of the community). Rio de Janeiro: FEEMA,1982.

Fundação Leão XIII. *Favelas: um compromisso que vamos resgatar* (Favelas: A commitment we will fulfill). Rio de Janeiro: Fundação Leão XIII, 1962.

———. *Morros e favelas. Como trabalha a Fundação Leão XIII. Notas e relatório de 1947 a 1954* (Hills and favelas: How the Fundação Leão XIII functions: Notes and reports from 1947 to 1954). Rio de Janeiro: Imprensa Naval, 1955.

Gay, Robert. *Popular Organization and Democracy in Rio de Janeiro: A Tale of Two Favelas.* Philadelphia: Temple University Press, 1994.

Geiger, Pedro Pinchas. *Evolução da rede urbana brasileira* (Evolution of the Brazilian urban network). Rio de Janeiro: Centro Brasileiro de Pesquisas Educacionais, 1963.

Germani, Gino. *Politica y sociedad en la época de las masas* (Politics and society in the age of the masses). Buenos Aires: Paidos, 1962.

Gershenkron, Alexander. "Economic Backwardness in Historical Perspective." In *The Progress of Underdeveloped Areas.* Edited by Bert Hoselitz. Chicago: University of Chicago Press, 1952.

Godoy Filho, Armando and Nelson Correa Monteiro. "Semana de estudos favelas: Resposta ao temario, apresentada, para o caso do Distrito Federal (Week of studies on the favelas: Response to the previously presented case of the Federal District). Rio de Janeiro, Comissão nacional de bem-estar social, subcomissão de favelas. 1952. (Mimeo).

Goode, William. *World Revolution and Family Patterns.* New York: Free Press, 1963.

Goulart, José Alipio. *Favelas do Distrito Federal* (Favelas of the Federal District). Rio de Janeiro: Ministerio de Cultura, Serviço de Informação Agrícola, 1957. Estudos Brasileiros 9. Appendix: *Censo de 1o-VII-1950.*

Guanabara, Comissão Executiva para o Desenvolvimento Urbano (CEDUG) and Doxiades Associates. *Guanabara, a Plan for Urban Development.* Athens: n.p., 1965.

Guanabara, Estado da. *O problema sanitário das favelas* (The sanitation problem of the favelas). Rio de Janeiro: Secretaria das Obras Públicas, Departamento de Saneamento, 1967.

———. *Rio de Janeiro em seus quatrocentos anos: Formação e desenvolvimento da cidade* (Rio de Janeiro in its four hundred years: Formation and development of the city). Rio de Janeiro and São Paulo: Distribuidora Record, 1965.

Guanabara, Estado da, Secretaria de Estado do Governo, Coordenação de Planos e Orçamentos. "Aspectos da geografia das industrias no Rio de Janeiro" (Aspects of the geography of the industries of Rio de Janeiro). Rio de Janeiro: SEGCPO, 1969. (Mimeo).

Guanabara, Governo da. *Boletim de informações* 5 (Information bulletin 5). (Rio de Janeiro) 1969.

Guanabara, Governo do Estado. *Rio: operação favela* (Rio: Operation favela). Rio de Janeiro: Governo do Estado da Guanabara, 1969.

Guanabara, Governo do Estado, Instituto de Engenheria Sanitária. *Levantamento sanitário de Lagoa Rodrigo de Freitas* (Public health survey of Lagoa Rodrigo de Freitas). Rio de Janeiro: n.p. 1969.

Guanabara, Governo do Estado, Secretaria de Serviços Sociais. *Alguns problemas sociais na Guanabara* (Some social problems of Guanabara). Rio de Janeiro: Secretaria de Serviços Sociais, n.d.

———. *Praia do Pinto*. Rio de Janeiro: Secretaria de Serviços Sociais, 1969. (Mimeo).

Guarnieri, Enny. "Uma experiencia de promoção social: Cruzada São Sebastião " (An experience in social promotion: Cruzada São Sebastião). Rio de Janeiro: Comitê Brasileiro da Conferência Internacional de Serviço Social, 1963. (Mimeo).

Guimarães, Alberto Passos. "As favelas do Distrito Federal segundo o censo de 1950" (The favelas of the Federal District according to the census of 1950). *Revista brasileira de estatística* (Rio de Janeiro) 14, no. 5 (July–Sept. 1953): 250–78.

Gunder Franke, Andre. "The Development of Underdevelopment." In *Dependence and Underdevelopment*. Edited by James Cockroft. New York: Anchor Books, 1972.

Hahner, June. *Poverty and Politics: The Urban Poor in Brazil, 1870–1920*. Albuquerque: University of New Mexico Press, 1986.

Ianni, Octavio. *Industrialização e desenvolvimento no Brasil* (Industrialization and development in Brazil) . Rio de Janeiro: Editora Civilização Brasileira, 1963.

Instituto de Estudos de Mercado. *A vida mental dos favelados do Distrito Federal*. The mental life of the favelados). Rio de Janeiro: IPEME, 1958.

Iutaka, Sugiyama, and Wilbur Bock. "Urbanização e família extensa no Brasil" (Urbanization and the extended family in Brazil). *Revista de ciéncias sociais* 6, nos. 1 and 2 (1975): 29–50.

Jelin, Elisabeth. "Formas de organização da atividade económica e estrutura ocupacional" (Organizational forms of economic activity and occupational structures). *Estudos Cebrap* 9 (July–Sept. 1974): 51–78.

Jesus, Carolina Maria de. *Child of the Dark*. New York: Signet Books, 1962.

Katzman, Martin. "Urbanization since 1945." In *Social Change in Brazil, 1945–1985: The Incomplete Transition*, edited by Edmar Bacha and Herbert Klein. Albuquerque: University of New Mexico Press, 1989.

Kliman, Mauro. " 'Acabar com as favelas': Parques proletários provisórios; uma intervenção na prática" ("Putting an end to the favelas": Provisional Proletarian Parks; intervention in practice). *Chão: Revista de arquitetura* no. 2 (June–Aug. 1978): 16–22.

Kowarick, Lucio. *Capitalismo e marginalidade na América Latina* (Capitalism and marginality in Latin America). Rio de Janeiro: Paz e Terra, 1975.

Kowarick, Lucio, and Clara Ant. "Slum Tenements in the City." In *Social Struggles and the City: The Case of São Paulo*. Edited by Lucio Kowarick. New York: Monthly Review Press, 1994.

Kowarick, Lucio, and Milton Campanaro. "São Paulo: Metrópole de subdesenvolvimento industrializado" (São Paulo: Metropolis of industrialized underdevelopment). *Novos*

Estudos Cebrap (São Paulo) no. 13 (Oct. 1985): 66–73.

Kriegel, Annie. "Generational Difference: The History of an Idea." *Daedalus* no. 107 (Fall 1978): 23–38.

Kuznesof, Elizabeth. *Household Economy and Urban Development: São Paulo 1765 to 1836*. Boulder, Colo.: Westview Press, 1986.

Kuznets, Simon. "Economic Growth and Income Inequality." *American Economic Review* 45 (Mar. 1955): 1–28.

———. "Underdeveloped Countries and the Pre-industrial Stage in Advanced Countries." In *Two Worlds of Change*. Edited by Otto Feinstein. New York: Anchor Books, 1964.

Lacoste, Yves. *Geografia do subdesenvolvimento* (The geography of underdevelopment). Translated by T. Santos. São Paulo: Difel, 1982.

Laslett, Peter, ed. *Household and Family in Past Time*. Cambridge: Cambridge University Press, 1972.

Leeds, Anthony. "Political Considerations and Social Effects of Producer and Consumer Oriented Housing in Brazil and Peru: A System Analysis." In *Latin American Urban Research*, vol. 3. Edited by Francine Rabinowitz and Felicity Trueblood. Beverly Hills, Calif.: Sage, 1973.

———. "The Significant Variables Determining the Character of Squatter Settlements." *América Latina* (Rio de Janeiro) 12, no. 3 (July–Sept. 1969): 44–86.

Leeds, Anthony, and Elisabeth Leeds. *A sociologia do Brasil urbano* (The sociology of urban Brazil). Rio de Janeiro: Zahar, 1977.

———. "Brazil and the Myth of Urban Rurality: Urban Experience, Work, and Values in the Squatments of Rio de Janeiro and Lima." In *City and Country in the Third World: Issues in the Modernization of Latin America*. Edited by Arthur J. Field. Cambridge, Mass: Shenkman, 1970.

Lefevbre, Lucien. *The Survival of Capitalism: Reproduction of the Relations of Production*. New York: St. Martin's Press, 1973.

Lewis, Oscar. *La Vida: A Puerto Rican Family in the Culture of Poverty—San Juan and New York*. New York: Vintage Books, 1965.

———. *The Children of Sanchez: Autobiography of a Mexican Family*. New York: Vintage Books, 1961.

Lloyd, Peter. *Slums of Hope? Shantytowns of the Third World*. New York: St. Martin's Press, 1979.

Lobo, Eulalia M. L. *História do Rio de Janeiro: do capital comercial ao capital industrial e financeiro* (History of Rio de Janeiro: From commercial capital to industrial and finance capital). 2 vols. Rio de Janeiro: IBMEC, 1976.

Lobo, Eulalia, et al. *Questão habitacional e o movimento operário no Brasil* (The housing question and the workers' movement in Brazil). Rio de Janeiro: UFRJ, 1989.

Lomnitz, Larissa Adler. *Networks and Marginality: Life in a Mexican Shantytown*. Translated by Cinna Lomnitz. New York: Academic Press, 1977.

Lopes, Valdecir Freire. "Duas favelas do Distrito Federal" (Two favelas of the Federal District). *Revista brasileira dos municípios* (Rio de Janeiro) 32 (Oct.–Dec. 1955): 283–98.

López, Juárez Brandão. *Desenvolvimento e mudança social: A sociedade urbano-industrial* (Development and social change: The urban-industrial society) 2 Vols. São Paulo: Nacional/MEC, 1976.

———. *Sociedade industrial no Brasil* (Industrial society in Brazil). São Paulo: DIFEL, 1964.

Louzeiro, José, ed. *Assim marcha a família* (Thus the family walks on). Rio de Janeiro:

Editora Civilização Brasileira, 1965.

Löwy, Michael. *The Politics of Combined and Uneven Development: The Theory of Permanent Revolution*. London: Verso, 1981.

Macedo, Carmen Cinida. *A reprodução da desigualdade* (The reproduction of inequality). São Paulo: Hucitec, 1979.

Machado da Silva, Luis Antônio. "Mercados metropolitanos de trabalho manual e marginalidade" (Metropolitan manual labor markets and marginality). Master's thesis, Universidade Federal de Rio de Janeiro, 1971.

————. "O significado do botequim" (The significance of the community store). *América Latina* (Rio de Janeiro) 12, no.3 (July–Sept. 1969): 160–82.

Mangin, William. "Latin America Squatter Settlements: A Problem and a Solution." *Latin American Research Review* 3, no.3, (July–Sept. 1967): 65–98.

Marx, Karl, *Capital*. vol. I. New York: Vintage Press, 1976.

Medina, Carlos Alberto. *A favela e o demagôgo*. (The Favela and the demagogue). Saõ Paulo: Ed. Martins, 1964.

————. *Familia e mudança* (Family and change). Petrópolis: Vozes, 1974.

————. "A favela como estrutura atomistica: Elementos descritivos e construtivos (The favela as an atomistic structure: descriptive and constructive elements). *America Latina* (Rio de Janeiro) 12, no.3 (Jul.–Sept. 1969): 112–36.

————. "Família e desenvolvimento" (Family and development). *America Latina* (Rio de Janeiro) 12, no. 2 (Apr.–June 1969): 53–69.

Medina, Carlos Alberto and Licia Valladares. *Favela e religião* (Favela and religion). In house document CNBB, CERIS, Rio de Janeiro, 1968.

Meillassoux, Claude. *Maidens, Meal and Money: Capitalism and the Domestic Community*. Cambridge: Cambridge University Press, 1981.

Mendes de Almeida, Angela, ed. *Pensando a família no Brasil: Da colônia à modernidade* (Thinking about the family in Brazil: From colony to modernity). Rio de Janeiro: Espaço e Tempo/Editora da UFRJ, 1987.

Minas Gerais, Estado de. Secretaria do Trabalho e Cultura Popular. *Levantamento da população favelada de Belo Horizonte* (Survey of the favela population of Belo Horizonte). Belo Horizonte: Secretaria de Estado do Trabalho e Cultura Popular, 1966.

Mortara, Giorgio. "O aumento da população das grandes cidades do Brasil entre 1940 e 1950" (The increase in the population of the large cities of Brazil between 1940 and 1950). In *Pesquisas sobre as populações urbanas do Brasil* (Investigations on the urban populations of Brazil). Rio de Janeiro: IBGE, 1954.

————. *Tábuas brasileiras de mortalidade e sobrevivência* (Brazilian tables of mortality and survival). Rio de Janeiro: Kosmos, 1946.

Mount, Ferdinand. *The Subversive Family: An Alternative History of Love and Marriage*. London: Counterpoint, 1982.

Moura, Vitor. "Favelas do Distrito Federal" (Favelas of the Federal District). In Academia Carioca de Letras, *Aspectos do Distrito Federal* (Aspects of the Federal District). Rio de Janeiro: Sauer e Filho, 1943.

Musgrove, Philip and Robert T. Ferber. "Identifying the Urban Poor: Characteristics of poverty households in Bogatá, Medellín and Lima." *Latin American Research Review* 14, no. 2 (1979): 25-53.

Nascimento, Erotides Arruda do, and Adel Cerqueira Alvim. "Luta contra a tuberculose na favela" (The fight against tuberculosis in the favela). Offprint of *Clínica tisiologica* (Sept.–Oct. 1949): 91–111.

Needll, Jeffrey. "Making the Carioca *Belle Epoque* Concrete: The Urban Reforms under

Pereira Passos." *Journal of Urban History* 10, no. 4 (1984): 383–422.

Nogueira, Oracy. "A organização da família no municipio de Itapetininga" (The organization of the family in the municipality of Itapetininga). *Educação e ciências sociais* (Rio de Janeiro) 6, no. 1 (1959): 61–112.

Notícias municipais. "Favelas: problema de planejamento" (Favelas: A problem of planning). 5, no. 43 (1960): 8–9.

Nun, José. "Superpoblación relativa, ejército industrial de reserva y masa marginal" (Relative overpopulation, industrial reserve army and marginal masses). *Revista Latino-Americana de Sociologia* (Buenos Aires) 5, no.2 (1969): 6–78.

Nunes, Guida. *Favela: Resistência pelo direito de viver* (Favela: Fight for the right to live). Petropolis: Vozes, 1980.

Observador Economico e Financeiro. "O censo retrata as favelas " (The census portrays the favelas). 16. No. 191 (1951): 68-82.

Oliveira, Francisco de. *A economia da dependência imperfeita* (The economy of imperfect dependence). Rio de Janeiro: Graal, 1977.

Oliveira, Francisco de, and Francisco Sà, Jr. *Questionando a economia brasileira* (Questioning the Brazilian economy). São Paulo: Seleções Cebrap, 1976.

Oliveira, Ney dos Santos. "Parque Proletário da Gávea—uma experiencia de habitação popular" (The Proletarian Park of Gávea—an experience in people's housing). Master's thesis, Universidade Federal do Rio de Janeiro, 1981

Pacheco, Maria Stella Bezerro. "Uma experiência de desenvolvimento e organização de comunidade no Parque Proletário Provisório no. 3 do Estado da Guanabara" (An experience in community development and organization in Provisional Proletarian Park no. 3 of the state of Guanabara). Rio de Janeiro: Pontífica Universidade Católica, Instituto Social, 1962. (Mimeo).

Parisse, Lucien. "Favelas de L'agglomeration de Rio de Janeiro: Leur place dans le processus d'urbanisation " (Favelas in the greater area of Rio de Janeiro: Their place in the process of urbanization). Ph.D. diss., University of Strasbourg, 1970.

———. "Bibliografia cronológica sobre a favela do Rio de Janeiro a partir de 1940" (Chronological bibliography on the favela in Rio de Janeiro after 1940), *America Latina* (Rio de Janeiro) 12, 3, (July.–Sept. 1969): 221–232.

———. *Favelas do Rio de Janeiro: Evolução e sentido* (Favelas of Rio de Janeiro: Evolution and significance). Rio de Janeiro: Cadernos CENPHA, 1969.

———. "Las favelas en la expansión urbana de Rio de Janeiro: Estudo geográfico" (Favelas in the urban growth of Rio de Janeiro: A geographic study). *America Latina* (Rio de Janeiro) 12, no.3 (July–Sept. 1969): 7-43.

Pastore, José, et al. *Mudança social e pobreza: O que ocorreu com a familia brasileira, 1970–80?* (Social change and poverty: What happened to the Brazilian family, 1970–80?). São Paulo: Pioneira, 1983.

Pearse, Andrew. "Integração social das famílias de favelados" (Social integration of favela families). *Educação e ciências sociais* (Rio de Janeiro) 2, no.6 (Nov. 1967): 245–78.

———. "Notas sobre a organização social de uma favela do Rio de Janeiro " (Notes on the social organization of a Rio de Janeiro favela). *Educação e ciências sociais* (Rio de Janeiro) 3, no.7 (Apr. 1958): 9–32.

Pedroso, José, and Adolpho Porto. *Rio de Janeiro: O estado e o município* (Rio de Janeiro: The state and the municipality). Rio de Janeiro: n.p., 1950.

Pereira, Luis Bresser. *Desevoluimento e crise no Brasil* (Development and crisis in Brazil). São Paulo: Brasiliense, 1970.

Pereira, Silvia Baptista. "O serviço social e a urbanização da favela de Jacarézinho" (Social service and the urbanization of the favela of Jacarézinho). Rio de Janeiro: Pontífica Universidade Católica, Escola de Serviço Social,1965. (Mimeo).

Perlman, Janice. *The Myth of Marginality: Poverty and Politics in Rio de Janeiro.* University of California Press, 1973.

Pinto, L. A. Costa. *O negro no Rio de Janeiro: Relações de raça numa sociedade em mudança* (The Negro in Rio de Janeiro: Race relations in a society in transition). São Paulo: Companhia Editorial Nacional, 1952.

Pontífica Universidade Católica, Escola de Sociologia e Política. "Tres favelas cariocas: Mata Machado, Morro União, Brás de Pina-Levantamento sócioeconômico " (Three Carioca favelas: Mata Machado, Morro União, Brás de Pina–socioeconomic survey). Rio de Janeiro: Pontífica Universidade Católica, 1967. (Mimeo).

Portes, Alejandro. "Latin American Class Structures." *Latin American Research Review* 20, no. 3 (1985): 7–40.

Portugal, Isaura Lembruger. "Favelas: Problema administrativo" (Favelas: Administrative problem). Rio de Janeiro: Pontífica Universidade Católica, Escola de Serviço Social, 1952. (Mimeo).

Prado, Regina de Paula Santos. "Conceito de família e domicílio " (Concept of the family and household). Rio de Janeiro: IBGE, 1982. (Mimeo).

Prado Junior, Caio. *The Colonial Heritage of Brazil.* Translated by Suzette Macedo. Berkeley: University of California Press, 1969.

Rainho, Luis Flavio. *Os peões do ABC* (The peons of the ABC). Petrópolis: Vozes, 1980.

Ramos, Donald. "Single and Married Women in Vila Rica, Brazil, 1754–1838." *Journal of Family History* 16, no. 3 (1991): 261–82.

Ravelo, Carlos. "Blessed Are the (un)meek for They Shall Inherit the Earth." *News From Brazil* 6, no. 104 (August 1994): 7–10.

Renault, Delso. *O dia-a-dia no Rio de Janeiro segundo os jornais, 1871—1889* (Day-to-day life in Rio de Janeiro according to the newspapers, 1871–1889). Rio de Janeiro: Civilização Brasileira,1982.

————. *Rio de Janeiro: A vida da cidade refletida nos jornais 1850–1870* (Rio de Janeiro: The life of the city as reflected in newspapers, 1850–1870). Rio de Janeiro: Civilização Brasileira, 1978.

Revista do globo. "'Cidade Maravilhosa:' onde a vida tem duas faces" ("Cidade Maravilhosa:" Where life has two faces). 11 November 1944: 22–56.

Rio de Janeiro, Governo do Estado. *Relatório de atividades do projeto de ecodesenvolvimento.* Vol. 2: *Favela do Jacarézinho* (Report on the activities of the ecodevelopment project, Vol 2: Favela of Jacarézinho). Rio de Janeiro: SOSP/FEEMA, 1980.

Rios, José Artur. "As favelas " (The favelas). In Associação dos Geógrafos Brasileiros, Secção Regional do Rio de Janeiro, *Aspectos da geografia carioca.* Rio de Janeiro: IBGE, 1962.

————. "Coordenação dos serviços sociais—projeto de financiamento do programa de recuperação de favelas e habitaçoes anti-higiênicas" (Coordination of social services—a project for financing the program of recuperation of anti-hygienic dwellings). Rio de Janeiro: Serviço Especial de recuperação das favelas e habitações Anti-higiênicas, 1961. (Mimeo).

Robert, Mauricio. "As favelas do Rio de Janeiro: Encaminhamento para a sua solução " (The favelas of Rio de Janeiro: Moving toward a solution). *Arquitetura* (Rio de Janeiro) 10 (Apr.1963): 7–9.

Roberts, Bryan R. *Organizing Strangers: Poor Families in Guatemala City.* Austin:

University of Texas Press, 1973.

Rocha, Helio. "Indústrias na Guanabara " (Industries in Guanabara). *Boletim Geográfico* (Rio de Janeiro) 24, no. 184 (1965): 65–66.

Rodrigues de Meida, Maria Leda. "Família e desenvolvimento: Uma analise bibliográfica (relatório final)." (Family and development: A bibliographical analysis (final report). Rio de Janeiro: Centro Latino-Americano de Pesquisa en Ciências Sociais, 1971. (Mimeo).

Romero, Breno Machado, ed. *O salário mínimo no Brasil de 1940 à 1977* (The minimum salary in Brazil from 1940 to 1977). Pôrto Alegre: Sulina, n.d.

Rosen, Bernard, and Manoel T. Berlinck. "Modernization and Family Structure in the Region of São Paulo, Brazil." *América Latina* (Rio de Janeiro) 11, no.3 (July–Sept. 1968): 75–95.

Russell-Wood, A. J. R. *The Black Man in Slavery and Freedom in Colonial Brazil*. New York: St. Martin's Press, 1982.

Saboia, João. *Salário mínimo: A experiencia brasileira* (Minimum salary: The Brazilian experience). Pôrto Alegre: L & PM, 1985.

Sachs, Celine. "Croissance urbaine et favelisation des métropoles—São Paulo et Rio de Janeiro." (Urban growth and favelization of the metropolises—São Paulo and Rio de Janeiro). In *Economie et humanisme* (Paris) no. 260 (July/Aug.1981).

Safa, Helen. "The New Women Workers: Does Money Equal Power?" NACLA *Report on the Americas* 27, no. 1 (July/August 1993): 24–29.

———. *The Urban Poor in Puerto Rico: A Study in Development and Inequality*. New York: Holt, Rinehart and Winston, 1974.

Sahlins, Marshall, and Edward Service, eds. *Evolution and Culture*. Ann Arbor: University of Michigan Press, 1968.

Salman, Lawrence F. "Housing Alternatives for the Carioca Poor: A Comparison Between Favelas and Casas de Cómodos." *América Latina* (Rio de Janeiro) 13, no. 4 (Oct.–Dec. 1970): 51–70.

Santos, Carlos Nelson Ferreira dos. *Tres movimentos sociais urbanos no Rio de Janeiro* (Three urban social movements in Rio de Janeiro). Rio de Janeiro: Zahar, 1981.

———. "Tres movimentos sociais urbanos no Rio de Janeiro " (Three urban social movements in Rio de Janeiro). Master's Thesis, Universidade Federal do Rio de Janeiro, 1979.

———. "Some Considerations about the Possibility of Squatter Settlement Redevelopment Plans: The Case of Brás de Pina. " Cambridge: Massachusetts Institute of Technology, 1971. (Mimeo).

Santos, Milton. *A pobreza urbana* (Urban poverty). São Paulo: Hucitec, 1978.

Schlesinger, Arthur. *The Cycles of American History*. Boston: Houghton Mifflin, 1986.

Schminck, Marianne. "Women and Industrial Development in Brazil." In *Women and Change in Latin America*. Edited by June Nash and Helen Safa. South Hadley Mass: Bergin & Garvey, 1986.

———. "Household Economic Strategies: Review and Research Agenda." *Latin American Research Review* 19, no. 3 (1984): 87–101.

Schurz, William Lyttle. *Brazil: The Infinite Country*. New York: Dutton, 1961.

Schwartz, Stuart. *Sugar Plantations in the Formation of Brazilian Society: Bahia 1550–1835*. New York: Cambridge University Press, 1985.

Shirley, Robert W. *The End of a Tradition: Culture Change and Development in the Municipio of Cunha, São Paulo, Brazil*. New York: Columbia University Press, 1971.

Silberstein, Paul. "Favela Living: Personal Solution to Larger Problems." *América Latina*

(Rio de Janeiro) 12, no. 3 (July–Sept. 1969): 183–200.

Silva, Adelaide Margarida Manso. "Estudo sobre um inquerito social realizado no Parque Proletário Provisório no. 1 (Study on a social inquiry undertaken in Provisional Proletarian Park no. 1). Rio de Janeiro: Pontífica Universidade Católica, Instituto Social, 1953. (Mimeo).

Silva, Maria Beatriz Nizza da. *Cultura e sociedade no Rio de Janeiro (1808–1821)* (Culture and society in Rio de Janeiro, 1808–1821). São Paulo: Companhia Editora Nacional, 1977.

Silva, Maria Hortencia do Nascimento. *Impressões de uma assistente sobre trabalho na favela* (Impressions of an assistant on work in the favela). Rio de Janeiro: Gráfica Sauer, 1942.

Síntese social. "Radiografia da favela " (X-ray of the favela) 6, no. 21 (Jan./Mar. 1964): 60–73.

Siqueira, Irmã Helena. "O centro Nossa Senhora das Graças como solução da favela de Esquéleto" (The Our Lady of Grace Center as a solution to the favela of Esquéleto). Rio de Janeiro: Pontífica Universidade Católica, Instituto Social, 1959. (Mimeo).

Smith, T. Lynn. *Brazil: People and Institutions.* Baton Rouge: Louisiana State University Press, 1954.

Sociedade de Análises Gráficas e Mecanográficas Aplicadas aos Complexos Sociais (SAGMACS). "Aspectos humanos da favela carioca " (Human aspects of the Carioca favela). *O Estado de São Paulo* (São Paulo) parte geral (Apr. 13, 1960), supp., esp. 1–40; parte especifica (Apr. 15, 1960), supp. esp. 1–48.

Souto de Oliveira, Jane. "Favelas do Rio de Janeiro" (Favelas of Rio de Janeiro). Rio de Janeiro: IBGE, 1983. (Mimeo).

———. "A reposição do suor" (The replacement of sweat). Master's Thesis, Universidade Federal do Rio de Janeiro, Museu Nacional, 1981.

Stein, Stanley. *Vassouras: A Brazilian Coffee County, 1850–1890.* New York: Atheneum, 1970.

Stolcke, Verena. "A família não é sagrada: Sistemas de trabalho e estrutura familiar. O caso das fazendas de café em São Paulo" (The family is not holy: Systems of work and family structure: The case of the coffee plantations of São Paulo). In *Colcha de retalhos: estudos sobre a família no Brasil* (Quilt of shreds: studies on the family in Brazil). Edited by Maria Suely Kofes de Almeida et al. São Paulo: Brasiliense, 1982.

Stone, Lawrence. "The Rise of the Nuclear Family in Early Modern England: The Patriarchal Stage." In *The Family in History.* Edited by Charles Rosenberg. Philadelphia: University of Pennsylvania Press, 1975.

Sutcliffe, Bob. "Imperialism and Industrialization in the Third World." In *Studies in the Theory of Imperialism.* Edited by R. Owen and Bob Sutcliff. Burnt Mill, U.K.: Longman, 1972.

Topik, Steven. *The Political Economy of the Brazilian State 1889–1930.* Austin: University of Texas Press, 1987.

União Pro–Melhoramentos dos Moradores da Rocinha. *Varal de lembranças: Histórias da Rocinha* (Clothesline of memories: Stories from Rocinha). Rio de Janeiro: Tempo e Presença, 1983.

Valla, Victor. *Educação e favela: Políticas para as favelas do Rio de Janeiro* (Education and favela: Policies toward the favelas of Rio de Janeiro). Petrópolis: Vozes, 1986.

Versiani, Flavio, and José Roberto Mendonça, eds. *Formação económica do Brasil: A experiência da industrialização* (Economic formation of Brazil: The experience of industrialization). São Paulo: José Olympio Saraiva, 1977.

Vianna, Oliveira. *Instituções políticas brasileiras* (Brazilian political institutions). 2 vols. Rio de Janeiro: 1949.

Villaça, Maria José. *A força de trabalho no Brasil* (The workforce in Brazil). São Paulo: Pioneira, 1967.

Violich, Francis. *Cities of Latin America: Housing and Planning to the South*. New York: Reinhold, 1946.

Visão. "Uma cruzada e um paladino " (A crusade and a paladin). (December 27, 1957): 20–23.

Willems, Emilio. "The Structure of the Brazilian Family." *Social Forces* 31, no. 4 (May 1953): 339–45.

Zaretsky, Eli. *Capitalism, the Family and Personal Life*. New York: Free Press, 1976.

Index

About the Author

JULIO CÉSAR PINO is Assistant Professor of History at Kent State University.

ISBN 0-313-30362-2

90000>

EAN

9 780313 303623

HARDCOVER BAR CODE